THREE MEN

THREE MEN
AN EXPERIMENT IN THE BIOGRAPHY OF EMOTION

JEAN EVANS

Introduction by *GORDON W. ALLPORT*

VINTAGE BOOKS
A Division of Random House
New York

FIRST VINTAGE BOOKS EDITION, *September*, 1966

VINTAGE BOOKS
are published by Alfred A. Knopf, Inc.
and Random House, Inc.

To EP

INTRODUCTION

WE ALL LIKE to read true stories about real lives. A few years ago I happened to read one that impressed me deeply. It was the story of a young delinquent girl who was trying to find personal security somewhere in the rubbery fabric of her environment. The sketch appeared in the pages of *PM*—a former newspaper that welcomed experimental ventures in feature reporting. The author was Jean Evans.

The piece impressed me because it represented a type of case-writing that I had never encountered, but had long wanted to see. As a psychologist I felt the need in my teaching and research for more authentic reports of lives as they are actually lived. To be authentic a report must set forth accurately the social context of the life, but must also center in the person's own image of himself. Above all, good case-writing must absorb the reader's attention, for if the portrait of a human life is not interesting it cannot possibly be true.

The qualities I sought in life histories I found in the work of Miss Evans. Like any novelist or biographer she is highly sensitive to the human material she deals with, but unlike the fiction writer she has a passion for fidelity to the actual case. And more than most biographers she lets her subjects do the speaking and thus reveal the images they hold of themselves.

All writers, to be sure, are forced to select incidents and to communicate them in a more or less orderly fashion, thus imposing some degree of structure and interpretation upon a case. But the difference between fictionized and authentic portraiture lies in the stricter constraints under which the portraitist works.

While Miss Evans has many of the attributes of the artist—being, for one thing, an excellent storyteller—she also has attributes of a scientist. Her chief loyalty is to the life as it is actually lived. She saturates herself in her material: holding innumerable interviews with her subject, reading his personal documents where such exist, checking her own impressions where possible against case records, with physicians, social workers, or friends. As patient as a chemist in his laboratory, she takes pains with her assignment, sifting her data and rewriting her results until they spell accuracy and fidelity. The product is fresh and absorbing; the reader cannot lay it down. It is not the author's artfulness that carries him along; rather it is the veracity of what he reads.

Good case-writing, as I have said, is hard to come by. After reading Jean Evans the reasons become apparent. Most writers of social and psychological cases are impatient. They do not let the client's whole story filter long enough in their imaginations. Usually, too, they are stilted stylists, being soaked in the professional jargon of sociology, social work, or, worst of all, psychiatry. It is not only their style of writing that is limited, but their minds are frequently overloaded with professional prejudgments. Case writers naturally reflect the bias of their specialties. In this respect they are not unlike novelists who project their own moral preconceptions upon the characters they create.

Literature and psychology are the two primary approaches to the study of human personality, each having distinctive advantages. Yet too often does the literary writer ridicule the psychologist, and too often does the latter scorn the insights and methods of literature. A very few autobiographers attempt to combine both approaches; among them one thinks of H. G. Wells and William Ellery Leonard. Still fewer are the instances where the writer of social case histories employs the art of the storyteller while holding himself within the constraints of science. Miss Evans does so, deliberately and with success. If she has not invented a new genre of case-writing, at least she has brought it to new high levels. Science and art are steeds of unlike temperament, and it is no small feat to ride both at once.

There are several important uses for the three absorbing cases presented in this volume. First of all, since they exemplify the blended approach to the study of personality, they will open new horizons to all students of human nature whether their own preference leans toward the scientific or toward the literary approach. The blended method will interest especially social workers, clinical psychologists, criminologists, and psychiatrists, and will, I suspect, inspire them to improve their own writing of case histories.

But chiefly, I hope, this volume will find its way into classrooms where students are being introduced to the study of child development and personality, to the study of social problems and policy, to the study of abnormal psychology and psychotherapy. The three cases offer precisely the raw material of which each of these fields of study is composed.

From firsthand experience I know their value for teaching purposes. For the past few years I have employed both "Johnny Rocco" and "William Miller" as material in a large elementary course in social psychology. Students eat them up. They ask: "Why can't we have more like them?" They say: "Learning from these cases is the most valuable part of the course." The follow-up data contained in this volume add a great deal to these studies, as originally published in the *Journal of Abnormal and Social Psychology*. "Martin Beardson" is a new case, and I have not yet used it in teaching. It likewise sets forth challenging problems, and in some ways is the most baffling of the three. Many readers will find Martin an unsympathetic character, but if they are able to transcend their subjective dislike they will learn much about a not uncommon form of mental disorder.

The principal reason, I think, why these cases are ideal for teaching purposes is that the author imposes a minimum of interpretation. The subjects live and breathe and enter the reader's comprehension as vivid problems of existence. They invite, and demand, the student's response and participation. Questions come tumbling out: How can we explain Miller's preoccupation with death? Was Johnny's delinquency due more to his misfortunes at home or at school? Is Miller's blindness hysterical or is it organic? What will happen to Johnny and to Martin in middle life? The first requirement in good teaching is to arouse greedy curiosity. These cases succeed in doing so.

We must admit that all three men are highly dramatic and colorful. They emerge from unfavorable environments; they are tortured by intense inner conflicts that in all cases spill over into serious friction with their social environments. Because of these underlying similarities it is profitable to view them comparatively, and to ask why, for all their basic likeness, such marked diversity also exists. We need not here raise the question whether the author has intentionally limited herself to the severely maladjusted type of case; or whether any life, however serene on the surface, would with equally skillful probing reveal equally poignant drama. Whatever the answer to this question may be, the intrinsic fascination of these three lives remains.

All three deal with problems that are central to child and adolescent psychology, and to mental hygiene. Miss Evans takes particular pains to depict the home backgrounds as seen by her three subjects, and to trace in frank detail their adolescent conflicts. Each has run into ructions with the law. The mental health of each has been damaged. For both diagnosis and treatment they require the combined efforts of criminologists, psychologists, social workers, and other specialists in the theory and rehabilitation of personality.

Since the author refrains from imposing professional interpretations, the teacher has maximum freedom. He may, if he wishes, label Johnny as a stubborn and intractable child, or Miller as hysteric and compulsive. In the case of Martin Beardson he can invoke a variety of diagnoses: character neurosis, schizoid personality, or psychopath—each with plausibility. But Miss Evans herself doesn't believe in tags. To her a human heart in conflict with itself and with society gains no clarification and no solutions from a label.

At the same time there are processes at work in these lives that are familiar to social and psychological scientists. The teacher will want to point them out, and to name them. The cases illustrate many principles of child training (and mistraining), the processes of compensation, projection, rationalization, and other psychoanalytic mechanisms; they highlight facts of social class, of social reference groups, of law enforcement. Particularly do they show much about the course of motivation, especially of the striving for love and security, so prominent in every life. In each of the present cases this striving runs against adamant obstacles, and as a consequence the character is badly bent. In all three the struggle for self-respect suffers defeat. One question the reader will ask is: "What, if anything, could have been done to avoid the disaster?"

The reader is invited to exercise his own insight, call upon his own relevant experience, and make his own predictions. The average student, to be sure, will want and need some guidance. The teacher, according to his own skill and preference, may give it in the way he chooses. The approach I have used in my own classes in teaching from "Johnny Rocco" has been described in a separate publication (Pauline B. Hahn: "Johnny Rocco —Teaching Material for Elementary Students," *Journal of Abnormal and Social Psychology*, 1948, XLIII, 384– 90). I shall not here attempt to describe the method, for I know that other teachers have employed other techniques with these cases with equal or greater success.

It is a temptation to comment in detail on Johnny, Miller, and Martin. They are so viable and so insistent that every reader will feel impelled to diagnose, interpret, and prescribe. But if I personally yielded to the temptation, I should be taking unfair advantage of the reader and of the author. Miss Evans introduces us with unique skill to three unforgettable characters. Let each of us make of them what he can. In pondering their troubled designs for living we shall certainly grow in our knowledge of human nature.

Gordon W. Allport
Professor of Psychology, Harvard University

AUTHOR'S FOREWORD

IN THESE PAGES are three studies. I should almost prefer to say "three lives," for it was my wish, not to present "cases," but to depict human beings.

In doing this work help came to me from many quarters, sometimes directly, sometimes indirectly. Wherever possible I talked with men and women who were in a position to observe my subjects in their everyday lives and relationships. I talked with experts in medicine, sociology, psychology. Social-work records, medical records, and other documents were made accessible to me.

In the case of "Johnny Rocco" there were put at my disposal the unusually sensitive records of several consecutive years of case work with this boy. For this I am profoundly indebted, not only to the research foundation under whose grant that study was undertaken, but also to Johnny's counselor, the man known as "O'Brien" in that story.

In the case of "William Miller" no such detailed records existed. Miller had lived a vagabond life and was brought to the "Institute" a blind man, from prison. But in the months that followed his remarkable recovery of vision I was generously assisted by members of the executive, teaching, and medical staff of that institution. Personal observations, medical data, and whatever background information could be assembled were placed at my disposal, and there grew up among us a highly rewarding collaboration of inquiry.

The good offices of still another agency made the study of "Martin Beardson" possible, and in this notable instance a paper [1] by Dr. William V. Silverberg was of inestimable help in extending my understanding of Martin's sexual problem.

Without such assistance this work could not have been done. It provided me with material, with documentation, with facts and checks on facts, and with ideas against which my own ideas and evaluations could be examined. But the formulation of final theories or the making of diagnoses is, in the end, the job of the professional psychologist and/or social scientist. Although I could not have presented my material with any logic without myself arriving at certain hypotheses, my function as a writer—though there are inescapable overlaps—was mainly to "depict." In the tradition of my craft I set out to "tell the story." More than this, I set myself the task, in so far as my capacities would allow, of presenting the human being and of permitting him, through his own words, attitudes, and reactions, to unfold and reveal what is, after all, for the writer the stuff of character delineation, and for the scientist the raw material on which hypotheses may be based. For this I went to the sources, the men themselves, and in the final analysis I depended most heavily on firsthand impressions and observations, and on the hundreds of pages of notes—the intimate dialogues of these men, with all that implies of subjective

[1] "The Personal Basis and Social Significance of Passive Male Homosexuality." *Psychiatry: Journal of the Biology and Pathology of Interpersonal Relations*, Vol. I, No. 1, February 1938.

coloration—that I accumulated in the course of personal interviews.

These studies then, for all intents and purposes, may be described as based on subjective accounts, and as written from the points of view of the subjects. Perhaps their spirit is best suggested by the following remarks contained in a letter I once received about another similar effort: "That story," my correspondent said, "might be sub-titled this way: 'Man, his Development and Decision, based upon History (as he is able to know it) and upon Circumstance (as he is able to recognize it).'"

I have sometimes been asked: "But how do you know if a man is telling the whole truth?" Or: "How do you separate fact from fantasy?" To ask this is, in a sense, to beg the question, for in the study of human personality there are limitations common to the scientist as well as to the writer. I would like to define for the reader, as it was necessary to define for myself, the inherent limitations as well as the aims of this work.

Beyond that broad framework of basic key data—the "vital statistics" of a life, which can be verified with reasonable accuracy, there are no absolutes. And in dealing with what is primarily the biography of emotion it would be foolhardy for anyone to think he could verify the details of every incident in a life. Were it possible to track down participants or witnesses, there would still be that well-known human factor. The story about the five different descriptions given by five different people who were involved in the same incident is a commonplace among students of psychology. And it goes without saying that subjective accounts, especially those of troubled people, are apt to be slanted.

Given these conditions, a particular emphasis of attention must first be placed on an understanding of the subject himself—his aims, the tack of his emotional and mental processes, his characteristic patterns of operation. *By his slants shall you know him.* I believe this to be especially important in cases like that of Miller, and even more so of Martin, where personal development is so very individual, where the proneness to fantasy is obvious, the dramas enacted often so removed from reality, and the personal "imagery" abstruse. There are rewards in the recognition first of those broad general outlines— of the particular style of outlook, and of the themes and infinite variations on those themes that emerge out of totalities of detail. These in turn become valuable criteria for further speculation.

Whether all the details in Miller's accounts of his woods life, and of his secret explorations of "nature," are facts or fantasy, or where they become a fusion of both, no one can say with certainty, perhaps least of all Miller, although it is indisputable that Miller has remarkable knowledge of the earth and of woods life. Even more significant, however, in the light of his total story, is the fact of his profound preoccupation with the earth, as well as with caves, graves, and "the secret of life and death."

Whether Martin was "poor" in quite the way he believes himself to have been or, speaking in another mood, was quite so "popular," "witty," and "entertaining" as it seems so important for him to believe—this can only be conjectured against our total picture of Martin, his general excessiveness, his fundamentally unhappy estimate of self, his grandiose aims. Martin himself produces many "coins," and reveals both sides of each of them.

I have tried to present these men as they presented

themselves to me, with all the paradoxes and dualities of their natures. And I have tried to let the material and the "tone" of the individual create the tone, style, and method of presentation. Although I have advanced themes and/or hypotheses—without those "threads" there could be no continuity and no story—all those are in the realm of conjecture. In undertaking this project I set out to prove nothing. It was rather my wish to take the reader with me on a series of explorations.

Wherever it was possible to write at "face value," presenting a maximum of raw material and giving a minimum of interpretation, I have done so. In the case of Martin a marked departure from this general policy was necessary. Where Johnny, and even Miller, live out their inner struggles in comparatively broad, comprehensible ways, Martin is more cerebral, complex, convoluted, his basic motivations hidden in layers upon layers of rationalization and fantasy. The study, "Martin Beardson," is more in the nature of a "translation."

I regret that I may not mention by name the agencies to which I am so deeply indebted for assistance in my researches. To do so would be to risk revealing identifying information about my subjects. But I am pleased to express my appreciation to individuals who assisted me:

Dr. Gordon W. Allport, whose idea it was in the first place that such a book should be written; Dr. Harry G. Schrickel, Dr. George W. Henry, Mr. Alfred A. Gross, Mr. Peter J. Salmon, Mr. George E. Keane, and Mr. Harry J. Spar, who, among other things, were instrumental in supplying me with essential documentation; Dr. Regina Gilroy, who clarified my understanding of certain medical phenomena, and who was kind enough to check the medical data in the study, "William Miller";

Dr. Percy E. Ryberg, for his sensitive and painstaking reading of "Martin Beardson," and for his many invaluable suggestions for the clarification of obscurities; my old friend and colleague, Lorimer D. Heywood, who read the first part of "Johnny Rocco" and contributed valuable editorial suggestions.

Much of the research for this volume was done on a Guggenheim Fellowship; I give thanks to that Foundation.

The first sections of "Johnny Rocco" and "William Miller" were originally published in the *Journal of Abnormal and Social Psychology*, a publication of the American Psychological Association. I wish to express my appreciation to that organization for many courtesies. Material not used in the original publication of these sections has been included here because of its bearing on later developments in these lives.

My greatest indebtedness is to the three men, "Johnny," "Martin," and "Miller," who gave so generously of their time, their thoughts, and their feelings that this book might be written, and who opened new dimensions of experience, knowledge, and understanding to me.

Names of people and of places, and other identifying data have, of course, been disguised.

Jean Evans

CONTENTS

THREE MEN

THREE MEN

JOHNNY ROCCO

W̲ᴀʟᴋ through the slum section of any American city some evening. Pause at the poolrooms, the gyms, the dingy bars, the candy stores, and certain street corners where boys and young men gather. Any one of them might be a Johnny Rocco.

Johnny is a short, chunky fellow of twenty. He looks older than his years. His hair, which is dark with a slightly reddish cast, is receding at the temples, thinning on top. His dark, heavy eyebrows, meeting over a slightly aquiline nose, give him an angry, somber look. His eyes are narrow, the skin underneath them tending to be baggy. There is a small narrow scar on his left cheek. His hands are stubby, the fingers square, the nails bitten short. Blue and red tattoos, their edges blurred, decorate both his forearms to just below the wrists. He carries his shoulders stiffly, walking with a cocky rolling gait.

At first contact Johnny seems tough—very tough. "I used to have a heart. I was chicken-hearted," he says contemptuously. "Now I don't give a damn for anyone. Everybody's out for himself. . . ."

"Cops? They're no good. Two-bit phonies and racketeers. I'm old now and I know the rackets they run. They beat the law themselves, and then they go out and arrest some poor kid. The guys outside the law, they'll gyp you, too. You got to watch your step. You can't trust anybody. Your own gang will insult you. Your own family they'll call you a jerk. I don't team up with anybody. I'm what you call—here today and gone tomorrow."

But as you get to know him, the brassy quality of what he has to say gives way to something else, and the real Johnny begins to emerge.

"All my life—as far as I remember. If I wanted to have something, to be something—No! Never! Not a goddamned lousy thing! Anything I wanted, I never could work it. I never could accomplish—"

Johnny was born in a large Midwestern industrial city. His parents, Italian immigrants, had settled there at the turn of the century. When Johnny was born, there were nine other Rocco children, each about two years younger than the preceding one. Regina, who was twenty when Johnny came along, was the oldest. Then came Francesco, Aldo, Sebastian, Georgio, Paul, Antonio, Carla, and Richard. Two more children came after Johnny was born: David, a year and a half younger than Johnny, and Mike. Mike died in infancy.

The neighborhood where the Roccos lived was known as one of the worst slums in the city. It was known, too, for its high rate of crime and juvenile delinquency. It was a neighborhood of factories, abandoned tumble-down shacks, junk yards, poolrooms, cheap liquor joints, and broken houses with sagging steps and paint peeling from their sides.

Johnny's father worked irregularly—as a bartender, teamster, or day laborer. Two things he did regularly: he drank and he gambled. In his drunken rages he often attacked the children and their mother. The little ones learned to scuttle across the floor like beetles and find shelter under tables or beds, where his kicking feet couldn't reach them.

Johnny's short, dark, excitable mother was always sick and complaining. She suffered from heart disease. The children fought. They were noisy and destructive. There was seldom enough food in the house. The rent was never paid, and Mrs. Rocco lived in constant terror of landlords and evictions. The Roccos moved frequently. They moved every nine or ten months, but never to a better house or neighborhood. They moved through a succession of drafty, sparsely furnished four- and five-room apartments, which were heated by coal or kerosene, the geography of their lives circumscribed by dirt, squalor, and factory and slaughterhouse smells and noises.

Johnny's memories of his early childhood are sporadic. He remembers that when he was a little boy, the family had a dog, Teddy. Teddy got sick and lay beside the kerosene stove, quiet and shivering. Johnny recalls that Teddy was still alive when one of his older brothers put Teddy into a sack half-full of trash, carried him to the garbage dump, and left him there to die.

Johnny remembers visiting another of his brothers at a reform school. That was a little later, and that memory has the quality of a holiday; the reform school, Johnny says, was in a "country-like" place.

Johnny remembers hiding in a snowbank once, when his mother was very angry. He remembers fights between his brothers when his mother stood in the middle of the room screaming, and blood ran from his brothers' noses. And Johnny remembers how his father died. A heavy, regular thumping awoke Johnny one night. He got up and, still dazed with sleep, wandered into the kitchen, where the family usually gathered. His father was lying on the floor.

"Some men my father was out with had dragged him up the stairs and put him there. There was blood on his face. Blood was coming out of his ears. He was holding the leg of the kitchen table with one hand, an' he was moanin', and he kept pounding his foot on the floor. One of my brothers called an ambulance, but he died."

Johnny was then five. One of the city's many social-work agencies through whose hands the Roccos passed has a notation in its records on the death of Johnny's father: "Killed in a drunken brawl by his best friend."

The rest of Johnny's memories, many of them more in the nature of a quality of feeling than of actual remembrance, flow backward and forward in time, a merging of history and experience.

Time out of mind there was trouble in the Rocco family. Johnny knows by a certain "lousy feeling" he's always had; by certain conditions that seem to him to have had no beginning or end; by monotonously repetitious happenings. There were sickness and violence. There was trouble with social-work agencies. The Roccos were known to twenty-five welfare agencies in thirty years. There was trouble with landlords, with the schools where the Rocco children went, with the police.

By the time Johnny's father died, four of the older Rocco children had married and moved away. (Johnny's oldest sister married a drunkard. Four of his brothers contracted "forced marriages" while still in their teens. Two of them have been divorced and remarried; one of them once, the other twice, though the family is Roman Catholic.) What was left of the Rocco family continued in its dismal course, the children getting into one difficulty after another and Mrs. Rocco, sick and confused, and inept, trudging from school to police station to court, listening to complaints about them, and from hospital to welfare agency, asking for help and still more help.

If the Rocco boys ever had any tender feeling for one another, that was lost somewhere in the maelstrom of accumulated want, frustration, and jealousy that was the lot of each of them. As much as possible, the members of the household moved in separate orbits, their paths converging under the family roof only when they paused to sleep or to eat their pasta. Of the seven remaining children only one boy, Georgio, assumed any responsibility toward the others, and that was thrust upon him. He was sixteen, the oldest son in the household, when his father died. If Georgio worked, he contributed part of his earnings to the family. When the rest of the children got so out of hand that Mrs. Rocco implored him to do something, he applied the only discipline he knew: he beat them brutally.

"My brothers— I don't despise them," Johnny says, "but the past I don't forget. They used to push me around. I wasn't afraid of them. I used to tell them: 'Go ahead. Hit me. Hit me. What do I care?' Except Georgio! The fear I had for my brother Georgio, if he threatened me—if he only looked at me—I'm scared of him, that's all."

Johnny slept in a bed with Richard and David. Richard, a dark, scowling boy who was born with a twisted foot, was two years older than Johnny. David, who was a year and a half younger, had congenital syphilis, and suffered from anemia. Johnny always felt that, because his mother was ill and Richard and David were sickly, the three of them were drawn into an alliance from which he was excluded.

"I was the strongest, so I had to sleep across the foot of the bed. Even if I wanted to swap places with them, it was no dice. They wouldn't. And, anyway, my mother wouldn't make them. Those brass beds! You know, they got bars at the end. Jesus! In the winter, those bars are cold. I used to lay there and they'd ball me up against the cold bars. They'd kick my face and my back and pull the covers off. I'd be—half of me out of the covers, freezing, or laying on those bars.

"Sunday mornings, hell, you wanted to sleep. It was cold. Then the fighting would start. They'd be crowding an' pushing an' I'd yell or kick them. It used to make me mad. Then my big brother, Georgio, he'd be laying in his bed in the other room, an' he'd yell: 'Johnny! Come here!'

"Whenever my brother Georgio said: 'Johnny! Come here!' Christ! I'd be scared. Walkin' to the sink or the table, wherever he was—to me, that was walkin' into a death house. I'd get out of the bed an' go up to the bed where he was an' bam! He'd let me have it. He used to give me charley-horses so's I couldn't move my arm. He broke my nose once. My head hit the door an' I went out cold."

The only person in that household Johnny loved was his mother. "Sometimes she was wrong," Johnny says, "but she tried to be good to us. She would just as soon take a meal out of her own mouth and give it to us. But she never favored me. She favored Richie and Davie. Davie—he's dead now—he was her favorite. I was trouble to her. I was always on the outside," Johnny says heavily.

"When Davie died she said she wished it was me instead."

Johnny was especially bitter toward David, who was the baby of the family. "I used to lick him. I used to fight and break things. I was always trouble. Even before he was sick, Davie was petted. He got everything, even a bike. I didn't get anything.

"I never went any place. If I went any place, I had to go on my own. My people never took me out to a show or any place with them. On Sundays when all the kids on the corner had money, I didn't. I'd go and clip it. I never had a birthday party. I never had a birthday present outside of what Mr. O'Brien, a friend I had when I was bigger, gave me. . . . Christmases, and I was always in the wrong. Maybe I cracked Davie, or I was yelling, or somebody complained. It was always something. My mother would get my brother Richie something and my brother Davie something. She'd tell me in advance I wasn't going to get anything. Yeah, it made me mad."

Johnny didn't want to be "always trouble" to his mother. He wanted to show her how much he loved her, but he could never quite reach her. He wanted to make her love and pet him, too, as she did David, but he didn't know how. He had a secret way of paying her tribute: "Money I stole, I would never give to my mother." He earned a little, periodically, selling *True Confession* magazines. He gave her that. Then she, in turn, would give him a dime.

Once, Johnny says, he borrowed a shoe-shine box, "hook-jacked" school, and worked from morning till night. "I made two bucks and a half. Boy! I was hungry, but I wouldn't even buy a roll. I wouldn't even spend something for carfare home. I wanted to give my mother all of it."

But even when Johnny was determined to make his mother love him, he was annoying, he was so insistent. He would rush home after school and make a great show of sweeping the floors or polishing the stove. He would urge and urge his mother to send him on an errand. Tense and watchful for the extravagant praise he craved, he'd even make overtures to David. But something always happened to burst the bubble; a quarrel with David, a rebuff from his mother—and Johnny, overcome with rage, frustration, and self-pity, would swing back to thieving, baiting David, and screaming savagely at his mother.

One of the subterfuges Johnny's fumbling mother resorted to in her efforts to pacify landlords, who were always hounding her, was to keep her screaming, battling children out of the house as much as possible. As soon as each child was old enough to shift for himself, she would turn him out on the streets. One after another the Rocco boys became known to the police. Their father himself had a long court record for assault, disorderliness, drunkenness; five of Johnny's brothers, who started in childhood, ran up police records covering charges of disturbing the peace, breaking and entering, larceny, perjury, assault and battery, bastardy, and malicious injury.

"I was in the police station, too. Plenty!" Johnny says. "Saturdays, they had Kid's Day. We'd be in this long corridor. There'd be all little kids sitting down, niggers and kids with their shoe-shine boxes who'd have to go out shining shoes afterwards. They'd bring us in an' those jerks, the cops, they'd be sitting there. They'd ask us—" Johnny's sentence broke off; then he continued on a new tack.

"Christ! I remember a lot of times I got picked up for something—or maybe staying out late, or suspicion. They'd round us up an' bring us in, an' this cop here, he was always insulting me. 'You little fresh—you little bastard!' He'd belt me or anything he felt like doing. I was just —— to him. . . ."

Johnny hadn't been running the streets long when the knowledge was borne in on him that being a Rocco made him "something special"; the reputation of the notorious Roccos, known to neighbors, schools, police, and welfare agencies as "chiselers, thieves, and trouble-makers," preceded him. The cop on the beat, Johnny says, always had some cynical smartcrack to make. Certain homes were barred to him. Certain children were not permitted to play with him. Wherever he went—on the streets, in the neighborhod settlement house, at the welfare agency's penny milk station, at school, where other Roccos had been before him—he recognized himself by a gesture, an oblique remark, a wrong laugh.

"Everybody always knew all about me," he recalls. "I always had a bad name. I felt cheap. Everybody gave me hell."

If Johnny was sinned against, he was also sinning. "Sure I was bad. I was fresh with my mouth. I stole. As far back as I remember I got in jams. There were things I never done, too, but I always got accused anyway. I didn't care. I didn't. Because I knew if I was in court and the judge said: 'You're free,' I was going to go right out stealin' an' getting in jams again. I was noted for a crook. I had it in me."

Most slum boys get a feeling of protection and prestige from membership in some neighborhood gang, but Johnny wasn't one of those. He knew members of various gangs in the many neighborhoods where he had lived. He rotated among all of them but remained always on the fringes of their society. Johnny wanted to be a fully accepted member of a gang, but he could never get along with any one group for long. Johnny was a maverick:

"I never fitted in. I never belonged any place. I never found anybody that liked me a lot, and that I liked, and could trust. I never played baseball, football—playing with the kids. I just had kids I clipped with—Bagdads, they used to call us—like the forty thieves. You know, a bunch of sloppy kids that ain't got nothing."

Johnny and a pal of the moment played around alleys and junk yards, or hung around the doorways of poolrooms. If the weather was right, they would swim in the oily waters of the river that runs through their part of the town. Sometimes they would hop on the back of a trolley to Green Hill, a suburb where people grew fruit trees. "We'd steal peaches and eat all day," Johnny recalls, "and then come home." Of an evening, they would break into the plant of a chain bakery near by and eat their fill of cake.

As a small boy, Johnny had one sport that he liked above everything else—going to the freight yards or parks to trap birds. "It's easy," he says. "You make—like a path with crumbs. Then you wait. If one goes in the box, a whole flock will go in."

One of the most urgent cravings Johnny can recall was his fondness for birds. He yearned to keep some of the ones he trapped, but he couldn't, his mother wouldn't permit it. She was afraid the landlord would object. "I liked birds. I was always thinking about them," Johnny says. "I got the nickname 'Sparrow.'"

From peaches, to cakes, to money, whatever the sequence, by the time he was ten, Johnny says, "It got so whenever I'd lay my eyes on something and want it, I'd just clip it." Then he and his cronies made a business of hopping rides on trucks. Johnny describes it: "A couple of guys would hop on an' throw the stuff off the side." They stole from cars, too, and broke into places at night. It was at about this time that Johnny began to make his appearance at the police station on "Kids' Day."

If Johnny's home and street life were turbulent, it was no different at school. He had entered kindergarten when he was four and a half years old. During the next seven years he had changed schools seven times, had been in at least fifteen different home rooms, and was only in the third grade. His reading was on a second-grade level; he was poor in arithmetic, and was almost completely unable to spell.

He was a trial to his teachers. They complained that he was "nervous, fidgety, sullen, obstinate, cruel, disobedient, disruptive." "Teachers can stand him for only one day at a time," one said. "He talks to himself. He fights. He insists on wearing his hat at school. When in Miss Clark's room, he attempted to kick her. He isn't going to be promoted. He knows this and refuses to make any effort to study. His present teacher is so tired she refuses to have it out with him. . . ." Another wrote: *He is the most difficult boy I have ever had. Does not belong in a classroom. He needs individual attention and a lot of it. He never applies himself. There is nothing in which he is interested enough to apply himself. He has more mentality than he seems to want to use.*

He is a showoff. I cannot keep him in any one seat. The other children do not like him. He has no regard for

*what belongs to anyone else. He wants to rip everything
out of everyone else's hand, to bully and to fight. . . .*

*The only things he cares for are stories, any kind of
stories. They seem to have a soothing effect on him. If
anyone makes a noise or interrupts a story in any way, he
jumps up and threatens to punch him. On occasion he
will bump his head hard against that of another boy for
no apparent reason.*

*There is just one period every day when he is not
troublesome. During that period he just wants to sleep.
It may come on him at any time during the day, but he
has it every day without exception. It may last ten minutes or it may last an hour. He just puts his head down
on the desk and goes to sleep for a while. Then he wakes
up and is a devil again.*

At this period of Johnny's life, it has been possible to
make a comparison of two members of the Rocco brood,
Johnny and his youngest brother, David, the boy who was
suffering from anemia and on whom the mother lavished
her affection. Both boys were students at the same school
at this time.

At the same time that teachers were complaining so
bitterly about Johnny's behavior, teachers who had David
considered him a "good, likable child." Observers noted
that though David had a violent temper and was sometimes harder to manage than Johnny, he was generally
sunny, studious, co-operative, generous, and popular with
the other children at school.

"David is a 'regular boy,' all in all," one of them stated.
"He likes to play and tussle. He is very well developed
and healthy-looking for a congenital luetic. He looks
clean and well cared for. He's quite independent, seems

more sure of himself than his brother John, and is better in his work despite frequent absences when he goes to the clinic. He has no serious fears or worries. He never does anything seriously wrong."

Undoubtedly David had less energy for mischief than Johnny, his illness (though not yet in its terminal stages) limiting the scope and intensity of his activities. But his health handicaps also brought him prestige and advantages that Johnny didn't enjoy: the demonstrated solicitude of his mother; sympathetic attention from members of the community; presents; regular vacations in the country provided by the local children's hospital. Doctors even prescribed that he get plenty of sweets.

Johnny, feeling himself neither loved, wanted, nor respected, was forever in competition with more favored children. He was always on the lookout for disparagement of himself. He was extremely sensitive about his scholastic standing. Above everything—it was his "best wish"—he wanted to be promoted. When special tests were given him at school, he assumed that was to find out "if I have any brains." He was obsessed with the fear that he would be placed in the "dummy class," thus proving once and for all, to himself, to the other children, and to the world at large, that he was different, inferior. (His IQ at eleven was 91, dull average—not so low as his scholastic achievements.) Yet Johnny didn't have the resources for concentrated effort. He was fighting on too many fronts at once.

With every new failure he became less tractable, more vindictive, and was compelled to some new misbehavior. Once, at the beginning of a new semester, he told his teacher: "I wasn't promoted. Okay. This year I'm going to make plenty of trouble." With every new dereliction and punishment, Johnny's conviction grew that his teachers, like everybody else, were "against him." Soon the most important thing was to harass his enemies. He did this at the price of pain and humiliation to himself.

He sneered at the other children, fought with them, guffawed at their mistakes, disrupted classrooms. He disobeyed school rules "deliberately, slowly, and with full intent," as one teacher noted. He smoked, swaggered, used foul language. He stopped trying to learn.

The public schools in Johnny's neighborhood are poor, the classes crowded, the teachers undertrained, underpaid, and overworked. Johnny remembers only one incident of kindness. "There was one once, she gave me a pair of ice skates." But Johnny, devoured by feelings of inadequacy, thrashing about in an effort to bring order out of chaos, to find one final object on which to pin all blame, cannot afford to keep kindnesses in mind. What stand out, still rankling, filling him with anger, hatred, and futility, feeding and yet justifying his sense of failure, are his grievances—grievances real and imagined, piled up over the years.

"Teachers! Crumbs! Bitches!" he says. "All the way back, in the King School—Miss Smith, she was the first-grade teacher; why, as young as I was then, Jesus! Jesus! I had a special desk. Not with the other kids or anything, but right up in front near her. I was special. All my life I was something special. I found right then that I had to show off, I suppose, or be proud of it, or something—

"Teachers, and the different mothers. They always pointed to me. I was the example. They'd ask the kids: 'You want to be like Sparrow Rocco?' Once when I went into a new room, at the beginning of the term, the teacher asks me: 'Is your name Rocco? I know all about you,' she says—Jesus, in front of all the kids! 'Don't think you're not going to be good in here!' Her name was Miss Wayman. The jerk! I'd like to—

"I felt cheap. I had that reputation. If something was missing—like going through the pockets in the cloak-room, whether I did it or not, I was always the first one accused. If the other kids did something, it wasn't so bad. But if I did it, yeah, that was the worst. In one school I had to go to the principal every morning, and every day after school, to tell him if I was a bad boy. When I was a bad boy he used to give me the strap.

"In the class, if there was a book—you know, as it goes up the aisles, kids read from it—and they came to me, they never called my name. I'd just be sitting there like this. The guy behind me would read, or the girl in front. But not me. The teacher didn't care.

"When the kids passed around the paper, to write something, it got so they just ignored me. Once a kid was passing paper, and when he came to me he asked the teacher: 'Should I give John some?' I said: 'Why ask the teacher? I'm in the room, too, ain't I?' It used to get me sore. I took the paper and wrote any god-damned thing on it. The teacher just looked at it and tore it up. The next time they gave me paper, I tore it into little pieces.

"Yeah. I used to feel bad. Seems like nobody wanted me around, neither the teachers or the kids. If they could avoid having me at a party, they didn't. I never had any real good friends. Once, in school, something happened. I cried over it. I know this girl. The bitch! Poletti. Mary Poletti. That's her name. I'm not forgetting her. It was Valentine's. She sent everybody in the room one except me. The teacher had all the kids to get up and say how many valentines they got, and to read them off and tell who they were from. I didn't get any. I was the only one. Then the teacher had little candy hearts she gave out. I didn't get one of them, either. Not because she didn't want to, but somebody, some visitors, I guess, came in, an' I was in the back or something, an' she didn't have any left. She asked me: 'You don't feel bad, not getting one?' What did she expect? That I should bust out crying and tell her? I said: 'Naw. I don't care.' Later I cried. I didn't get anything that day.

"I was dumb, too. I know it. Everybody knew it. I was just a jerk to everybody," Johnny says fiercely. "Maybe I *am* stupid. Maybe that's because I always felt so bad. It wasn't that I didn't have the brains to learn like everybody else. But teachers! Teachers! That's who I blame and no one else."

Before he was twelve, Johnny's attitudes toward society had crystallized in a hard, bitter core of rancor. He had his reasons: he felt that he had always been treated badly. He felt no one had ever loved him. Everyone was his enemy—his mother, his brothers, his teachers, the cops, even the other kids—all were against him. Okay, he was at war with them.

That was Johnny Rocco at the age of twelve, when something very important happened in his life. That year Jim O'Brien, a tall, pleasant-faced man in his middle thirties, became Johnny's friend. O'Brien was a counselor in an organization devoted to work with problem boys. Before he even approached Johnny, O'Brien had familiarized himself with the Rocco family history by talking to police, hospital, and welfare authorities, and by visiting the Rocco home.

Sad Mrs. Rocco, now fifty, tired and bedraggled, received him in her dingy kitchen, which was festooned with lines of drying clothes. Yes, yes, she was worried about her Johnny. She "couldn't do nothing with him." Only Georgie—he was twenty-one now, poor boy, and wanted to get married, but she needed him at home— only *he* had any control over Johnny. Johnny was at school now, but she didn't know when he would be home. Every morning, after a breakfast of bread and cocoa, he went away and didn't come back until ten or eleven o'clock at night.

She was doing the best she could, but there was so much—the cleaning, the washing, the cooking; the worry about money for food, for rent and coal. The Welfare Department only gave her thirty-eight dollars every two weeks for herself and the seven children. Jobs were hard to get and didn't pay much. Yet if one of her boys did get a job, whether he contributed to the family or not— and a boy *had* to have some spending money, she knew that—it always made trouble.

Just last month one of her boys had got a job as a messenger, seven dollars a week. Seven dollars doesn't grow on trees. If she had reported that income to the Welfare Department, they would have deducted it from her allotment. She didn't report it, but they found out, and her allotment was cut off entirely. Now the boy didn't have that job any more, but she was still being penalized. She was getting three dollars a week less than her original allotment. It was almost better, Mrs. Rocco told O'Brien, if the children didn't try to work.

Then there was David. He was having trouble with that anemia. He had to be taken to the clinic regularly for X-ray treatments. (At that time she had no idea of the seriousness of David's illness.) There was Richie, with his retracted toes. The condition was getting worse all the time, but she couldn't make him go to the clinic for help. Carla, the only girl in the household, was sixteen now. She had bleached her hair and was staying out late nights. Only God knew what would happen to her.

It was too much, too much, Mrs. Rocco cried. She was sick herself. Her teeth were bad. Her heart. Sometimes she felt so faint and dizzy she didn't think she could go on. Then what would happen to the children? See, her joints were swollen. She couldn't fasten her shoes. She held out her arms to show her swollen wrists.

O'Brien went to Johnny's school. He talked with the principal and Johnny's teachers, and then observed Johnny himself—"a sulky, hard-faced boy, intent on making trouble"—through a small window in the classroom door. Then when he felt he had a firm grasp of the situation he made himself known to Johnny.

Mr. O'Brien's friendship brought Johnny a sense of importance he had never known before. If Mr. O'Brien dropped in for talks with Mrs. Rocco and the other children, or performed small services for them, Johnny knew that was because Mr. O'Brien was *his* friend.

It was Johnny whom O'Brien took for drives in his car. Sometimes as they set out for a drive and Johnny saw some kids he knew on the corner, he yelled and gesticulated wildly so they would see him. It was Johnny whom O'Brien took to a museum and on a week-end camping trip. He bought Johnny a white scarf, embroidered with his initials—the first birthday present Johnny had ever got. He even interceded with Johnny's mother and the landlord so Johnny could indulge his passionate interest in birds by having some of his own.

On their rides, or during walks they took, Mr. O'Brien encouraged Johnny to talk. Johnny told him about the gangs and their hangouts, about his troubles on the street, at school, and at home. Mr. O'Brien made it clear when he disapproved of things Johnny was doing, but he never harangued him as his mother did, and he never stopped being Johnny's friend. He told Johnny he only wanted to help him, so Johnny could make friends and keep out of trouble.

If O'Brien's friendship was a source of pleasure and comfort to Johnny, it sometimes brought him worry and embarrassment, too. The neighborhood kids began wondering what a man like O'Brien wanted with a kid like Johnny, anyway.

"If I told the kids he was trying to find out why I stole," Johnny says, "and why I was so dumb in the school, they said: 'He must be trying to find out if you're bananas' [crazy]. If I said he was just my friend, they got wise. 'Yeah. He's a fruit.' "

Johnny himself was dubious about Mr. O'Brien's motives sometimes. He really couldn't understand, either, why an important man like O'Brien bothered with him. Once, when Johnny had been particularly difficult and Mr. O'Brien got stern, Johnny had a sneaking suspicion that O'Brien was really a cop and was spying on him. Occasionally the thought crept into his mind that maybe Mr. O'Brien *was* trying to find out if he was crazy and wanted to "put him away." He worried about that especially after Mr. O'Brien took him to a clinic for a series of special examinations and tests once, and when he learned that his mother, too, harbored that suspicion.

It wasn't long before Johnny realized that there were implicit in that friendship responsibilities and obligations that Johnny found hard to fulfill. Mr. O'Brien's friendship had introduced a new and befuddling factor in Johnny's orientation to society, a society that heretofore he had known as a collective enemy: it split his offensive. His skirmishes continued, but for the first time he felt constrained to distinguish friends among the foe. This led to more formidable encounters—encounters to be kept alone, and with himself. It was no longer so easy to justify some of his behavior.

After he had started winning Johnny's confidence, Mr. O'Brien arranged to have Johnny attend classes in the morning at a special educational clinic, while going to public school in the afternoon. When Johnny had been at the clinic for about two months, Mr. O'Brien discovered that an instructor there had given the boy a rosary and that Johnny always carried it with him. Johnny was also overheard urging another child to pray every night "because you might die before you wake up." He had given the other child his own definition of the horrors of hell: "It's a place where you're cold and hungry all the time and you never get anything to eat."

On the strength of that manifestation of interest in religion, Mr. O'Brien got Johnny a scholarship in a parochial school where he would be able to attend classes in the afternoons while continuing to attend morning sessions at the clinic. Mr. O'Brien reasoned that Johnny's interest in religion might be an effective tool in dealing with him. In addition, Johnny had exhausted most of the public schools available to him, and it had become increasingly clear to O'Brien that Johnny's teachers in the public school he was now attending had accumulated such a backlog of hostility toward the boy that they were cynical and unco-operative. The sisters at the parochial school, given an understanding of the boy's problems, might handle him more sympathetically.

Before he had embarked on these plans, Mr. O'Brien had considered a foster-home placement. Johnny, he believed, was a boy whose heredity was questionable, but who was also a victim of the worst possible environmental influences. Should he not attempt to transplant Johnny to a healthier soil? Though Johnny's feelings toward his mother were full of conflict, he was still deeply attached to her, and Mr. O'Brien questioned the wisdom of severing that attachment. He could try to help the boy in the school situation, he reasoned. If Johnny could develop good behavior and work habits at school, it was possible, O'Brien wrote in his case records, that "those adjustments would carry over in terms of a healthier outlook and satisfaction in other phases of Johnny's life."

About three months after Johnny entered the educational clinic, the clinic reported him doing well. His improvement in reading seemed to give him great satisfaction. The report noted that he had an "excellent" memory, but it also stated that Johnny would become suddenly impatient and discouraged. This seemed to occur when he was confronted with tasks like naming words in quick flash devices that demanded mental alertness. He appeared pale, tired, and tense. Perhaps fatigue was a factor in his inability to respond quickly.

A short time later the director of the clinic told Mr. O'Brien that Johnny's behavior had become so poor that she did not think she could keep him in the clinic school any longer. She now realized the boy had never really adjusted to the group. She believed that that was mainly due to the deprivations he suffered, which set him apart from the other children. Most of the children at the clinic school came from comparatively comfortable families. Johnny's clothes were different, his speech was different, he carried no pocket money. He was aware of these differences and seemed to feel them acutely.

Johnny's misbehavior had begun with little "fights and fusses" in the classroom and had gradually mounted to such hyperactivity that at times he was uncontrollable. What worried his teacher most: Often during a spell of wild, uncontrollable behavior he asked to go to the bathroom. When he returned, his face was "pasty-white, his eyes narrowed down to mere slits." Walking as if his equilibrium had been disturbed, his body would knock against both sides of the door as he re-entered the room. His teachers knew that Johnny smoked. They were afraid he was smoking "doped" cigarettes, but could not substantiate that fear.

Mr. O'Brien visited the educational clinic to see if Johnny couldn't be kept on. Then he took him to a medical clinic for a complete physical examination. It is likely that Johnny's suspicion that Mr. O'Brien was trying to find out if he was "crazy" was strengthened by the way in which he was handled during that examination. Johnny, already harboring the fear that his scholastic standing and his inability to conform to socially acceptable behavior had something to do with the state of his "brains," was examined in the presence of several medical students. To Johnny's mortification and Mr. O'Brien's chagrin, the examining physician and the students discussed Johnny's peculiar behavior at length in the boy's presence. Johnny, who may also have harbored the belief that masturbation causes insanity, was questioned searchingly about masturbation too. Afterwards, he was given an electroencephalogram test, mysterious and frightening to Johnny, to determine whether his behavior was due to the presence of epilepsy.

The general examination ruled out the likelihood that Johnny had been smoking "doped" cigarettes. The explanation for the "doped" states, the doctor said, more likely lay in a combination of deficient diet, fatigue, smoking, and possibly excessive masturbation. The electroencephalogram indicated some slight irregularity in Johnny's brain waves, only faintly suggestive of epileptoid tendencies.

"All we can say is that here we have a boy who shows certain behavior and reactions which are similar to epileptic attacks although not truly epileptic in their manifestation," a specialist commented. "The encephalograph findings are consistent with this behavior in that there, too, we find indications of an epileptiform brainwave which is not, however, perfectly clear as true epilepsy."

As a result of Mr. O'Brien's efforts, Johnny managed to stay on at the educational clinic three more months—six in all, after which he attended parochial school all day. During the rest of his time at the clinic his behavior continued to be sporadic though the peculiar "doped states" seemed to disappear. At times he seemed to be struggling desperately to study and be "a good boy." At other times he would break into a crescendo of poor behavior that spilled over into every area of his life, at school, at home, and on the streets. Mr. O'Brien noted that these outbursts usually coincided with some condition of unusual pressure, often a crisis at home.

Despite Johnny's tumultuous emotional problems, the clinic reported, just before he left the clinic to go to the parochial school on full time, that his reading level had been raised from the second to the fourth grade. His work in arithmetic, though weak, had improved. His spelling was still very poor.

Johnny's behavior at the parochial school, where he remained for a year and three months—longer than he had ever stayed in any one school before—followed a pattern like the one he had set at the clinic. The children there came of comparatively comfortable families, too, and Johnny was troubled by the difference in his social and economic status.

"I never had clothes like the other kids," he says. "My people didn't have to pay for me. I didn't even have to pay for my books or pencils. When they'd come with the box and call the kids to put their money in, they'd never call me. The other kids got ideas about me. You know, I was different."

There was a special problem in connection with his size and age, too. Johnny was in the third grade when he was twelve, and again when he was thirteen. His classmates were all about nine. Johnny felt shabby, lumbering, and conspicuous. When the children lined up to march out of the classroom, he would run away and hide, or slip out of the room early. But Johnny also wanted to conform. Once he worked up courage to fall into line and march with the other children down to the street. He kept at it for more than two weeks. Then some boys he knew who were his size, and who went to the public school near by, began to lie in wait for him. They mocked him with mincing gestures and called him sissy. Johnny sprang out of line and into a fist fight with one of them one day. After that he didn't march with his classmates again.

At times Johnny was extremely hostile to the other children in his class. He tripped them up, stuck gum in their hair, broke their pencils, and crumpled their papers. He was especially cruel to the "good little kids." At other times, swinging to an opposite extreme when he yearned to be accepted as one of them, he made overtures to them. But the other children feared or shunned him.

"They didn't make fun of me," Johnny says fiercely. "If they did, I'd floor them. But they used to look at me in a certain way. The way they looked at me, Jesus— like they were scared. It was worse than if they said it. They all thought I was tough. I *wasn't* tough. I *wasn't*. I'd try to show them—'I'm *not* tough'—the bastards! The way they looked at me, it used to get me mad. I'd be so mad, just trying to tell them—yah! yah! yah!—trying to get it in their dumb heads. I never could make them see it."

At one point, after he had been at the school for quite a while, he succeeded in gathering a gang of admiring little boys around him. He reacted extravagantly. He swaggered, swore, defied school discipline. He encouraged them to break school rules, too, and incited them to trip or grab and hug girls. The sisters, O'Brien noted, would have liked to see Johnny make friends, but Johnny was far from a wholesome influence and they had begun to get complaints from parents of some of the other children that Johnny was teaching boys to steal and say bad words. Johnny's gang was finally broken up.

"In that school," Johnny says, "they didn't have no playground. They used to block off the street. Once I went up in a tree with some kids. I guess I was showing off. It was the kind of a tree where you strip the leaves off one of the thin branches and make—you know, like a switch. All of us kids were doing it, hanging in the tree, swinging the switches around. The sister caught us. She didn't do anything to the other kids. She said I was the biggest and I was getting the other kids in trouble. She took all the switches away and she took me in all the rooms, in front of all the classes, and she whipped me with those switches. To make an example of me—a jerk, you know—in front of all the kids. I let them know right there that I didn't care what they done to me. I hated them all. I didn't care. I didn't.''

One day Johnny folded his arms and, with face ugly and sullen, refused to do any work. The only thing he would say to the sister was that he wanted to return to public school. When Mr. O'Brien came to discuss this with him, Johnny, sitting stiff and upright in his chair, would neither speak to him nor look at him. Lips tightly pursed, his face set in a hard belligerent expression, he stared straight ahead.

Mr. O'Brien talked kindly to Johnny, but Johnny wouldn't answer. He tried talking sternly, but Johnny merely tightened his lips and shrugged his shoulders. O'Brien knew Johnny was unhappy because he was a big boy in a class with little kids. He pointed out that in public school the boys Johnny's size and age were in the upper grades and that there, too, Johnny would be among small children. Johnny indicated that he knew this, but still wanted to go back to the public school. Then Mr. O'Brien reminded him of some of the things the public-school teachers had said to Johnny—that he would never learn to get along anywhere. "I don't agree with them," O'Brien said to Johnny, "but maybe I'll have to admit that I'm wrong and they are right."

Finally Mr. O'Brien rose as if to leave. "All right. I'm sorry about all this," he said. "I'm not mad at you, but I'm a little disappointed. I want to help you if I can, but no one can help you if you don't want to help yourself. All the same, I know you've tried hard. I think you're a good kid."

As he patted Johnny's shoulder in a departing gesture, Johnny grabbed his arm and, burying his face in it, burst into sobs. Mr. O'Brien said Johnny clung to his arm and cried until the material of his coat was crinkled and the tears soaked through. Then he went back to his classroom.

Afterwards O'Brien learned that Johnny had been particularly difficult at home during that period, too, and that he was reporting regularly to the police because he had broken some windows. When Mr. O'Brien asked about that, Johnny burst out: "What am I gonna do? If I play with the big kids, they get me in trouble. If I play with the little kids, I get them in trouble. What am I gonna do?"

Mr. O'Brien, who had a thorough appreciation of Johnny's dilemma, reflected: there is more than one Johnny. There is the winsome, puppy-like boy, grinning, garrulous, grateful for attention, and full of high resolve. There is the "bad" Johnny, cruel, self-centered, his chunky body rigid, "his face set in a hard expression of pure hatred like a little god of evil." Somewhere between the two was the unhappy and perplexed Johnny, impelled by conflicting drives within himself, besieged by conflicting influences from the outside.

There were the gang kids, cocky, street-wise, and seemingly invulnerable, whom Johnny could not help admiring. Though he wanted the prestige of being one of them, he didn't "fit in." There were the "good kids" at school, whom Johnny despised because he was barred from their society, but by whom he wanted to be accepted. There was the paradox of his mother, who, Johnny said, "lived like a saint," yet found lying, cheating, and chiseling from the relief bureau a necessary part of the war for survival. There were the cops, the men who stood for law and order, but who Johnny knew had their little rackets, too. Finally, there was Mr. O'Brien, Johnny's friend and the "big man" whom Johnny wanted to impress and emulate.

Mr. O'Brien realized that in giving Johnny his friendship and help he had also brought Johnny new challenges and conflicts. He realized, too, that in trying to win Johnny from the influences and effects of his environment, he was working against formidable odds.

"The more I learn about this boy and his background, the more convinced I am that it is going to be extremely difficult to achieve any betterment in him in his present environment and home situation," he wrote in his records. "It is going to be a constant fight to keep Johnny from following the pattern so well grooved by each of his brothers."

Johnny hadn't been in parochial school long when Mr. O'Brien realized that immersion in this religious atmosphere served merely to increase Johnny's anxieties and conflicts. That was revealed as a result of the following incident: One morning Johnny appeared in his classroom wearing a bracelet to which a religious medal was attached. It was exactly like some others that were on exhibit on a small table in the church. A day or two before, two altar boys had seen Johnny kneeling in prayer beside that table, and the sisters had noticed that some of the thumbtacks holding the cellophane that covered the religious trinkets had been removed. No one accused Johnny of theft, but when the sisters saw Johnny wearing the bracelet they expressed the suspicion, among themselves, that Johnny had stolen it. Later that day, when Johnny was sent to the office on some errand, the Sister Superior admired the bracelet and asked him where he had got it. Johnny flew into a rage.

"You think I stole it, don't you?" he asked.

The Sister Superior said no, she didn't believe in accusing people of things she could not prove.

"But you know I *would* steal it, don't you?" he insisted.

"I know no such thing," she said.

"Well, I would. I would," Johnny cried. "You know I would. You think I'm a crook, don't you? Everybody knows I'm a crook. I'm even a worse crook than you think I am," he told her. "I'm worse than everybody says. I steal on the outside. Don't think I wouldn't steal in church, too. I'm no good. Everybody says I'm no good."

His family had been nagging and yelling at him, he went on. They kept "throwing it up to me" that he was the only one of all the children who had ever got a "break." He went to a Catholic school, and still was no good. "Okay. I'm a crook. I'm no good," Johnny said. "I'm not going to church any more. Anyway, the church is a fake."

Speaking in a low, tense voice, Johnny told the sister how he had arrived at this conclusion. A boy he knew—he wouldn't tell his name—once heard of a sinner "way back" who took the Holy Host (communion wafer) and, in order to find out if it really contained the body and blood of Christ, desecrated it by urinating on it. Immediately blood flowed from the wafer. Then the sinner was struck dumb. So the story went. Well, the boy who had told him this story had disbelieved it, so he'd made the test himself. Nothing had happened, either to the boy or to the wafer.

He'd had an experience, too, which proved it was all a fake, Johnny went on. He had seen a photograph of what was purported to be the authentic shroud of Jesus Christ. He had been told if he looked carefully he would see the outline and imprint of Christ's body. Well, he had looked. There was nothing, nothing there.

Then Johnny told the sister something that was, perhaps, the underlying reason for his need to repudiate the church. He had committed a sin that was so terrible he had not been able to face going to confession for six or seven months. A couple of months ago he had become so worried and upset about this sin that he forced himself to go to confession. He began by telling the priest that he had not been to confession for a long time. The priest became angry. "Are you one of those boys from the parochial school?" he asked. When Johnny said: "Yes," the priest, Johnny claimed, violated the secrecy of the confessional. He had asked Johnny to give his name; then, ordering him out of the booth, he told him, in future, he was to come to confession regularly, and whenever he came he was to give his name. He would never go back. "Never!" Johnny declared. A priest wasn't supposed to ask who you were. Confession was between you and God. No priest need expect him to go in there and identify himself and then tell him all his sins. But, just the same, the awful, unconfessed sin weighed heavily on him.

The first stages of a troubled adolescence came upon Johnny while he was at the parochial school. The sisters noticed, one day, that Johnny had begun to dress very cleanly and that he was paying a great deal of attention to girls. One day he came to school so doused in perfume that the air for yards around him was saturated with the odor. Johnny was also writing notes to some of the little girls in the class. The sisters, who intercepted several, said they consisted mainly of "I love you." The trouble was, they said, that Johnny chose the "best little girls" as the objects of his attentions, and that they were "scared to death of him."

One afternoon Johnny followed a little girl he knew from her home to the grocery store. It was late and getting dark. When the child realized that Johnny was following her, she became hysterical. The next day when her mother went to school to make a complaint Johnny denied vehemently that he had meant to harm the girl. "She was one of the little girls to whom he had written 'I love you,'" the Sister Superior said.

During this period Johnny was having similar troubles at the neighborhood settlement house where Mr. O'Brien had encouraged him to go for after-school and evening recreation. Johnny never felt that he was welcome there. He made himself extremely unpopular by harassing the other children. He was especially hostile to the *good* children, who made a great point of avoiding him. He also antagonized settlement-house workers by intruding into classes and club rooms where he didn't belong. He had been asked to leave the settlement house several times, but he kept returning. He deliberately committed acts of vandalism. Once he emptied a bottle of ink on a desk, then rubbed the ink into the wood with some gravel and stones he had brought with him. On another occasion he pulled all the notices from a bulletin board and tore them into little pieces. One day, according to another complaint received by O'Brien, he walked into a meeting of Girl Scouts and broke up their gathering by exposing his genitals. When one of the workers caught him, the record states, Johnny said a boy in his gang "showed him that trick." [1] Johnny was sent to bring the boy to the settlement house. A half-hour later he returned with a small army of urchins and they stormed the building with bricks and stones. The police had to be called.

Mr. O'Brien interceded with the police and persuaded them not to take any official action on condition that Johnny would never return to the settlement house. A few weeks later, though, he went back. He was treated coldly, but was permitted to stay so long as he bothered no one. Gradually, starting in little ways, he began to misbehave again. One evening Johnny went into the office of the settlement-house director, where she had visitors. She ordered him out. A few minutes later he poked his head inside the door again. He was asked to go away. After the third time, Johnny was put out of the building and the outside door was locked. Johnny began to kick and throw himself against the door as if to break it in. When one of the workers came to chase him, Johnny slipped in through the open door, ran to the

---

[1] Johnny denied none of these allegations at the time, but some time later he was to deny, bitterly and furiously, that he had exposed his genitals. Worse than thieving or brawling, in Johnny's milieu, is the sexual offense, particularly that smacking of the "irregular," and Johnny wanted to "get this straight." That story, he declared, was one of the "dirty lies that they used to make up about me to give me a dirty name."

center of the room, and threw himself on the floor. He had to be carried out bodily.

Johnny was nearly thirteen when the Sister Superior told Mr. O'Brien that the boy could no longer be kept in parochial school. Two or three times before, she had yielded to Johnny's pleas for "one more chance," but now she had made her decision. It was final this time, not because of any new outbreak by Johnny, but for the sake of the school, and because she had become convinced that all her efforts, Mr. O'Brien's efforts, and the boy's efforts were in vain so long as he remained in his present environment.

"I don't want you to give this boy up," she told O'Brien. "I think he is trying a lot harder than we know sometimes. Often it seems he just can't help doing some of the things he does." She pointed out that, despite Johnny's many complex emotional problems, he had shown he was capable of at least "fairly good work." Indeed, on some occasions he had shown "good, quick intelligence."

She realized that Johnny's road to self-improvement was made immensely more rough because everyone—the police, the parents of the other children, and the children themselves—condemned him so much that it amounted to persecution.

The police picked Johnny up at any hour of the day or night for questioning about any delinquencies that had occurred in the neighborhood. It didn't matter whether there was direct evidence against him—he was a target of suspicion.

The parents of the children at school had overwhelmed the sister with complaints. Why did she keep that awful boy in the school? When she questioned them as to why they called him "an awful boy," the reply was usually no more specific than "Well, everybody knows he's no good, and that his family is no good."

Johnny couldn't walk down the street without being pointed out or gibed at by the other children. In the classroom he was left almost entirely alone. As for his "going straight," in talks with the sister Johnny had revealed how the boys in his neighborhood, the only companions he had, taught the younger children to lie, cheat, and steal. They stole not only because it was lucrative; in Johnny's circles it was a major form of recreation and a way to prove one's mettle. If you didn't do as the others did, you lost caste. Johnny had also indicated to the sister that there was a great deal of sex talk and sex play among the boys he knew, and that he felt guilty and uneasy about this.

She knew that during the preceding summer O'Brien, thinking in terms of possible foster-home placement, had arranged for Johnny to spend a vacation on the farm of a childless German couple who hoped to find a boy they would want to keep permanently. Johnny, missing his mother and the excitement of his street-corner life, had insisted on returning home after ten days. Just the same, the sister repeated, the only hope for Johnny's salvation lay in removing him from the environment in which he lived.

The next month, Johnny left the parochial school and went back to public school. During his first months at the public school Johnny's teachers found that he was making a tremendous effort to behave, but that he was "like a kettle of boiling water with the lid about to blow off."

Johnny managed to get through that term at school

without too much trouble, but school had not been out long before he fell into trouble with the police again, this time for breaking into a house with two other boys and stealing fifty dollars' worth of jewelry. Before he appeared in court Mr. O'Brien had a talk with Johnny. Johnny, he reported, seemed "unhappy, but stolid and apathetic, though once or twice, as we talked, he verged on tears."

Johnny did not deny the theft. The jewelry, he said, had been taken to the Widow Hatfield, a neighborhood woman, whose eighteen-year-old crippled son, who pushed himself about on a cart, was leader of a gang of smaller children. Mrs. Hatfield had told Johnny and the other boys that the jewelry was brass, not gold, but had given them a nickel apiece for it.

Mrs. Hatfield had lived in the neighborhood for years, Johnny went on. Her place was a kind of hangout. There was always a gang of kids hanging around. He had got to know her a long time ago, he said, when she had called him into her house through a window and given him lunch with her son. Within a week he had stolen a flashlight for her. He had stolen lots of other things for her after that. There had been a fancy umbrella and a camera, which he took from parked cars, and for each of which she gave him a quarter. Once, when he and some other boys had shoved a side of beef off a moving butcher's truck and taken it to her, she had given them three quarts of wine.

Sure, she bought from all the kids. Georgie Minetti had stolen a dress for her once. The dagger-like letter-opener with which she peeled potatoes had been brought to her by a kid named Micky. She never turned anyone away. The kids knew she cheated them, but when they balked she told them: "I've got enough on you to put you away." Since he had been arrested and had talked, Johnny continued, Mrs. Hatfield had been trying to get him to say he had sold the jewelry to her son, because she didn't believe the police would be hard on a crippled boy. As this confession poured out, Mr. O'Brien asked: "Even when I thought you were being a good boy, Johnny, were you stealing all the while?" Johnny, verging on tears, replied: "Yes. But lots of times I *didn't* steal because I thought of you."

At Johnny's hearing, late in August, Mr. O'Brien discussed Johnny's case with the judge and suggested that Johnny be sent to a state-supervised foster home instead of to a school for delinquents. A police officer who had known Johnny for years and had noted the improvement in his behavior during recent months also spoke for him. Johnny was sent to one of three temporary homes in the neighboring town of Baldwin where delinquents were placed until more permanent arrangements could be made for them. This was the strictest of the three homes, and Johnny was sent there because he was the toughest-looking of a group of boys who were being committed that day. Mr. O'Brien, knowing how Johnny responded to discipline, anticipated trouble, but there seemed to be no alternative solution.

A few days after Johnny's arrival at the home he ran away after becoming involved in a series of thefts from parked cars, along with two older boys from the home. In court, at Baldwin, Johnny cried continuously for three quarters of an hour. He had been treated roughly, he said, had been glared-at at the table and whipped for picking grapes from the vines in the yard. He had not wanted to stay in this place, so he had committed the thefts in the hope that he would be transferred immediately. Then he had become frightened and ran away.

The judge who heard the case ruled that Johnny had not yet had a fair trial at foster-home placement, and, recommending that another home be tried, returned him to the juvenile authorities in his own town. Early in September Johnny was sent to a second temporary foster home, run by a Mrs. Baker.

Johnny stayed at Mrs. Baker's for nearly two months while more permanent arrangements were being made for him. Except for a flurry of poor behavior during the first few days, Mr. O'Brien reported "an amazing change for the better in his personality and behavior." Mrs. Baker, whom O'Brien described as a "very loving, affectionate woman who doesn't resort to measures of strict discipline," did not send Johnny to school with the other children during his first two weeks there because she thought any day he would be transferred to another home. Mornings Johnny stayed at her side, helping her with the household chores. In the afternoons he went to a park near by to watch the ball games.

Mrs. Baker was touched by this thin, tough-looking ragamuffin, whose brittle surface seemed to melt under the warmth of attention. When he ate voraciously, she ignored his manners and praised him for his good appetite. Johnny exclaimed: "I never had such good things to eat."

Johnny had never been in such an attractive place, either. He noticed the flowered cretonne curtains at the windows, the bright oilcloth on the table where meals were served, the potted plants scattered lavishly through all the rooms. He was outraged when one of the boys spit in a flowerpot. Mrs. Baker remarked: "I've never had a boy who seemed so impressed with little touches of beauty."

Sometimes Mrs. Baker kissed him. Johnny still squirms with pleasure and embarrassment as he recalls this. "She used to kiss me in front of everybody. I used to be embarrassed. She was all right. She was nice to me."

When the state gave Johnny some clothes—a suit, underwear, and shoes, and Mrs. Baker added two brightly colored lumber jackets—Johnny was beside himself. His happiness was complete when on Sunday afternoons, well fed, well scrubbed, and well dressed, and with the money that Mrs. Baker gave him because he was such a good boy jingling in his pocket, he started for the movies. He was happy and incredulous, too, because he was getting along with the other children. "I guess they like me," he told O'Brien.

When Mrs. Baker finally sent Johnny to the neighborhood school, Johnny got along perfectly. His teacher, who sensed his need for importance, asked him to help a smaller, badly retarded youngster with his lessons. Johnny took great pains with his charge. "He ain't dumb outside school," he told Mrs. Baker. "He knows how to get along, and the kids like him. But his lessons—well, I keep trying and trying to explain it to him, but I can't get it in his head. If I tell him six apples and six apples is twelve apples, and then I asked him another question, about, maybe, eight bananas, he always gives me the answer I told him before: 'Twelve apples.' I try my best, but like I tell the teacher, there's some kids that just can't learn."

During his stay at Mrs. Baker's, Johnny often spoke of his mother, expressing love for her and saying he wanted to see her. One day Mr. O'Brien took him home for a visit. During the drive Johnny asked O'Brien about the length of his "sentence." O'Brien tried to explain the difference between an adult prison sentence and the placement of a child in a foster home, but Johnny found it difficult to understand the distinction. He was very happy where he was, he assured O'Brien, but just the same he wanted to see his mother. His eagerness, O'Brien thought, came from a mixture of affection for his mother and his pride in what a good boy he had become. He wanted a chance to show his mother.

When they got to Johnny's home, O'Brien said, Johnny's mother was wonderfully happy and excited. So was Johnny. Georgio, who had married and moved away but was visiting his mother, found the change in Johnny "almost unbelievable." He had grown and gained weight. His face was clean, his hair carefully combed. The bags had disappeared from under his eyes; he was almost handsome. David and Richie clustered around Johnny, examining and envying him his new clothes, especially his bright new lumber jacket. Johnny, who had never had so much attention from his family before, grinned happily.

But when his mother asked him to stay for supper, Johnny told her he had to get back to the Bakers'. When his mother began insisting, in a manner that formerly would have brought from Johnny an explosion of nerves or ill temper, O'Brien became a little apprehensive. But Johnny, calm, poised, perhaps a little self-important, repeated that he had decided to be back at the Bakers' for supper. Before he left, his mother tried to give him a box of chocolates. "Nah," Johnny said, "the kids at the Bakers' would eat it up in no time; better keep it for Richie and Davie and Carla." She offered him some money. "I'm not supposed to have any money," he explained, then added grandly: "Anyway, you need it more than me."

Johnny went back to the place he liked so much, but within two weeks an official order came transferring him to a farmhouse on the outskirts of town. Mrs. Baker and Mr. O'Brien both tried to have the order rescinded. They pointed out to the authorities the wonderful progress Johnny had made in his new school and home, but their plea was in vain. Mrs. Baker's home was not for permanent placements, but a way-station, and now a permanent home had been found for Johnny; it was not wise to disrupt established procedures. The authorities argued also that the steady flow of delinquent boys through Mrs. Baker's temporary home was bound to prove disturbing to Johnny.

Within three days of the time Johnny arrived at his new home on the farm he was whipped for breaking a house rule, and then ran away. He was returned to Mrs. Baker's while the situation was being investigated, but this time almost immediately ran away from Mrs. Baker's too, with another delinquent boy who had recently been placed with Mrs. Baker on a temporary basis. On the morning after his disappearance from Mrs. Baker's Johnny turned up at the police station in his own neighborhood. He pleaded to be permitted to stay at home. He knew he had been a bad boy, he said. He didn't want to be bad ever again. If they would only give him a chance, he would never get into trouble again. Please, would they let him try?

A police sergeant took Johnny before the judge who had sent him to the foster home. Johnny made a very good impression. Before he was through, the judge was smiling and nodding. He placed Johnny on probation and sent him home.

Johnny didn't go straight home from the court. He went to the school where he had been a student before his arrest and asked to be readmitted. He made a good impression there too, and was permitted to go to his class. Later that day, when Mr. O'Brien learned what had happened, he went to the school and he, Johnny, and the principal had a long talk. Johnny told them about the school near Mrs. Baker's where he had got along so well. At that school, he said, because it was so hard for him to "get" the lessons in the regular classes, he had been given a lot of "handwork" to do. He had done that well. He didn't want to go on being "dumb" in his classes. Would it be possible for him to be transferred to the vocational school where the work was mainly "handwork"?

The principal pointed out that a boy had to be fourteen to go to vocational school and that Johnny wouldn't be fourteen for several months. In addition, vocational-school work required at least a sixth-grade education. Johnny was only in the fourth grade. In Johnny's case though, the principal said, every effort would be made to arrange it. Perhaps there Johnny would find a niche into which he would fit more comfortably. In the meantime Johnny was to go back to his regular classes.

Johnny made a brave start at being a good boy. During several visits to the Rocco home following this discussion, Mr. O'Brien learned that, though the Roccos were beset with many troubles, Johnny for the first time had no part in them. Mrs. Rocco reported that he was helping around the house, that he was not staying out late nights, and that he was not associating with the known "bad boys" of the neighborhood. Johnny's school and his probation officer also gave good reports of his conduct.

But, like the bright lumber jackets he had brought back from Mrs. Baker's, Johnny's brave resolutions soon became worn and dingy: he was swallowed up again in the old familiar conditions. He became nervous and surly. The bags came back under his eyes. What little sense of dignity he had acquired disappeared.

When the day of his entry into vocational school came, Johnny was miserable in mind and body. His head was twisted to one side because of three large boils that had developed on the side of his neck, and a badly infected finger had caused a pus-pocket to form in one of his armpits, but he had not seen a doctor. He had not been in school for more than a few days when he realized that here, too, he was to be "the big jerk."

"In the carpenter work, to figure out the size of the wood or something—I couldn't do it. I didn't have the knowledge in arithmetic. They put me in the printing-room. I couldn't spell to print. In electricity, the teacher would tell the kids an' you had to write it down. I couldn't. He talked too fast. Half the time I didn't know even what he was saying.

"Yeah, nobody respected me. The principal—he was a big phony, a sneak. He thought I was dumb, but I'd know when he was making fun of me. He used to pinch me on the cheek. He talked a certain way—

"One time they had a concert up there. The girls from St. Theresa's School—they saved a bunch of seats for them in the auditorium. I went like everybody else. When everybody was there—the bastard—he got up an' he said: 'I know you girls thought Benny Goodman was coming, but he couldn't. But I've got somebody that's better.' Then he made me get up in front of everybody and bring a chair and sit in the middle of the aisle where the girls were. The dirty bitch! I don't forget. He made a fool out of me."

During the next few months Mr. O'Brien made the following entries in Johnny's case record:

John is showing some significant changes of adolescence. He has grown larger and heavier. The word "grosser" occurs to mind as descriptive of the change in him. Almost overnight, it would seem, his features have grown heavier and he has lost the occasional flash of boyishness that used to redeem his appearance. . . . There have been evident personality changes also. He is sullen and unresponsive. He merely grunts out responses to me, his mother, or Mr. Thompson [the school principal]. . . .

Mrs. Rocco continues to be very ill. Sometimes she is all puffed up about the face and swollen at the wrists and ankles. Her heart is giving her a great deal of trouble. . . . She has had several attacks of flu and has been in bed about every second day. . . .

Brother David's blood count is about one-fifth of the normal blood count. Recently he spent ten days in the hospital. He was put in the adult male ward and was quite unhappy all the time he was there. . . . The doctors say his case is hopeless, that he will die in a few months. Somehow or other this information was given in front of David and I discovered, to my horror, on one visit, that he and his mother were talking quite openly about it. It was shortly after this statement was made that the mother took him out of the hospital without permission. His condition seemed to improve markedly al-

*most as soon as he came home . . . but the other day it
was necessary for him to have a blood transfusion. . . .*

*Since Georgio's marriage, the last vestiges of control
have left this home. Not only Johnny, but his older
brothers as well, come and go as they please. . . . The
mother continues to have her usual troubles with the
welfare authorities over one of the older boys working.
On several occasions this month this family seemed to be
in actual need. I had the allotment restored by telling the
welfare department I thought the need was very real.
Perhaps one of the older boys is working, but certainly,
if he is, the money is not coming into the home. . . .*

*Since John's return from the foster home, he has not
been involved in any known delinquency, nor has there
been any suggestion that he has been verging on delinquency. . . . Yet, paradoxically, I felt more apprehensive about him than I used to when he was getting into
trouble with the police more frequently. I suppose that is
mainly because I can see his increasing resemblance to
the older Roccos.*

In August of that year, when Johnny was fourteen and
a half, he and another boy robbed a store. They were
caught by police as they left with the stolen goods, and
Johnny was sentenced to a reform school for a term of
six months. During his first month there his conduct was
so stormy he was placed in the "disciplinary cottage."

"When you get in there," Johnny says, "you got to
stand a long time with your arms folded. If you move,
they'd just as soon slug you. Other times you've got to sit
on a bench with your feet stuck out so's they're on another bench. Boy, does that hurt! Some of the masters,
they're bitches. Some of those kids got all bloody they

were beat up so much. One master there, he had a habit
. . . He put his fingers in a boy's neck, I don't know just
where, and he'd do something. . . . The boy's nose
would bleed."

When he got out of "disciplinary," the officials, having
learned of Johnny's fondness for birds, decided it might
be helpful if he were put to work in the hennery. His
work there consisted, largely, in slaughtering hens. The
method used was one in which the bird's throat is pierced
by thrusting knifelike pincers into its mouth. During one
of O'Brien's visits Johnny described this work for him in
all its "bloody detail." Coming from a boy who so many
times had expressed his love for birds, that description.
O'Brien commented, struck a "gruesome note."

Johnny also worked on a milk-delivery detail. His conduct for the remainder of his term was beyond reproach.
He earned the maximum number of credits for good work
and conduct, lost none for infractions of rules. O'Brien
noticed striking changes for the better in Johnny's appearance. He had gained height and weight, held himself
straighter, and seemed generally more attractive. But his
perfect behavior, according to Johnny, did not grow out
of miraculously achieved habits of relaxation.

"In Hartford School, Jesus Christ, how I suffered. I suffered, an' I mean I suffered," Johnny says fiercely. "I was
good all right. That was 'cause I didn't even let myself
breathe. The work part, that was all right," he goes on.
"I could move around an' I was away from the masters
an' the other kids. I wanted to be away from everybody.
I was afraid if I mixed with someone I might do something—lose my temper, or do something wrong.

"The evening. That was the worst time," Johnny continues. "In the evening when I would go back to the

cottage, the kids would be jumping around . . . fellas playing cards an' things. They'd say: 'Come on an' play.' I wouldn't. I just kept my mouth shut. I would just fold my arms, and I would leave my arms folded, an' I wouldn't even move. I was in misery, but I was scared. I had to have the points to get out of there. I had to get out of there, that's all. I can't stand being cooped up anywhere."

One day, early in November, Mr. O'Brien made one of his customary calls on the Rocco family before visiting Johnny at Hartford. David, who was now failing rapidly, had been asking to go for a drive in a car. His doctor had said, since the boy was going to die soon anyway, he should be permitted to do anything, within reason, that made him happy. When Mr. O'Brien came, David pleaded to be permitted to go along when he visited Johnny. Mr. O'Brien consented.

Although David was very happy that day, O'Brien said, his "white waxlike" face looked as though death could not be far off. Two of the reform-school instructors, sitting on the porch of the administration building when the car drove up, were visibly startled by David's appearance. When Johnny, who had been expecting Mr. O'Brien, ran up to the car and saw David, he was startled, too. His face twisted momentarily, Mr. O'Brien said, but after that he was careful to give no indication that he had noticed the change in his brother. He climbed into the car beside him and, chattering incessantly, engaged him in a conversation about their neighborhood, the public school, and the boys they knew. As the three of them sat there in the car, a group of boys in the "disciplinary line" marched by. Johnny, dipping his head in their direction, said: "Look at them. They think they're wise guys. They'll learn their lesson, just like I did."

Then turning eagerly to David, he said feelingly: "I'm through with all that stuff, Davie. I'm gonna come home an' I'm going to be a help to Ma, not a headache. Nobody's gonna get a chance to call me a crook again." David, the brother whom Johnny had always resented so bitterly, replied with vehemence: "They'd better not call you a crook in front of me. They'd better not, and me hear it." When David said that, O'Brien reported, Johnny stared at him dumbly.

David died a few days after that visit and Johnny was permitted to go home for the funeral. When he arrived, O'Brien said, his face was swollen from crying and he wept all morning at the church and later at the graveyard. He returned to Hartford worn and depressed, but eager to complete his sentence and go home for good.

On the eve of Johnny's departure from Hartford, one of the boys in his section came down with a case of mumps. "Jesus, my time was up!" Johnny exclaims. "I had to stay there three weeks more because this kid, he gets the mumps. Then two days before I was supposed to go home, another kid gets the mumps. I thought I was blowing my top." Only on his last day, despite these trying delays, did Johnny relax his terrible self-imposed discipline. "It was the first rule I broke. I light a cigarette, and I'm caught! Boy, I was scared. I mean I was *scared*— but they let me go home anyway."

Johnny's sentence to six months had stretched into more than seven. He returned to vocational school, but it was tacitly agreed by everyone concerned that there was no hope now that he would ever fit into its program.

There was nothing for Johnny to do but "wait out" the months until he was sixteen and permitted by law to leave school, or to find some job that would justify his getting special permission to leave. Johnny, who was miserable at school, tried several jobs, but none of them was satisfactory. He worked for a while as a part-time janitor in an apartment building, receiving fifty cents a day for five hours of work. He hated the job. In addition, his mother kept nagging at him. Such a job, she kept telling him, was a waste of time and did more harm than good. His earnings only cost her the free "welfare milk" the family had been receiving, and so what was being gained? He quit.

He tried working as a farm hand for a while. This job paid twelve dollars a week, and room and board. But Johnny could neither get along with the other workers nor adjust to the isolation of farm life. He quit that, too.

He was comparatively happy for two months in a woodworking shop where he had been employed on a temporary basis, but he stepped on a nail one day, injuring his foot, and had to stay at home until it was healed. When he returned, he was no longer needed. Between jobs, Johnny spent his time at school. He was not expected to go to classes. He swept floors, ran errands, or just sat around in the office.

When Johnny was fifteen and a half, Mr. O'Brien found him a job as a truck-driver's helper, and Johnny got an official release from further attendance at school. He was overjoyed. It seemed to him this job was less menial than anything he had ever done, and it would give him a certain freedom. He was elated that he would not be "cooped up." Finally, the salary was to be fifteen dollars a week, a lordly sum to Johnny. He would be able to help at home, to buy some clothes, and have a little money in his pocket besides.

O'Brien went with Johnny for his final interview about the job on a Saturday afternoon. Johnny was told to report for work on Monday morning. "Never have I seen this boy so happy and yet so poised, calm, and sure of himself," O'Brien said. "When I left him on his corner after the interview he was enthusiastically telling a group of boys of his age about his good luck." But on Monday morning Johnny was in jail. The night before, with another boy, he had broken into a store near his home and stolen twenty-one dollars.

O'Brien visited Johnny in jail a few days later. He said Johnny was pale and lifeless and looked as if he had been crying a great deal. "My first remarks to him," O'Brien continued, "brought forth a slow but continuous flow of words."

"I don't know how anyone will believe me," Johnny had said. "It wasn't like it was me at all that did those things on Sunday. Ever since I came out of Hartford, you know, I was scared to do anything wrong. If someone even mentioned Hartford or stealing it made me feel scared. It made me sick. I didn't even want to talk about it. . . . I'm scared to be locked up.

"Saturday night, I went to sleep an' everything was fine. Sunday, I woke up, and it was not me. It was just like somebody else. It was that crazy old way, back when I wanted to go out and walk around and not come home for supper or anything. . . . I knew I was going to do something bad. . . . I wanted to do something . . . to hurt people. . . ."

Johnny had got out of bed, dressed, and gone wandering around in the center of town. There he ran into a friend named Mike. They had gone into a number of penny arcades. They had tried to shake money out of the machines. When that failed, Mike had said: "Let's go snatch pocketbooks." Johnny had put him off—"I don't know why I said no"—but suggested that they meet on a certain corner that evening and "go out and break into some stores."

That night Mike didn't show up. Johnny prowled around for several hours. Then he met another boy he had known only slightly. "He told me he was going to join the Merchant Marine an' we talked about that for a while. Then we got to talking about stealing an' this an' that. He'd done it, too, from cars and everything. He said there was one store where he worked once. They always left money there on the week-end. We went over an' we got in and took it."

The police caught Johnny and the other boy as they were coming out of the store. Then, Johnny said, "a crazy thing happened. I wanted to laugh an' I laughed an' laughed. . . . I don't know what I was laughing for." After a while, though, he began to cry, and he had been crying incessantly ever since. "I don't know how it happened. Everything is all screwy," Johnny said heavily. "I'm always behind the eight-ball."

Later Mr. O'Brien discussed this occurrence with a psychologist who was familiar with Johnny's case. "The psychologist and I agreed that it was no mere coincidence that this delinquency occurred at this particular time when John was about to be incorporated into the workaday world," he wrote in his records. "Our belief was that it was related in some way to this imminency of being absorbed into a life of work in which he presumably would be protected against such likelihood of

delinquency as had existed for him in the past. We felt
as though 'the bad Johnny' within the boy had risen in
last rebellion, determined not to be thus 'saved.' In any
event we were sure that its happening just at this time,
after such a long period of good behavior, had some
special significance."

Because of Johnny's "good behavior" during the preceding months, he was again placed on probation, but he
lost the job that had been promised him. According to
O'Brien's records Johnny had two more brushes with the
police. The first occurred when he was sixteen. He went
back for forty days in Hartford Reform School voluntarily and under conditions that Mr. O'Brien protested
vigorously were prejudiced and unfair. The charge was
"violation of probation," but that, Johnny explains, was
not the real reason. There had been a wave of "breaks"
(breaking and entering) in the neighborhood. As always,
Johnny was among the first to be picked up for questioning. Mr. O'Brien protested again that it was necessary
to Johnny's rehabilitation that he not feel forever suspect. The police considered O'Brien's attitude foolish,
quixotic. Finally, Johnny recalls, Mr. O'Brien said:
"Okay. Maybe the only way to get them to leave you
alone is go back to Hartford. That way they'll see you've
got nothing to do with these breaks." A few months after
his return Johnny was questioned once more about a
theft, but was released.

Mr. O'Brien had been Johnny's counselor nearly five
years by now. At this time he left his position with the
boys' work agency and moved to another city, about
thirty miles away. They met from time to time and
O'Brien continued to keep a watchful eye on Johnny's
affairs, coming to his aid on a number of occasions. But

the old close relationship that Johnny valued so much was to taper to a close.

Since that time Johnny has worked in a wholesale fish market, a slaughterhouse, a meat-packing plant, a black-market butcher shop, as assistant to an embalmer, and in a couple of factories. "I never can get a good job," Johnny says miserably. "I can't spell. I can't even spell to write an application. My father's name—Alexander. I know it, but I can't write it down. My mother's name; Italy, the place where she was born; Humphrey Avenue, a street I lived on once—I'll be a bitch if I can write it. I can read all right. Hitler—Europe—things like that. But I can't spell. I can't be that dumb," he says significantly. "There must be something wrong.

"When I do get a job, I can't keep it," he continues. "I can't seem to stay in the same place and do the same things, all day, every day, all hemmed in. I have to feel like I can keep moving. A factory! That's captivity. I just go crazy. . . . In Hartford School I was in misery. I suffered. An' I mean I suffered. I could never stand to feel like I'm locked up. . . ." Johnny has developed an acute claustrophobia.

He has had one or two jobs that he has liked, but he didn't keep those either. Johnny cannot endure to reveal himself as fallible. On one of those jobs, whenever his employer asked him to take a package to the shipping-room and address, weigh, and stamp it, Johnny was plunged into a fever of anxiety. Sometimes he pretended he hadn't heard the order. Sometimes he managed, by devious ways, to get someone else to do it. "Plenty of times I got in positions where I'd have to write and refused. The guy would say: 'Why? Why don't you write?' I'd say: 'I don't want to, that's all.' 'Cause I couldn't,"

Johnny says angrily. "An' I couldn't tell him I was that stupid. There must be something wrong."

On another job, where he had been very happy driving a station wagon for a large industrial concern, he quarreled with another worker, who accused him of an oversight. When the quarrel came to the attention of his employer, who reprimanded him for his violent profanity, he quit—"because now I was ruined there.

"I have to do everything just right," Johnny explains. "I don't want anybody to have something on me. I try so hard, I get nervous. If somebody says something to me, if they insult me, I fly off the handle. Maybe I *am* stupid but I've got pride," Johnny says. "Nobody makes a jerk out of me.

"I don't know what's the matter," Johnny continues in a burst of exasperation. "I'm changed now. I don't steal. I don't do wrong. But they still say it. I'm always 'wrong.' Even if I'm changed, I feel like I'm guilty—like I'm not as good as the next one. Whether I done something or not, it's like—like everybody thinks I'm a crook.

"There's this teacher—the crumb! I was out of that school for years! Some kid was acting up—I've got a cousin in the class that told me: 'You want to be like Sparrow Rocco? Go to reform school?' she asks.

"This cop I know," he continues. "I won't mention names. He's the miserablest cop that ever walked—

" 'What are you doing on this corner?'

" 'Nothing.'

" 'What's your name?'

" 'Rocco.'

" 'You Sparrow Rocco?'

" 'Yeah—'

" 'Get the —— out of here,' an' he walks away.

" 'Aw ——,' I say."

And Johnny, observing a group of young men and women, members of a motorcycle club, important in their high-laced boots, goggles, bright scarves, and leather jackets, wants a "motorbike" too. He wants it with the same clamoring intensity as, when a small boy, he wanted to "keep birds."

As soon as he turned seventeen, Johnny, the last of the Rocco boys to leave home, joined the Navy. He managed to fill out the necessary applications by copying from a paper prepared for him by a friend the night before. No official information is available about Johnny's conduct during the few months he was in the Navy, but by his own accounts he was a problem.

Johnny's real troubles began when he hit a winning streak in a running crap game. "I won about a hundred an' seventeen dollars. I had a shoe box full of money." Two men whom Johnny describes as "cokeys" were among the heaviest losers. "They would go an' borrow a few bucks, an' come back an' roll the dice, an' then go and borrow again." One evening Johnny "heard the two of them, in a huddle, talking about how they would take it away from me. I took my belt," he says with deliberation, "I was just with my shorts on, but I took my belt an' I strapped it around me with all the money in it, an' I walked right past them." The "cokeys" did not accept his challenge. Instead one of them asked: " 'Will you let me have five bucks?' " Johnny was disarmed.

" 'When am I getting this back?' " he asked.

" 'Two weeks from today,' " the "cokey" replied.

Two weeks went by and "the cokey didn't pay up."

Another week passed. Johnny had warned him, "so now I had a big jam with him. Then," Johnny continues, "this other fellow comes up. He was a big sonofabitch from Duluth, Minnesota. I'll bump into that bitch yet! 'What did you hit him for?' he asks me, an' he lets me have it. . . .

"I was on the main gate then. I stood guard. Every time this fellow passed we would have words; we'd fight. It wasn't the money part—to hell with that! I wanted to show him I could lick him, because he was *wrong;* he was in the *wrong.* . . . He knocked the hell out of me all the time, but I wouldn't quit. It got so bad we were going to have a court martial. . . ." Johnny's day was saved when his sister Carla, who had married a soldier, died in childbirth, leaving Mrs. Rocco completely alone. Mrs. Rocco was ill. She petitioned the Navy for Johnny's discharge. The Navy complied quickly.

"I feel bad," Johnny says. "I feel bad about things I done. I used to cry over my brother Davie when he died. Now I only cry over my mother. I feel bad about things I done to her. . . ."

When he went into the Navy, he says, "I didn't fix it for her to get the allotment. I didn't even tell her when I was going. When I came home I *wanted* to do right. I gave her a hundred dollars from the money the Navy gave me. She just spit on the floor an' said 'Baffa anculo!' That means like 'I don't care if you are home or not.' I know she was sick, but, Jesus, she used to nag me. She nagged an' nagged me. I couldn't keep a job. I was a bum, no good. I always brought her trouble. Whenever I came in the house she used to give me hell.

"I was going with my girl, Judy, after I came home. I

loved my girl. She was the only one that ever went for me like I always wanted. I used to see her every night. When I took my girl out, I'd have to leave my mother alone. If I brought her home my mother yelled and hollered.

"My mother was plenty sick then," Johnny, as if impelled by a need for confession, continues. "She had to sit in a chair day an' night. She had heart trouble an' dropsy an' they had to give her needles to drain the water out. She was suffering all the time. Once my girl was there an' I wanted to take her to a show an' my mother said no, but I went anyway. It was raining that night. She turned the gas on. When I came home she was passed out. I feel bad. I feel bad about things I done. Even when I was a kid—even up till the day she died—for everybody—for everything—I was wrong, I was always wrong."

Johnny's mother died in the fall, about a year after he was discharged from the Navy. The next March Johnny and Judy were married. He was nineteen, she seventeen. Judy's parents were bitterly opposed to the marriage, but Judy was pregnant and they saw no other choice. Johnny's first child was born in August of that year. A few months later another baby was on the way.

For Mr. and Mrs. Necro, the marriage of their daughter Judy to Johnny Rocco was a tragedy. For Johnny it was a solemn and promising event. "I had to marry her, but that was all right. I *wanted* to marry her. If she hadn't of been innocent when I met her," he puts in stoutly, "that would be different. Because a woman that will do it before will do it after she's married, too." But Judy had been a "good kid. I *loved* her," he explains.

So important was this marriage to Johnny that he even went to confession. "I went an' I told everything. I wanted to do everything right—so our marriage would be blessed." Johnny also bought "a book about marriage . . . I couldn't read it but I gave it to my wife. I told her she should read it. She should know about those things."

Johnny felt strongly the obligations of his new status. "I want to make a nice home, have respect. I want to raise my kids right. I love my little baby." He was pleased that his baby was a girl. He hoped the new one would be a girl, too, because "a boy has a tough time. A girl, she's more in the house," Johnny says earnestly. "You can take care of a girl better. . . ."

But hand in hand with such tender aspirations came the old anger and frustration. The world, which Johnny felt had always been set against him, continued to dog him, even into his marriage. The blessedness that he sought to ensure, it seemed to him, was already leaking away. If he could, Johnny would have built a bulwark around his Judy—"the only one that ever went for me the way I always wanted"—to shut out everything that might lower him in her eyes. But he could not shut out his own fears, suspicions, and feelings of inadequacy, or his uncompromising demands for repeated proofs of Judy's unwavering regard.

"It used to be at night when I went to sleep I would think about her. In the morning I was thinking about her. She was in my mind. You know? The reason I felt so good—she was my *girl*," he explains. "She had respect for me."

That Judy's parents disapproved of him Johnny learned during his courtship. So strong was his wish for acceptance by her family that this came as a shock to him. "One night after I brought Judy home I heard her mother yelling. What she was calling me—I'm not saying, that's all." After the marriage Judy's father suggested: "Let bygones be bygones," and once in a while, Johnny says, "the old man invited me: 'Come on, Johnny, let's go see a fight.' " Mrs. Necro, too, made an effort to be pleasant. Johnny liked that; against his better judgment he wanted to trust the Necros. Then it happened again.

One evening during dinner at the Necros', the entire family decided to have an evening out. Johnny rushed home to change his shirt. When he returned the Necros were having a quarrel. "He was saying he was going to knock the hell out of her—that she took some money he put away in the drawer. She was yelling she didn't. She was calling him names. They were arguing, you know? I couldn't stay there. I *had* to get out. Because I knew," he says, with hatred, "I was going to get blamed. The next day, I'll be a bitch, they come an' accuse me that I took the money."

Johnny had protested: "May you never believe a word I ever say—Jesus, let me die the worst life there is if I took it." Nobody seemed to believe him. "I know I didn't take it," he exclaimed. "For Christ', they got me feeling as if I took it anyway. My own wife—she was standing right there. She didn't say anything. A wife is supposed to stick up for her husband!"

Things have not been the same between the Roccos since then. "My wife has hit me, an' I've hit her. She's called me a crook, too . . . I *try* to control myself. I know it isn't right to hit your wife; but I get mad. For Christ', I get so mad I have to hit the wall."

Things are not the same between Johnny and the Necros, either. He has knocked down his father-in-law.

"Him and his wife come over yelling and hollering. In my own house he calls me a yellow bastard! He says: 'Come on, Judy, I'm taking you home, but not that god-damned kid of his.' About his own grandchild, about my little baby!

". . . Once I asked my mother-in-law: 'You think your daughter is too good for me?' She said yes. I said: 'What is she that I ain't?' My mother-in-law, she says: 'She's better than you.' I said: 'I love Judy, but she's no prize. She can't cook. She can't sew. She isn't even a good wife. She's got no money. She's just like me.'"

But privately Johnny wonders. And Johnny is afraid. Every day, it seems to him, the hostile world wedges deeper into his relationship with Judy. He recognizes the futility of demanding that Judy give up her parents. "They're no good for her, an' they're no good for me. They think the worst of me. . . . Well, I don't go, but I let her go to them. The mother loves the daughter. The father loves the daughter. They all love each other," he comments bitterly. "I used to like them a lot, myself."

But Johnny is not so lenient about Judy's friends. "Near Factory Street—that's where her people live. I know that street. I used to live there myself. There's a gang of women there—I hate them worse than any bunch of slouches. They get talking about this an' that. Once my wife comes home. We have a little argument, an' she busts out crying. I ask her: 'Now what did they say?' She says: 'Everybody says you're no good.'

"My wife's just a kid! She don't do wrong things, you know, that make a husband look bad. But she's *young*. I know more about life than her—I try to teach her something. I try to tell her: 'Those women, they're bums; they're fighting with their husbands; they live a tough life; they haven't got much, an' won't have it, an' they know it.' They buzz her wrong!" Johnny exclaims. "They give her wrong advice! I *try* to explain it to her: 'They'll put you twenty years ahead in your marriage! It's no good hanging around with a bunch like that!' A young girl," Johnny cries insistently, "should be thinking about other things; she should be happy! No good!" he glowers, "she's stubborn; she's *thick—*"

Well, one thing Johnny knows, and he repeats it fiercely, insistently, and in infinite variation: "A wife should have respect for a husband. She should keep a clean home. . . ." Let Judy go to her parents, let her hang around with her gossiping girl friends, "just so's when I come home she's got the supper on the table." Even a dirty dish in the kitchen sink is an affront to Johnny. "A husband goes to work; a wife's got to do her part. . . .

"She's a funny kid. She's just a god-damned kid," Johnny muses. "If I stay home after supper, *try* to be nice, you know? An' I tell her: 'Hang up my coat,' she says: 'Do it yourself.' If I get mad—I have to get real tough—then she'll do it. Well, even if I'm disappointed—she don't find me very happy," he puts in—"sometimes I buy her something. Like tonight. I said: "Here's your valentine.' I had a little money, so I bought her a box of candy. Well," he adds roughly, "I help her eat it—"

February 1947

JOHNNY ROCCO

FOLLOW-UP: *September* 1952

SHORTLY after my return to my home city in February 1947, I received word that Johnny's first baby had died after a sudden illness. Several months later his second child, another girl, was born. Still later I was informed that Johnny's old friend O'Brien had helped him obtain a hack license and that Johnny was driving a taxi. In the spring of 1951 another daughter was born to Johnny Rocco. When I returned to the Midwestern city where Johnny lives, to talk with him again, Johnny was twenty-five years old. His wife, Judy, was twenty-three. Maude, his oldest child, was five, and Betty was one and a half.

The first impact of Johnny Rocco's personality after five and a half years was a jolting experience, despite my knowledge of him. His face, with its dark and brooding look, had perhaps settled into more mature lines, but Johnny had always looked too old for his years. The chunky, muscular body seemed even more powerful than I had remembered. There was the familiar rolling gait, the defensive stance. But all these, combined with a quality of immense control and, at the same time, Johnny's way of bolting his remarks as if anger, accumulating under pressure, escaped with compounded force, brought home a new impression: that here was a reservoir of fury and the hair-trigger possibility of violence. But soon there was the other Johnny I had come to know, too, who had protested again and again: "I'm not tough, I don't want to be tough," and out of whose glowering face there suddenly flashed a wistful and desperately engaging boy who questioned, made his overtures to understanding, and then rounded the circle again to frustration and anger.

"I'm not happy." The remark exploded out of him like a furious accusation. "I don't know what kind of a person I am. I don't get along. I feel irritated all the time. If I have to go on in life all the rest of my life like that—"

Did he have friends? Good times? "With some I get along, an' some I don't. What do you think, that I've got all enemies?"

His brothers and sisters? "I don't bother with them. Maybe only in death, at a funeral, like that." His last meeting with one of his brothers had taken place three years before, when he wanted to get into the truckdrivers' union. Johnny had appealed to his brother Antonio for guidance. Some weeks later Antonio, acting the "big man," turned up with an application for Johnny to sign; he would fill in the rest. Antonio also collected Johnny's dresser-drawer savings: "Fifty-two dollars. For the initiation," Johnny explained. Johnny didn't get into the union, and it took him six months to get his initiation fee back. "You know what my brother did. He took the money and went out to the race track and blew it all on the horses."

His relations with his in-laws were little improved. "Once in a while we go out with them, have a couple beers. I know they don't like me," Johnny stated, lest he seem to be taken in. "I used to mind. Now I don't care. But I don't forget," he added vehemently, "when I was going with her. I don't forget they accused me of stealing from their house—I remember plenty.

"Once I asked my father-in-law: 'Remember you accused me of stealing?' He said: 'That's all over.' It's not all over. I wish it was, but it's still there. I don't say I'm grouchy; I get a few laughs like the next one. I try to be nice, to forget things. I'm sitting in a bar. Everything's okay. I'm happy. You know? Then I think about something, an' Jesus Christ, it burns me. It's there, it's still there. It just lays there in my mind."

Johnny's job problem, too, was still with him. In the past five and a half years he had worked as a laborer, attendant of a parking lot, cab-driver, had driven a truck, a delivery van, and had gone to sea three times. Now he was again driving a taxi, but not in the large city where he lives. Johnny had lost his hack license there. He was driving for a private owner in a small town near by.

"I *want* to better myself. I can't get ahead. I've got nothing. I*'m* nothing. I live from day to day. I'm looking for something an' I don't find it. . . . I'm driving my taxi. I go out for it," he declared. "It's not just the money I want, but I want the money, too. I can work nine, ten hours an' bring home five dollars. How are you going to take care of a family with that? What else do I want? I want—" Johnny couldn't go on. His mouth worked and he glared with impotent rage. "Happiness," he burst out. "Happiness. I want to wake up happy."

Johnny's marital relations had improved to the extent that both he and Judy had learned to accommodate themselves to a difficult situation. Their quarrels were nòt so raw and violent as in the past. "I haven't belted her now in maybe a couple of years." But he had also given up trying to explain himself to his wife, and to re-gain that unqualified allegiance which promised so much in courtship. Johnny has the feeling that he is constantly falling short in Judy's eyes, and for this he is unforgiving. He seldom stays at home in the evenings. "After supper I go sit in a bar, I take in a show." Their sexual life is sporadic. "I don't sleep with her." He nurses old griev-ances against the temptations of weakness—to turn to Judy again. He is touchy, authoritarian, secretive. Judy knows how to hit back where it hurts the most.

"I don't talk to her. I tell her nothing—what I do, where I go. Nothing. If I have a good day or a bad day I don't like to say anything. My wife, she'll say: 'Mon-day you'll need money for the rent.' I know I need money for the rent. I don't need her to tell me. I don't talk to her because if I try to explain something, when she gets mad she throws it up to me. Plenty of times my own wife has called me a crook. 'You're no good. You're crazy,' " he quoted. " 'You can't even read or write. Your own mother didn't like you.' She's talking about when I was going with her. I feel bad. My mother was sick. I didn't buy oil for the stove."

Only two days before, on my reappearance in the city, Judy had expressed curiosity. " 'Now what does she want with you?' "

Johnny had been pleased to see me. He had a need for friendly attention. And he co-operated generously and with a touching pride, as he had on those previous occa-sions more than five years before—"to help people un-derstand other kids that have troubles like I did." But it is not so simple as all that. Judy's questions touched off anxieties that Johnny preferred to keep at bay. They not only existed in his relationship with me, but had troubled his relations with O'Brien. It was the same taunting question, it seemed to Johnny, that the neighborhood kids had asked when he was a little boy: "Why should a man like O'Brien be interested in someone like you?" And it was the same question that, despite his wish to be friendly, Johnny had once put to me: "But why *me*? Because I'm special?" And: "What's in it for you?"

Savagely Johnny had brushed Judy's question aside. "She's my friend. She's interested in me." Beyond that he would not go.

"I know," Judy had countered. "Because you were a criminal, a delinquent. Because you're an unadjusted person. That's why those people are interested in you."

As for the society in which he lives, Johnny is convinced more than ever that "everything's a racket." He wouldn't steal again, he said with aggressive bluntness, "because I'm afraid of being caught." The mere thought of being confined in a prison again makes him sweat. "I want to be good. I want to be so good," he exclaimed with urgency, "I would never do anything wrong. I wouldn't smoke. Drink. I wouldn't go out nights. Nothing. Because if I ever do wrong again—to be locked up— I would—" He made a violent and distraught gesture. "They would have to put me in a mental institution."

But there is vindication for Johnny in lawfulness, too. With the exception of a few traffic violations, Johnny's police record shows no court appearances since he was sixteen. The nickname Sparrow, which he despised, has faded from the memory of the neighborhood, and Johnny is no longer driven from street corners by policemen. Ironically, nowadays, the situation is somewhat reversed. "*I'm clean*," he glowers. And it is Johnny, a beat-up angel with flaming sword, who polices his world and discovers at every turn, with a bitter and cynical triumph, that there is no honest man.

In the neighborhood club where he spends many evenings, "a bunch of fellows there, *they* pull crooked deals. Just last week they did a hi-jacking. I wouldn't touch it, but I wouldn't squeal on them either."

There were those commonplace practices of cabdrivers: "Plenty of times they will take a fifty for a five. . . . I wouldn't roll a drunk," Johnny declared, "but I'll tell you the truth—I've 'short-changed,' myself."

There were the crooked ward heelers, the system of bribes. "If you want a better job, maybe a civil service, it's 'Who do you know? How much have you got?'" Even Eddie, a respectable man for whom Johnny ran the parking lot. "A man maybe leaves his car. Moving it, Eddie bangs a fender. The man comes back. 'What happened to my fender?' This Eddie, he can talk all around you," Johnny said, not without admiration. "First thing he's got the owner thinking that dent was there all the time. I *like* him," Johnny stated, "but that's not what you'd call exactly reliable either."

There were the bars where cab-drivers gather in the small hours of the morning. "Saturday, twelve o'clock midnight, they should be closed till Monday morning. That's the law in this town. And cops! Crooks!" Johnny amended. "I see them come in, four, five of them. They hang around in the barrooms. Sunday mornings. They get drunk. They gamble. I see them take money off pimps and hustlers. They take their pay right on the spot. I've been shook down myself."

Johnny was driving a delivery truck when one day his car and another hooked bumpers. After the cars were disengaged a policeman came over and wanted to see his papers. Johnny had all the necessary papers for the truck, but he had left his own driver's license at home.

The policeman shook his head. " 'I can prove I'm John Rocco,' I told him. 'Just a phone call. Or let me go get my license.' 'You're in hot water,' he says, an' he tells me meet him ten thirty tomorrow with my license."

The next day Johnny returned with his license. " 'I hope there's no trouble,' I said. He says: 'If the station finds out, it's gonna go hard with you,' an' he starts hinting around that ten dollars will fix it up."

Johnny was fuming as he went on with his story. "I said: 'Jesus, all I've got is five dollars—less than five.' He says: 'I've got kids to feed.' I tell him: 'What in hell do you think I've got?' I tell him: 'I'll give you three. Jesus,' I says, 'I need a couple bucks in my pocket.' He says: 'I'll take what you got.' He takes every penny from me."

But the real pay-off came that evening when Johnny was describing this incident to a couple of other drivers and he learned that he had been twice a sucker. "It wasn't even a fix," he raged. "Because if you're driving for a company—a cab or a truck or like that—if you don't have it with you, you're supposed to have twenty-four hours to produce your license.

"I had a cop once challenge me," Johnny continued. "I've seen that pig drunk more than once." The policeman had joined a poker game in the neighborhood club. By three or four in the morning most of the men had quit. "I was going to quit, too," Johnny said. "The game was over. He says: 'Let's play showdown.'

"I said: 'What for? You won an' I won. I'm satisfied.'

" 'Let's play showdown,' he says.

"I told him: 'I don't want to play showdown with you.' Then he says: 'Let's go for a drink.' I didn't want

to drink with him either, so he left. When he went out I
said: 'I'd like to kill that ——, I'd like to ——.' I was
cursing him out. It got back to him. A couple of days
later I'm driving an' he stops me.

" 'You say you want to fight me?'

" 'Sure.'

" 'Now?' he says.

"I said: 'Are you kidding?'

" 'Get your ass out of that car,' he says, 'an' I'll take
you on.' "

Johnny appealed to me. "I couldn't fight him. It burns
me. I said: 'With what you've got in your car an' on your
side, I'd be dead. I'd be in the pen for striking an officer.
I know you've got the drop on me.' That burns me."

Johnny can forgive the barroom proprietors, the chiselers, thieves and hi-jackers, even the pimps and hustlers, "but a cop—maybe he's not supposed to be better
than anybody else, but he's supposed to abide by the law
more than the next one." He ticked off the policeman's
offenses: "Playing cards with me, that's against the law.
Going in bars Sunday morning. *That's* against the law.
He takes money from the hustlers. He was driving his
car drunk. . . . I can't stand it to have somebody pull
their superiority when I know they're doing worse than
I am. Dirt—dirt. . . . We see each other now an' give
each other dagger eyes, but I know he's got the drop
on me."

One of Johnny's greatest worries has to do with the
frequency with which he changes jobs. "It's not the work.
I like to work. If I have a boss that respects me, I'll work
my—I'll work *hard*," he substituted. Some jobs, like
"pick-and-shovel work," he admitted he didn't like.
"Other things, I *know* I could do them, but I'm afraid to

go after them; I can't even write the application." He
had liked working on the ships, and that paid well, but
"I missed my kids." He had enjoyed running the parking
lot. "Eddie, this fellow that built it up, he was nice. He
was good to me. He didn't pay me much, but he liked
me." But too much of a good thing had made Johnny
fidgety, too.

Eddie had helped him to get the motorcycle he had
wanted for so long. Each week he deducted something
from Johnny's salary toward the down payment, and
added some money of his own, "so he could ride it, too."
He let Johnny use his car. "He was good to me," Johnny
repeated, "but he was the kind of a fellow that likes to
call you up at home every night just to talk. 'Did you get
home okay?' That would be when he let me use his car,"
Johnny put in with a rare grin. "Or 'How are things?'
'Okay, okay,' I would say. 'Now what in the hell are you
calling me up for now?' Sundays," Johnny continued,
"he liked to call up an' have the husbands and wives get
together an' go for a ride in the car. He liked to pal
around with me alone, too. His biggest hobby was to go
to a movie and eat hamburger. I don't go for that, that's
all." When the motorcycle came "he wanted to ride in
the back with me all the time. He could have it any time
he wanted." And: "I *liked* him," Johnny protested. And:
"He wasn't a queer, if that's what you think. He just
liked to hang around with me all the time. I don't care
for that. I don't go for it, that's all."

Then there was Johnny's quick eye for a disparagement
which spoiled so many jobs. "If somebody, like, insults
me—I can't let it go." There was his burning sense of
injustice. And there were the mysteries of human relations.

A fist fight with a fellow cab-driver precipitated the loss of his hack license. At the hearing at the Hack Bureau, Johnny's old police record was brought up. Johnny argued: "But I haven't had anything brought against me since I was a kid. . . . 'License revoked,' " he quoted. " 'The matter is closed.' "

He had gone sour on another job after this occurrence. He was driving for a man named Lorenzi who owned two cabs. Johnny's first fare one evening was Lorenzi's nineteen-year-old daughter and her boy friend, a soldier. "They were having a fight. He starts slapping her around. I warned him: 'Cut it out,' but he keeps on belting her." Johnny stopped the car and told them, "If you're going to fight, it's not my business, but you can't do it in my cab." The girl stumbled out, the man following her, "an' he starts hitting her again, right on the street!" For a moment Johnny was torn by an impulse to drive away. Then he stepped out of the cab and knocked the soldier down.

Many things about this incident still perplex and agitate him. Was he right to "protect" the girl? "I know it wasn't my business, but I can't stand to see somebody knocked around. He was hitting her *hard*. She was *crying*— I know I've done it myself," he put in, defensively, "but my wife has hit me, too. An' he wasn't even married to her."

Of Lorenzi he spoke with biting indignation: "When I told him: 'I got hurt protecting your daughter,' 'To hell with her,' he says. What kind of a father is that?"

And: "It cost me money. I hurt my hand. I lost three weeks' work. A man like that, he could have said: 'You protected my daughter. I can't pay you what you would make, but here's a few dollars to help out with your family.' "

But what perplexes and agitates Johnny most is the suddenness of his temper, with its complete blackouts of control. "When I get mad like that, I don't know what I'm doing. . . ." Johnny is literally afraid of his own strength.

"That time I floored my father-in-law—an' he's a young man, strong—I split his mouth. His eye was cut. He was bleeding. I took pity on him myself." The soldier, Johnny continued, lost three teeth with his one blow. "I broke a bone in my hand, an' I didn't even know it. I *must* of hit him hard to do that. I'll tell you the truth," he confided, "I'm afraid of what I might do."

For most of his outbursts Johnny can show provocation. But only a short time ago something had happened that seemed to happen by itself, that he couldn't explain at all. He was walking on a deserted street late one night, smoking a cigarette, when a drunk loomed out of the darkness. He asked Johnny for the butt. Johnny had been startled. In addition, he said, he has a feeling of revulsion for "lushes." Still he had thought that he was taking the situation in stride. "I wouldn't give him a butt. I took out the pack. I gave him a whole." But as the man reached for the cigarette he suddenly lurched toward Johnny. The next thing Johnny knew, he heard the crack of a head on cement, and the man was lying in a pool of blood. "I don't know why I hit him—it was the way he moved, all of a sudden like that—I got scared. Do you remember that test they gave me," he asked a little later, "the one where they strap all those things on?" He was speaking of the electroencephalogram test that he took when he was a boy. "Is that," he asked, too non-chalantly, "to see if you are crazy?"

On the face of it, this was the same Johnny I had known before, fearful, angry, suspicious, and with the bitter, cynical pall that overcast everything, enveloping even his old friend O'Brien. So prone was Johnny to the expectation of rejection that he seemed unable to assess even the obvious external circumstances that had finally severed his relations with O'Brien. Johnny could see only an abandonment, and he gnawed these questions over and over again: Could O'Brien ever have been truly his friend? Could he have liked him for himself? Then what were his real motives? He argued: "He helped me, yes, but he got *paid* to see me." And: "I gave him knowledge. He was studying me. He's a big man now. Now he has no use for me."

Even the promise left him by O'Brien, an image of a better life than this, it seemed to Johnny, had served only to mislead him. "When I was a kid, those talks we used to have—'If you try hard, be honest, work'—they used to give me hope. I'm big now. Nothing! Nothing's produced!"

Yet Johnny had never given up that promise. And he was also able to talk like this: "He did a lot for me. He was like a father to me. If it wasn't for him I'd be a criminal today. . . . I know he's a busy man. He lives far.[2] It's my fault, too. I guess I've got—" he grappled for the word—"an inferiority. Because if I want to write a letter, keep up a friend, I'm ashamed. I have to ask my wife— I *want* to make something out of myself, have respect—I don't know if I can do it. I guess I try too hard to be liked. When I was a kid I always wanted to be in a

[2] O'Brien now lives in another state.

nice crowd, get in with them. You know? If they didn't like me, it used to get me mad. . . ."

More than this, more than Johnny himself realizes or can give himself credit for, he has achieved something of the respectability and of the satisfactions in life for which he always hankered. That there have been no further flare-ups of stealing, even though at the possible cost of other controls, is worthy of note. Despite his work difficulties, he has managed to meet his economic responsibilities to his family. Johnny, his wife, and his two children live in the four-room half of a two-family frame house. It is true that the cooking is done by kerosene and the neighborhood is humble, but the street is pleasantly clean and his home is far above the type of slum into which the large family of Roccos were crowded when he was a little boy.

Nor was his marriage without covert joys.

In spite of his angry accounts of difficulties with Judy, Johnny's dark eyes glowed when I commented on the tidiness of his house, his pretty wife and attractive children. "She keeps a nice home. I couldn't stand a dirty home," he said with stony pride. Then, in a burst of confidence: "We don't get along, but I don't by any means mean my wife is bad. She's the mother of my kids. She's *good*. I know I get her mad all the time. I don't treat her good. I don't talk to her, I keep a grudge, I'm grouchy. She's mad," he added, "because I don't stay home nights. She nags me a little, too—she wants security. I don't blame her. I'd like to have security myself, regular pay, a chance to go some place. . . . Well," he continued, "I try to do my part.

"When my little baby died," Johnny said, "the undertaker told me: 'It's not the same as a grown-up person.

You can have a plain box.' I told him no. It was my kid. I wanted her laid out right. . . ."

He had bought a "parlor set," a new stove for the kitchen—"the one the landlord gave us, that was just a piece of junk." A couple of years ago he had painted the kitchen and bathroom. Now they needed paint again. He had done nothing about that yet, which made him feel guilty; but on the back porch was a plastic wading pool, "so my kids can cool off when it's hot. When I sold my motorbike," he added with a touch of self-importance, "I bought a TV for the home." Getting that motorcycle had brought him satisfaction—"it was the first thing I ever got that I wanted, except for little things"—but he hadn't liked the motorcycle crowd. "They were too fast. They were heavy drinkers. An' reckless! The girls—when you find a girl like that, she's worse than the boys." Besides, he had a hard time keeping up the payments; his wife was complaining. And motorcycling was dangerous. "I saw two people killed. When I was a kid I didn't care how reckless I went, but now I'm older. I have to think twice about things. I have to think about my family."

When Johnny talks about his contributions to his home, his spirits rise. When he talks about his children, especially five-year-old Maude, he is an almost happy man. "She's smart. She likes friends. She wants to play with them all the time. She talks a lot. She's just a nice, normal girl. . . .

"She *wants* to go to kindergarten. She's not afraid, but she's been talking to her friend, Mary. Mary is six. She's a little dominating. I've watched them," Johnny put in, "but Maudie takes care of herself pretty good. Mary told her the nuns are too strict. She was a *little* worried, but she wants to go to school."

Had Maude asked about the facts of life? Johnny's first reaction, as if this question suggested a poor opinion of Maude and perhaps of himself as well, was to bristle: "She's a little young for that yet, isn't she? If she asks me, I'll tell her you buy them in the hospital." But on second thought he permitted himself to relax. "I think she knows *something*." He smiled reflectively. "Once she says to me: 'The girl across the street, she can't be married yet. She hasn't got a big belly.' I asked her: 'How do you get a big belly?' " Johnny's eyes were absolutely merry. " 'From eating too much,' she tells me.

"When I'm going out, she'll say: 'Where are you going, Daddy?' Sometimes I don't answer. Then she says: 'I know. You're going for a beer.' She hears my wife complaining I don't stay home," he went on. "I say: 'All right. Is it all right with you?' She's cute. Sometimes she's a little fresh, but she's cute.

"That's another thing I hold against my wife." Johnny retraced his thoughts to pick up that dropped thread. "She insults me something terrible in front of the kids. I tell her, 'For Christ', if you have to tell me something, don't tell me in front of the children; if we *have* to argue, why do you bring it out so the kids will hear?' Is it bad," Johnny asked anxiously, "when a father goes out every night?" And: "Is it bad if you lose your temper with a kid? She loves me, my Maudie. She hugs me an' kisses me. She's not afraid. She's afraid of me at times," he corrected, "like when I tell her to keep quiet. I can't stand it when a kid is fresh to me. . . . Well, even if I lose my temper, when she's in bed I go in to her. 'Do you

want to kiss Daddy good night?' I know the answer will
be no, but I ask her. I grab her an' kiss her anyway. I
want to show her I love her even if I was mad."

Another source of friction in the Rocco household is
Johnny's feeling that Judy shows partiality for the baby.
"When I lost the first one, well, she was still young. Then
Maudie was born. Maudie *grew* on me. I love both my
kids," Johnny said defensively, "an' I know my kids love
me. But the older one—she *gets* me."

So strongly does she "get" him that, as if standing in
Maudie's shoes, Johnny grows fretful and irritable because "the younger one, she's in my wife's arms all the
time. Before the other one was born"—Johnny never
refers to the baby by name—"my wife just catered to
Maudie. You can't love a kid so many years and then,
when you get another one, not have time for her. You
can do it," he cried belligerently, "but it isn't good for
her. Maudie's jealous! Even if she's older, Maudie *likes*
to be petted. . . ."

Johnny talked long and hard and intensely. He shut-
tled from Maudie to himself when he was a little boy,
and back and forth again. He remembered his difficulties
at home. "A kid, if he turns against the home, he's got
nothing. A kid should be taught a home is a place to get
love, understanding. My Maudie, she gets more love in a
year than I got in my whole life. When I was a kid it used
to take me three, four hours to beg for one dime. To go
to a show—*I* had to suffer for it. I treat my kid to an
allowance, a nickel a day. Sometimes I treat her to a
dime. I hug my Maudie; I hug her an' kiss her. In my
whole life I don't remember my mother to kiss me."

He remembered experiences in schools, on the streets,
and experiences with doctors, hospitals. When he was

about ten he was playing along the river one summer day. Other boys were swimming, but he didn't want to go in. The water was too dirty. Johnny's older cousin, Rico, ordered him to dive in. When he refused, Rico picked him up and threw him in. "I must of hit something. My leg was laid open. I was drowning. They had to pull me out." Johnny showed me the deep scar along the kneecap of his chunky, hairy leg. It was still an angry red.

Johnny had gone into the water thrashing, cursing, and crying. Wet, streaked with blood, dirt, and grease from the river, he was still struggling, crying, and spewing obscenities when, imprisoned in Rico's arms, he was brought into the emergency ward of the city hospital. Johnny knows he wasn't a pretty sight. Still, he cannot refrain from protesting: "I was just a kid. . . .

"The interns looked at me. They just looked an' walked away. They were arguing who was going to do it! I was hurt, mad. . . ." When another intern came up, Johnny gave him the full measure of his wrath. " 'I'm not bothering with you,' he says, an' *he* walks away. Later, Johnny continued, "they just threw me on a table like I'm a sack of dirt. They sewed up my leg without even an anesthetic."

Johnny remained in the hospital for three weeks. "I was crying all the time. My leg was strapped to a board so it wouldn't bend. It was hurting me something terrible. This nurse, she was one of those mean bitches, she would come in an' say: 'If you don't behave yourself I'm gonna give you a needle.' " He cried so much he had to be moved into a private room where he wouldn't disturb other patients. There, though his leg injury mended, other hurts remained. The thing for which Johnny cried the most (and perhaps has never stopped crying) was no more to be had in a busy, impersonal free hospital than in a crowded, anxiety-driven home. "I was hurt—mad. . . . Nobody talked to me. I was all alone." He needed no books to know this—"all you've got to know is the fundamentals! A kid isn't supposed to be abused."

Well, things were going to be different for his kids. He was there to see to that. Only the other day Maudie had "a little fever." He called the doctor. Maudie is a pert, spunky little girl. In my brief conversation with her she did not strike me as a child who would be overly afraid of a doctor. But Johnny was at the door when the doctor arrived. "I took his hat. I told him: 'She's a little afraid of doctors. Her name is Maudie.' "

Johnny was close at the doctor's heels as he went in to Maudie. No word or gesture that followed between the doctor and his child escaped his watchful attention. "The doctor said: 'Hello, Maudie—' He was making out like he knew her name. He took her temperature. . . . He was nice. Then he said: 'Can you take medicine?' He was going to leave her some penicillin pills. Maudie said sure, she could take medicine."

In all our talks Johnny has never laughed aloud. But as he recounted this conversation he flushed, his eyes glowed, and a slow smile that seemed to start somewhere at his center gave his face almost a look of gradual diffusion. "She was showing off a little bit. She's cute. That kid," he remarked, "won't take medicine in any shape! I told him: 'Doctor, she won't take medicine.' He said: 'Do you want me to give her an injection?' "

Johnny went on to describe how, playfully, the doctor told Maudie he was "putting a dime on her little fanny" while he rubbed a spot with alcohol, and how "the first thing, it was over! He handled her fine." Any kindness to Maudie was a kindness to Johnny. If Maudie was a credit, he was a credit, too. If Maudie was winsome, charming, then Johnny was likable, too. It was as if in Maudie lay, not only the possibility of correction of all the indignities of his own childhood, but even of restitution. "All it takes," Johnny declared with urgency, "is a little bit of kindness. All you need—you just have to use a little psychology. Yeah," he added, "an' money. Money talks."

And yet it was not that simple. There were so many conflicts, paradoxes, so many irreconcilables. Beginning within himself, and in the minutiæ of his everyday life, they radiated outward until they encompassed his whole world. The question of spankings, for instance, distresses Johnny, as any suggestion of violence must do. But there was an additional, a moral question that had attached itself to this. "When my wife punishes Maudie—I don't know what it is. I can't stand it to see my wife punish her. But sometimes I give her a worse spanking than my wife. . . ."

There was his sense of sin and guilt. "I know the difference between right an' wrong. I feel guilty to myself about a lot of things. I've committed adultery too, plenty, since I'm a married man." This was troublesome enough, but whenever Johnny thinks about his adulteries anxiety is compounded by anxiety: "What if Judy committed adultery, too?

"I don't know why I think about that," Johnny exclaimed. "I *know* my wife is good!" But even as he said this, he became distraught. "That's one thing— A woman that will do that! I would leave her!" And then there was that nagging sense of contradiction: "But I've done it— I do it myself!"

There were dilemmas like this one. "There's a kid in my neighborhood. She sits on the sidewalk alone. She lives with her grandfather, an' the son, her father, he lives upstairs with his second wife. They mistreat that kid something awful. Well, I told Maudie to play with her."

But Maudie came home with lice in her hair. Judy was furious and Johnny couldn't blame her. "I had to tell Maudie: 'Better not play with her.'" But that didn't seem right either. "It makes me feel bad. I feel bad. Nothing," he declared, "is so bad as a lonely kid." And "Is that," he asked earnestly, "what makes a girl go wrong?"

Five years before, when I had talked with Johnny, the girl who was "a tramp" was an object beneath contempt. He had looked on the Negro with his legendary virility and "animal" ways with an almost superstitious revulsion. Jews, too, were peculiar. They were "rich," "stingy," and possessed of an almost preternatural shrewdness. "You got to look out for them. They cheat you all the time."

Johnny still had "no use for tramps." He wanted that understood. Yet he had found something of warmth and companionship with some "loose" girls he has known, and now the little girl who "sits on the sidewalk alone"; a woman who gave him friendship as well as sexual gratification; girls he knew and condemned when he was an adolescent, all sometimes merge in Johnny's mind and set him to pondering.

He talked about prejudice, too—prejudice against Negroes, Jews—and about brutalities he had witnessed. It was confused and arduous talk in which Johnny's accustomed attitudes battled with his own logic and with his concepts of right and wrong. He still sometimes felt "a little funny about Jews," though "an Italian will cheat you, too." And he still "wouldn't want to live next door to 'a colored' "; but of one thing he was certain: "It's wrong to push somebody around, to be against him just because you don't like his face or his religion or something."

When he shipped to Brussels in 1951, he had observed that "the people there are not so prejudiced against foreigners like me, although they're very prejudiced against the Americans. Over here" (he was referring to his own little world) "it's Guineas! Everything is Guineas! I've got prejudice myself. I know it's wrong. But cops, politicians—the Irish! They're cheap! They take advantage! They're drunks, too. Although Flannagan," he granted, "he's a cop that lives on my street—he's a nice fellow."

There was also that paradoxical world of law and order, so much like a part of him, and in which both law and corruption could be bound up in a single policeman. Johnny's city is traditionally Democratic and traditionally corrupt. The presidential conventions had only recently taken place. The air was filled with talk about dishonest government, graft, and corruption. Johnny had been listening to speeches on radio and television. "Maybe," he said, "it would be better if the Republicans got in. As bad as they are, maybe the Republicans would be more honest. Because a Democrat—" he spoke haltingly, searching for the words that would make his thought come clear— "they started at the *bottom*; they're from the wrong side of the tracks. All they know is how to cheat an' connive. The Democrats, they *had* to cheat an' connive to get so high in politics. With the Republicans—they've been up there all the time. Maybe with the Republicans it would be better, more honest—"

Finally there was his complaint about the church,

which, like his own autocratic conscience, "laid down the law but didn't explain in English."

". . . I know I don't believe in the Catholic Church the way you're supposed to, but I believe in *good*, I have faith. I know if you do wrong, you're gonna pay for it. But sometimes I wish I was brought up in another religion. With the Catholic Church, you go to church an' the priest is talking in Latin. You sit in the house of God, but it would be better if they talked in English. It would be better if they would explain different things—people need somebody to explain. In the Catholic Church," he remarked, "everything is a sin."

Johnny's difficulties in writing and spelling have always been a major preoccupation. But now he spoke of "education" as of that other religion in which he wished he had been brought up. It was as if all his dilemmas were dramatized in this problem. "Do you think if I'd of had an education I would be a nice person?" he asked. And ". . . you can always tell when you see an educated person. They look clean-cut. Educated people *must* be happy."

Johnny has not been without opportunities in recent years. Five years before, at the time of our first set of interviews, he had been offered tutoring, but there was Johnny's painful sense of inadequacy. Even more arresting was his ferocious pride. He had accepted eagerly; but to Johnny, being a Rocco, or a thief, or unable to write and spell—all seemed to have the same humiliating weight, and he had been no more able to expose himself to a teacher than to avail himself, by confession, of the absolution offered by his church.

Yet Johnny had not been idle. The obscenities that had

so aggressively peppered his speech in the past were markedly reduced. He was showing an enhanced sense of the fitness of things. Many times when he was sitting in a bar with a girl, he took the trouble to tell me, he had been forced to call out: "Watch yourself! I'm sitting with a lady."

His vocabulary was miraculously improved. Such words as "fundamental," "produced," "psychology," "dominating," if used with self-consciousness, were also used with real comprehension.

On my last evening in the city we took a walk together. He was in a trustful, expansive mood. He spoke of an interest in "history," a desire for "knowledge." He recited the major facts in the life of Abraham Lincoln. "I like to sit down an' hear somebody talk on things in the past. TV," he acknowledged, "has done a good bit for me."

He spoke again about his trip to Brussels. "I enjoyed it very much there. I saw the sights. I saw the Mene— the—" He was referring to the Manneke-Pis, the famous fountain sculpture of a little boy urinating. He had taken the trouble to memorize that name, but now the pronunciation escaped him. "The people there," he commented, "they're more broad-minded there."

He demonstrated his reading ability on a display card in a music-shop window: "Barbirolli . . . Flagstad . . ." He did surprisingly well. He summarized an article he had read "about the cemetery racket. They're trying to correct that," he said. He confided his dream of glory, "to be able to write an application, a letter—not to have to ask my wife; to have a job where, if I have to write something down, not have to be ashamed; to have some books or papers to take when I go home at night. . . ."

At one point he asked me: "Do you think my speech is improved?" He showed me his bitten fingernails: "Is it a bad sign to bite your nails?" He described several Italian films he had seen: *Pagliacci, Open City, Shoe Shine*. He remembered particularly a sequence in *Paisan* in which a ragged boy steals a pair of shoes from a Negro soldier. He was highly pleased when I remarked that the Italians were making some of the finest films in the world. He asked: "Do you think I've got good taste?"

Before we said good-by, Johnny himself raised the question of outside help. He would not go to a "foreigners' class" in his neighborhood, because "a lot of people around here know me." Besides, he wasn't "that dumb. I'm good enough to pass the registration to vote. That's all they teach you in the 'citizen classes.'" He rejected the idea of a regular adult education class, too. He labored to explain. "Different people, they know different amounts. I have to start from the bottom. I need somebody that will show me the fundamentals—that will explain by the syllables." He wanted to know whether the tutoring we had once offered him was still available. When asked if he could make some contribution toward the cost, he nodded gravely. "I think so," he said with dignity. He made only one stipulation: that any correspondence having to do with this need of his for schooling be sent by registered mail. He did not want this secret to fall into the hands of his wife.

That was in September. Early in October Johnny was notified that if he would go to see a Miss Young at the psychological clinic near by, he could make the arrangements for the lessons he wanted. Late that month I received word that Johnny had gone to see Miss Young, but failed to find her, "and then had a couple of other miscarriages." Miss Young would now take the lead and invite him to come back. Whether Johnny would make this contact or, after making it, would be able to follow through is still a large question in the minds of those who are familiar with his history and problems. But in November I received, for the first time, a letter written by Johnny:

Dear Mrs. Evans: I do hope this letter finds you in best of heath [struck out] heatlh as for myself of [struck out] and family are fine. I recieved a letter from Miss Young today and I will get in touch with her tomorrow. sorry I did not write sooner. I am writing this letter alone and I am copying from [struck out] from a spelling book. not bad?

It is not necessary to send registered letter because I donot mind my wife rieding them. When you write send it regyl [struck out] regular mail, so it willnot cost [struck out] cost you so much money.

I am saying [struck out] staying home at night and feel much better now. business is not veyr [struck out] good I do hope I can pay for the lessons I am anxious to begin as soon as possible. I would like to say more but [struck out] but my spelling. Untill [struck out] until I hear from you

Good luck
John Rocco

THREE   MEN

WILLIAM MILLER

A<small>T</small> about one a.m. on Wednesday, January 19, 1949, William Miller, forty, who had begun going blind six years before and had been totally blind for the past two and one half years, woke up in his second-floor furnished room with a dreadful headache. The sharp pain, just above his eyes, was so severe "it felt like something splintering inside my skull." He saw "millions of tiny pinhead blue dots," which grew larger and whirled into wide, colorful circles, "orange and blue and red, like fire." When he thinks of it now, what he saw that night reminds him of "some kind of spectacle, like a big celebration, with fireworks." But at that time, he points out, "I was in terrible pain, and I was scared. I was frightened in a way I've never been frightened before."

Miller fumbled for his Braille watch, which he always keeps under his pillow at night, partly for convenience, partly for company. ("I love to hear the motion inside my watch. It's like something alive. I just seem to cuddle that thing.") Moving gingerly, the watch gripped in his palm, Miller inched his legs over the side of the bed and sat up. He felt for the time: it was one thirty.

"So much seemed to be happening inside my head, I was almost listening to it. The headache seemed to lighten up as the circles got bigger and bigger. Then I noticed a change in my darkness. I got up."

Miller has no idea how long he stood there. He was still in considerable pain, and his head was full of color and whirling motion. Then everything seemed to slow down, melt, begin to condense into images, and he saw, swimmingly, "squares with light in them beginning to take form in front of my eyes."

"The squares got closer and brighter," Miller continued. "Even before I recognized what they were, they reminded me of lights in windows at night. My bed stands alongside a window and I was looking out. I began to shiver and shake and I got the damnedest cold sweat. I started to cry. I didn't know what was happening. I had been told I would never see again, and I realized I could see."

Miller didn't test his vision further by turning on the light in his room. He knew where the switch was "in case I ever had company," he explained, but he was afraid a false move might plunge him back into darkness. He let himself down to a sitting position on the edge of his bed and, pulling the bedclothes over his shoulders, waited.

As the day came in he saw, for the first time, what his room was like. It was a small, neat room—he prides himself on his neatness. There was a table, a chair with wooden arms, an old-fashioned chiffonier with a white embroidered scarf on it. The ceiling and woodwork were white. The walls were powder blue.

He picked up the *Matilda Ziegler Magazine*, in which, the night before, he had been reading an article on the successful blind. His eyes could make nothing of the curious-looking raised dots. He closed his eyes, read a fragment with his fingers, put the magazine down again. He opened his left hand, in which his watch was still gripped, felt for the raised dots, glanced down, and saw with a start that the watch had numerals as well as Braille by which to tell the time. It was six forty-five.

Miller dressed hurriedly. He knocked against the side of the door in his hurry to get downstairs. At the head of the stairs he was horrified, they looked so narrow and steep. He went back to his room, grabbed his cane, closed his eyes, and, "like a blind man," went downstairs and into the kitchen, where his landlady, Mrs. Rudolph Canzoneri, was preparing breakfast.

"Mrs. Canzoneri," Miller cried, "I can see."

Mrs. Canzoneri ran into the hall and yelled to her husband, who was dressing in the bedroom. "Rudy, come here. Quick. William can see."

Rudolph Canzoneri, buttoning his pants and followed by the nine Canzoneri children, rushed into the room. He grabbed Miller by the shoulders, turned him to the light, and looked searchingly into his eyes. He shoved a hand, the fingers spread wide, in front of Miller's face.

"How many fingers?" he demanded.

Miller backed away, focused, and told him: "Five."

Canzoneri held up two fingers. "How many?" Then ten, eight, and then one. "What color is my shirt?" he challenged. "What's that?" he asked, pointing to the family cat. He took Miller by the arm and propelled him to the back door. "What's out there?"

"Well, fer Chris' sake," he commented when Miller had passed all the tests.

Miller was too excited to eat breakfast, but set out immediately for the Institute for the Training and Rehabilitation of the Blind, where for the past eight weeks he had been undergoing training in adjustment to blindness. Only two days before, he had made the trip alone by bus for the first time, but now he didn't trust himself to try again. Nor did he trust to his vision, which opened him up to a too opulent and confusing juxtaposition of impressions. Sunlight, color, and movement filled him with an excitement very like terror. Eyes closed tightly and right hand conscientiously placed in correct position with index finger along the shaft of his cane, he started by the "foot route" he had traveled as a blind man—two blocks south to Parker Avenue, a right turn and seven blocks east to the far corner of Palmer Park, another right turn and four blocks south along Grange to Grace Avenue, where, just around the corner, was the institute.

Excitement, perhaps, contributed to his feeling of confusion, but already, Miller said, something had happened to the orientation of his senses to blindness. The familiar signs and landmarks by which he had learned to assure himself that he hadn't gone astray—a shoe-repair shop located by its distinctive sounds and the odor of polish and leather; a bakery recognized by "a gorgeous yeasty smell"; intersections recognized by changes in air currents, the sudden opening of the sky and the feel of the sun, the ebb and flow of traffic "like the sound of surf," and at which he'd learned to "locate" himself by the position of letter boxes, fireplugs, or distinctly textured walls—all became somehow disarranged and Miller, the facilities of blindness as well as vision failing, was forced to ask directions several times before arriving at his destination.

At the institute Miller was rushed to the eye clinic. Examinations previous to his referral to this agency had produced a diagnosis of ". . . advanced optic atrophy . . . prognosis for improvement hopeless." On arrival, an examination by an institute doctor had also shown him to be totally blind. The doctors now conjectured that the condition might have been caused by a blood clot, pituitary cyst, or other foreign agent pressing against the optic nerve and shutting off the flow of blood necessary to the life of the nerve tissue. A secondary vascular spasm, removing the blood clot, or the bursting of the offending cyst, might have released the flow of blood to the nerve, but the revitalization of a nerve atrophied for as long as Miller's had been was, at the very least, remarkable. To make matters more perplexing, examination still showed unmistakable optic atrophy and, physiologically speaking, Miller had no right to see. Yet Miller *was* definitely seeing. Five days after the return of vision Miller's actual acuity was 20/40; with the aid of glasses he had regained more than eighty per cent of normal vision, and with the lateral fields, the record stated, improving.

A complete medical workup threw no light on this strange phenomenon. X-rays of the skull were negative. Neurological findings were negative, except for optic atrophy. Ears, nose, and throat showed no signs of infection to account for optic atrophy.

Further ophthalmological and neurosurgical consultations corroborated the diagnosis of optic atrophy, etiology unknown.

On February 10 the consultant ophthalmologist, suggesting the possibility of "a large mental factor," summarized his findings to the head of the institute's eye clinic: "There was a primary optic atrophy of each nerve, more pronounced on the right, with a definite atrophic cupping of the right. . . ."

The day before, the neurosurgeon had written: ". . . pallid nerveheads. . . . There was inequality of the pupils in both size and reaction. The right pupil did not react to direct light but there was consensual reaction on this side. The reaction of the left pupil was prompt, but there was very little, if any, consensual reaction of the left pupil with the light shining into the right eye. In other words, it looked as if he were blind in the right eye although this is not true. I cannot interpret this. I certainly do not think he is in need of any surgery. How about getting some of the psychiatrists to have a look at him?"

In the meantime Miller gave his own explanation of what had occurred: "A miracle has happened. It's like Lazarus, who was dead and came back from the tomb," he exclaimed. "It's like being born again."

William Miller was born of Danish parents in a modest frame house in Steinbeck, Pennsylvania, in June 1908. When he was five days old his mother died. His father, John Miller, a man in his late forties, who drove a truck, died of a stroke six months later. Miller spent the next fifteen years in a succession of public institutions.

The only family William ever knew consisted of a half-brother and half-sister, John Jr. and Clara, born of his father's first marriage, and of his sisters, Angie and Lucy, aged eight and five respectively, when they accompanied him to the city orphan asylum after their father's death. His memories of the adult members of his family, like those of a childhood lived in one of Grimm's fairy tales, are touched with terror and sorcery. He was afraid of his half-brother, John, who was his legal guardian, and whom he saw only on rare and always unpleasant occasions, Miller said. John was "a big giant of a man," who drank heavily and was given to brooding and violence, and who lived alone in the house where the younger children were born. He died, a bitter and solitary bachelor, at fifty-eight. Clara, whom he remembers as a "beautiful, slender creature," was a loving but ephemeral figure. As a small boy he had never been able to visualize the house where Clara lived—"where she came from, and where she went"—but for several years running, on visiting days, she appeared, miraculously, at the gates of the orphanage, bearing apples and jelly beans, and then disappeared again.

Miller's relations with Angie and Lucy, who shared his life at the orphanage were more substantial. Differences in age and routines separated William from his sisters for the greater part of each day, but as far back as he can remember, he was dependent on the knowledge that they were near. At mealtimes in the huge dining-room, where the children were divided according to age and sex, William knew they always kept a watch over him. During recreation periods they always sought him out.

He remembers them as fiercely protective, Valkyrie-like little girls with red cheeks and dark, flying hair, Angie as "the one who used to mother us kids," and Lucy, to whom he was especially devoted, "because she used to protect me and play with me, too." He recalled that once, at dinner, when an exasperated attendant, pulling his hair until his head rested in the crook of her arm, tried to force some stew he had refused down his throat, Angie, shrieking like a calliope—"You leave my little brother alone"—came running to his side. Lucy, he said, used to throw stones at the bare feet of the big boys when they were annoying him, and squatting before him as he sat on a stair of the schoolhouse, she taught him that one and one are two.

Once Lucy suggested: "Willie, you close your eyes.

I'll turn you around and around, and you keep your eyes closed, and then you walk around; I'll tell you when to stop." As William, dizzy and with eyes still closed, staggered about the grounds he ran into a post. "She laughed. She got a kick out of that, poor kid," he commented, "but I hit my head an awful bang. I made a big commotion. Lucy ran over to me and began to hug me and kiss me and say: 'Shhhh' because the attendant was coming." When the attendant asked what happened, Miller recalled, "I said I fell down; I wasn't going to get her in trouble." After that, "every day for a month she would kiss me on that spot on my head."

Only the appearance of their half-sister, Clara, could slacken the loyalty of the children to one another. When she came, Miller said, they became jealous.

"We used to fight to hold her hand. I remember, we used to jump up and down and hang onto her and ask her: 'Who do you love the most?' "

When he was about five, Clara didn't appear one visiting day. For a long time afterwards the children continued to watch for her, but she never came again. Later, as if by tacit agreement, they stopped talking about her. But on Thursday afternoons they invariably found themselves playing in the vicinity of the gate where visitors entered. That habit persisted even after they had learned the reason for Clara's disappearance—that she was dead.

The loss of Clara was the first of a series of bereavements for William. It was a custom at the orphanage, as the children grew older, to place as many as possible with private families where they could earn their keep. The girls were generally placed in homes where they were taught to serve as housemaids, the boys on farms where they helped with the chores. About a year after

Clara's last visit Angie, now a young lady of thirteen, was taken away. Then Lucy, when William was about eight.

"I was left all alone, when they took Lucy away from me," Miller said, "and I grieved for her like she was the last person left in the world."

William was ill for a time after Lucy's departure, and when he returned to normal routine, "the whole world was just changed. In school I just couldn't seem to learn anything. Whenever I'd dream off, I'd get rapped on the head with the pointer. I was always in a corner with the dunce-cap on."

A solitary child, he liked to pry into odd corners. There was a fascination for him in trash piles, under stones, in heaps of compost at the edge of the garden. He remembers being severely "disciplined" once when, exploring a garbage can, he disinterred a moldy cherry pie. Most painful and humiliating were the punishments he suffered for what happened to him because of his fear of thunder. He doesn't know when that fear began, but as far back as he could remember, whenever there was a thunderstorm he became so terrified, he lost control of his excretory functions. By the attitudes of those around him, he came to know himself as a "peculiar, dirty kid that just didn't fit in any place." During his secret hours he consoled himself by making "little boys and girls" out of hollowed-out acorns, fastened together with toothpicks. Among his acorn family, there were always a "Good Pinocchio" and a "Bad Pinocchio." He didn't know why he gave them those names, he said, but he had been familiar with the story of Pinocchio: "I used to cry because he was disciplined so much."

He also enjoyed assembling families of insects. "I liked

to play with bugs, especially big ones, like beetles, because they were alive and you could pick them up. I'd pet them and let them crawl on my hands. I wanted to keep them in the worst way. Sometimes I'd sneak them inside, in a handkerchief. I'd bring them crumbs from the table and try to take care of them. But I'd get caught and whipped for bringing dirty things in the house. Or they'd smother or starve to death, and I'd cry."

When William was eleven years old his half-brother, John, was notified that the orphanage could keep him no longer. John boarded William with a Widow Cross, a few blocks from the house where he was born. About a month later Mrs. Cross sent word she couldn't keep him either, and one morning John took him to court, where, in order to have him committed to a second institution, it was necessary for him to swear before a judge that he was unable to care for the boy himself. This was William's first encounter with the police and he remembers, as he sat in a corridor beside the big-boned, taciturn John, wretchedly waiting to "stand up before the judge," that he thought: "I must be a bad, terrible kid—because nobody wanted me."

At the County Home, where the regime was more rigorous and discipline more stringent, as William's reputation for being a stolid, sullen boy of peculiar habits increased, so did his stubborn need for the solitary pursuits which gave him that reputation. He would sit on the ground in the woods behind the home for hours looking at a rock, a leaf, or a bit of bark from a tree. He liked to dig in the earth—he became a good gardener—the only activity that brought him any approval; and he used the earth as a hiding-place for things he treasured—hickory nuts for solitary feasts, unusual bits of glass, wood, and rock, and "those beautiful old-fashioned giant agates," which he buried in separate little caches, according to color.

The agates "came from boys who had folks to bring them presents. I became a terrible little thief," Miller said. "I used to watch those kids playing, then follow them like a ghost till I found out where they kept them. I'd steal them and bury them. Then when I'd be down in the dumps, I'd just go and dig one up and play with it. I'd spit on it and shine and polish it, and baby it for hours. The prettiest ones were the ones with the different wavy colors streaming through them. Sometimes I'd keep just one wrapped up in my pocket handkerchief. When I'd get tired of that one, I'd bury it and dig up another one. I got more comfort out of a square foot of earth than all the kids' games in the world."

Soon after entering this institution William began building himself a stone hut in the woods. This was the first of countless huts the building of which was to engross him during the three years he remained in this institution. His first attempts, near a partly swampy area, were no more than a series of piled-up rocks, held together with layers of mud, which fell into rubble before he could even complete them. Later, having studied the stone fences in the vicinity, he abandoned the use of earth as a cohesive and, with crudely chipped stones, began to "build dry." He succeeded in building a number of rough, fortress-like structures, about four feet high, with peepholes in the direction of the orphanage, with tunnel entrances, and strong enough to hold their roofs of boughs. He was happy with each for a while, but invariably became dissatisfied, moved, began to build again.

With the passing of the seasons, he learned that the

earth, expanding in freezing weather, will "toss" a flimsy structure; that contracting with the first spring thaw, the earth will expel boulders and the strongest roots of trees, gradually leaving them homeless. He began to anchor the walls of his huts by building from deep beneath the earth's surface. He learned to cut stone "so each one would link with the next one, like a chain, and ride with the heave of the earth, and settle with it when the earth settles." Other boys from the home came into the woods and built huts too, he said, but "building with stone was the one thing I could do best. I became an artist at cutting stone," he declared. "I can build a stone wall that will stand a hundred years."

About three months after his arrival at this institution William made a discovery, which led to frequent expeditions to the city. It happened when he and a group of other boys were taken to church, in town, to be baptized and confirmed. As they straggled, two by two, along the avenue in their high shoes, long black stockings, serge knickerbockers, and white shirts, provided for special occasions, they passed Woodgreen Cemetery. There, behind an iron fence, William saw a tombstone, presiding over a family plot, and bearing the name Miller. "Seeing that name," he said, "was like something just grabbed me. I couldn't stop thinking about it."

William had thought a great deal about his parents, and especially about Clara. He knew that the dead were placed in the earth, but was unable to grasp the fact of death itself. He had puzzled about "souls" and what they looked like and how they left "the mortal body"; about the whereabouts of places like heaven, purgatory, hell— the vast, insubstantial hereafter.

"I never dreamed about my mother coming back, because I never knew her," he said, "and I never dreamed about my father. But I used to dream about Clara all the time."

He recalled that childhood dream: He was walking alone in a dusky, heavily wooded forest when he came to a tiny, crudely made cabin and entered. There, sitting on a rough stool made of an upturned log, sat Clara.

"She had beautiful long, black hair and a little bit of a pinched-in waist, and she was wearing one of those stiff wire collars, like my mother wore in a picture Angie showed me once. I ran up to her and I said: 'Clara! I thought you were dead!' " Clara, he said, had turned her face slowly to him and replied: " 'I'm not dead, Willie. I'm just resting.' " He had placed his face against hers and kissed her—"in that dream was the only time she ever kissed me on the mouth. Her lips were stony cold, but I didn't care. I was so happy to see her."

Soon after seeing the tombstone bearing his family name William paid his first visit to the cemetery. His mother's name, Alice, and the dates of her birth and death had been cut into the granite stone. But that his father and Clara had ever existed and now lay here, too, was unrecorded. The slightly sunken graves were overgrown with weeds. A battered and rusty metal flower-container lay on the edge of the plot on its side, and a Florabunda rosebush, on one of the graves, had been untended so long that it had grown raffish, "with suckers coming up from the old, wild root."

Moved by pity and indignation, William began breaking the dead wood from the rosebush, scratching his hands badly on the thorny stalks. "I broke away as much as I could with my bare hands. The next time, I pruned it up nice with a knife." He weeded the graves. He

searched the fields, roadsides, and picnic ground near by
for old whisky bottles and on subsequent trips, having
broken off their tops, sank them into the graves as con-
tainers for flowers. From his four-by-four garden at the
home he brought zinnias, cosmos, and asters—"the three
flowers I could raise the best. . . . I can't explain the
feeling, knowing the ones that brought me into the
world were laying there under the ground." On each
grave he planted a pink geranium, which he had raised
in boxes from cuttings.

He had no fear of "ghosts or things like that," he said.
The cemetery was, to him, a comfortable, friendly place.
He was on familiar terms with all the marble angels, the
doves, cherubs, weeping naiads, the granite urns and ob-
elisks, the polished and rough stone crosses. Several times,
caught in the vicinity of the cemetery by the superintendent of the home, he had refused to tell what he was doing there. "The more he twisted my ear, the less I'd say.
So he'd take me back and I'd get the cooler." The cooler,
he explained, was a tiny windowless room with an iron
door and a peephole in it.

At fourteen William was placed in a disciplinary farm-
institution where it was thought the stringent work-
regime would straighten him out. Here the boys slept in
dormitories of from thirty to forty beds, rose at six,
cleaned the buildings, attended school from three to four
hours daily, and worked on the farm, in the kitchen,
laundry, or cannery, until supper time. For those who
didn't adhere to the program there was "a regular
prison"; for incorrigibles, beatings with a rubber hose.
Homosexuality was common, and if a boy rebuffed the
advances of an older, stronger boy, he was forced to ac-

cept the alternative—"You just let him beat you up. You couldn't snitch on anybody or your life would be miserable," Miller explained. "You couldn't fight back or you'd get in trouble with the attendants for making a commotion."

In this place where there were no opportunities for isolation or freedom of movement, where his aggravated fear of thunder brought him unspeakable punishments and, from the other boys, the treatment afforded a buffoon, William's penchant for stealing became more persistent, and he became a chronic runaway.

On most occasions when William ran away, his absence lasted no more than a few hours or a day. A posse of inmate monitors sometimes brought him back or, frightened and miserable, he returned voluntarily. But one day he hitchhiked all the way to New York City. As he walked along the river front in the strange city, studying the barges and tugboats, he was "picked up" by Mike K—, a burly glib-talking man, who invited William to stay with him on his coal barge.

"He was real nice to me," said William, his bland face glowing with the memory. "He took me to the movies. That was the first time in my life I ever saw a movie. And he gave me good things to eat." The trouble was that Mike was "like those big bullies at the institution, who used to jump on the poor kids and ride them, and ruin them for life. Why, in those institutions, kids get ruined," Miller cried. "They get ruined for life."

The thought of relinquishing the movies, the comradely visits to the Forty-second Street "museum" with its side shows and flea circus, and the cosy little suppers of pork chops, potatoes, and doughnuts on the barge was almost unbearable to William. But he had also become so worried and upset by Mike's propensities that he couldn't sleep at night.

"Don't think anything happened," Miller protested anxiously. He wanted to make this very plain. "Nothing happened," he repeated. "I played dumb—I held him off that way."

Early one morning, about a week after joining Mike, William wandered away from the barge. He walked north along the river, turned west at Forty-second Street, to the Times Square area. He window-shopped and examined the pictures in front of theaters and movie houses. Hunger and wretchedness overtook him as the day wore on, and the desire to return to the cosy friendliness of the barge, but with it came anxiety, which bathed his palms with sweat and made his heart pound. That afternoon, after standing a long time on a street corner, watching a policeman direct traffic, he placed himself under the protection of the policeman. He was provided with a meal and returned to the institution.

Most of the objects William pilfered were of little intrinsic value—an elk's tooth, a fountain pen, a jack-knife with mother-of-pearl handle. It was not for their monetary or practical value that he wanted them, he said. The pen might be defective, the knife minus blade, "but I didn't have *anything*. It seemed like the only pleasure I got in life was from things I stole."

William had passed his fifteenth birthday when he slipped into the office of the superintendent one day, took two gold rings, each set with an opal, and ran away. For two days and a night he hid in the woods, lived on crops growing around the countryside, and enjoyed the opals, which were "like those agates I always loved, only a thousand times more beautiful." During the second night, anxiety mounting, he buried the opals as he had done with all things he valued, and began to consider his position.

Knowing from previous experiences the punishment awaiting him, William dismissed the thought of returning to the institution. He dismissed the thought of appealing to his half-brother, John, too—"I was afraid of him." As for Angie and Lucy, they had abandoned him. Angie, now the mother of two children of her own, had neither written nor visited him for more than two years, he said. The last time he had seen Lucy—an unexpected visit, and Lucy's first in about four years—she had been "a different person; she was all dressed up like a lady; she had pigtails down her back, and two ribbons on them, with big bows, and glasses with big rims." William had been summoned from the playground with the message: " 'You have visitors. Your sister is here to see you.' " He had looked at her, sitting prim and proper in the reception room, and asked: " 'You're my sister?'

" 'Don't you remember me, Willie?' " she had asked.

Then the wealthy Mrs. Reik, who had taken Lucy into "service" seven years before and had brought her back for this visit, remarked: " 'My, you have dirty ears! Don't you wash your ears and brush your teeth?' "

William had resented that as he resented this immaculate Lucy before whom he felt so constrained, "but I didn't talk back. I got hit so much," he put in, "I learned never to talk back. When they left Lucy kissed me," he continued, "but I felt like it was a stranger kissing me."

William found a barn, where he spent the remainder of the night. The next day as he walked aimlessly along a road about fifteen miles from the institution, William was picked up by a posse made up of John, the superintendent of the home, and an inmate monitor—"a great big bully of a kid"—whose chief duty was the dispensing of "discipline." Back at the institution, in a locked room in the "prison," William was grilled and beaten, but wouldn't admit that he had taken the jewelry. Throughout the grilling the superintendent kept demanding: "Where did you sell those rings?" That question still seemed preposterous to Miller: "I wouldn't have sold those opals for anything. The darned things were too precious," he exclaimed. "They're still out there someplace where I buried them."

That night, nose broken, eyes swollen, and body a mass of bruises, William was confined in the "prison," where he remained for thirty days. One morning, a few days after his release, he met in a cornfield the monitor who had wielded the rubber hose. "I picked up a hunk of wood—that was the first time in my life I ever fought for myself—and I laid it all over him. I beat him helpless—I thought that I had killed him—and then I lit out of that place for good. This time I knew it. I would never go back any more."

William fled to the house where he was born. The house was locked. His half-brother, John, had not yet returned from work. William hid in the yard. When John got home and saw the boy lurking behind the outhouse, he knew William was in trouble again. "I certainly wasn't a welcome guest," Miller commented. "The profanity was awful; I wouldn't repeat what he said. I got whacked with a shovel. He chased me all over the yard. He broke the shovel swinging it around. Then he went into the house and locked the door, but later, when it was dark, he took me in and gave me supper and let me sleep there for the night."

In the morning John gave William the choice of returning to the institution or joining the Army. They falsified his age, and William joined the Army. Army life was a torment to him.

"We had to stick a bayonet in a straw dummy: every time we had to charge I would throw up. I was scared to shoot a gun. The darn thing was made to kill somebody and I was scared to touch it." And, like thunder when he was a little boy, the sound of gunfire made him lose control of his bladder.

"Everybody laughed at me. Everybody had me down for a nitwit. It was 'Miller, get in step. Get the gun on your shoulder, Miller. Get in step.' I was always out of step with everybody." Then, Miller continued, a couple of men began making sexual advances to him.

Miller spoke of this with the same strident anxiety as when he had described the sexual practices of the boys at the institution, and as when describing his flight from the barge captain into the arms of a policeman. "I thought the world must be mad. I had been a bad kid, but I didn't know the world. One of the men offered me money. I wound up giving him my first pay to stay away from me. Then I stole a civilian suit that I found hanging in a barracks and I went over the hill."

For the next four years William traveled haphazardly through ten states, walking, hitchhiking, occasionally riding the rails; sleeping along the road or in barns and stables; begging or stealing his food from fields and orchards, or pausing to work on a ranch, farm, or plantation to earn it. Convinced that both the police and the Army were searching for him, he considered himself a hunted man. He had also been hunting for something.

For a long time before making his final break from the institution, he had been wondering what "the real outside world was like." He had certain notions about it, based on fleeting observations, on things he had been told or had read in books. "I knew people outside lived in families, and had jobs, and loved kids, and loved their neighbors, and like that," he said earnestly, "but I never could picture it for what it really was, because I never really saw it. Now I wanted to see it."

He traveled from San Antonio to Texarkana; crossed the muddy Red River by mule-drawn barge, and made his way to the vicinity of Little Rock, Arkansas; went on through Memphis and Nashville, Tennessee; then went to Kentucky, Ohio, Indiana, Ohio again, West Virginia, Pennsylvania.

What he saw and experienced was seldom what he had expected. He was appalled by the poverty he saw: "In the South, whole families with seven, eight kids slept on straw pallets in a one-room shack. They worked from morning till night; but mostly they only had corn bread and rice and beans to eat."

He was puzzled by the social divisions: "The boss on a plantation where they parceled out the land would call the white croppers trash. The white croppers called the colored people niggers. The boss would cheat them and treat them both like dirt, and they both hated him, but they would just 'mister' him to death."

It seemed curious to him, too, that "most of my food came from poor colored people that didn't have anything. They never turned me away, even if they could only give me a piece of dry corn bread." As he pushed north, poverty seemed to diminish and white people along the roads to become increasingly friendly and generous, but nowhere could he find the place, the people, or the state of being that mirrored his concept of the "outside world."

The closest he came to what he was looking for in terms of human relationships was on a plantation and ranch near Texarkana, where, in return for food, clothing, and a cot, he herded cattle, cared for a thousand chickens, and sometimes looked after the commissary where the sharecroppers bought supplies on credit. His first and closest friends had been a Negro sharecropper family of eleven, of whom the father and five of the children were deaf-mutes. He began to bring them eggs and chickens, which he had stolen, when he came calling in the evenings. "If I knew in advance the boss was going to town, I would tell them to come to the commissary and I'd give them what they needed, or put things down in the books at half the price." As he made friends with others, he helped them, too.

"My name spread all around," Miller said. "All the people knew me. In the evening when I'd go for a walk, the little kids used to hang on my hands. Every place I'd go, the people would want me to come in and visit awhile. The way those people lived, it was wicked. I used to tell them some day I'd tell the President of the United States how they were treated."

That episode ended one rainy evening about three months after his arrival when a herd of cattle for which he was responsible broke through a fence into a field of alfalfa. "The boss was in town and the workmen had gone home. I was all alone on the place, and the smell of that wet alfalfa just made those cattle crazy," Miller said. "I lost my head. I didn't think to get help from the tenants. I just rode up and down along the fence opening, trying to keep them out, when they'd break through in another place. I'd no sooner drive a bunch of them out, and go after some more, when they bloated up and started to drop like rocks. When the boss came home, he got three vets and they worked all night puncturing holes in the stomachs of those cows to let the gas out—the stink was something awful. At that, thirty or forty head of cattle had dropped dead and before morning the buzzards were all around. When it was all over, the boss said he was going to have me arrested for negligence, and he kicked me off the place. I hated him, but I was just heartsick about those cattle." Almost tearful as he described his departure, he said word got around quickly, and when he reached the main highway, about four miles away, "a whole bunch of my friends, whole families with their wives and all the kids, and even a little brindled dog that liked me, were waiting to say good-by, and they all sure hated to see me go."

With the exception of that experience, wherever he went, Miller said, he was nagged by discontent. In Jeffersonville, Indiana, the farmer for whom he worked had been "a drunkard," and "brutal to his wife and the animals." In Kentucky, where he dug wells, built fences, and helped harvest crops, he'd felt himself "a stranger." In Okalida, Ohio, where he painted a house, his employer "cheated" him. In Washington, Pennsylvania, a Mrs. Grayson—"I remember her name so well because she was so kind"—offered him a job on her sheep ranch, but by that time, he said, "I was so homesick I didn't know what to do. I wanted to go back to Steinbeck in the worst way."

When Miller returned he went directly to the Wood-green graveyard. "It was late afternoon, and not later than June—I know because the roses were out," he said. He weeded the graves, made a mental note to return later in the season to prune the rosebush, took a walk around the city. He made no attempt to get in touch with his sisters. He was afraid that if the police were still looking for him, "they might try to catch me through my sisters." At night he returned to the cemetery and went to sleep "on a large, flat stone that had been warmed all day by the sun. I felt as safe and comfortable as if I was in my own house."

William had just passed his twentieth birthday when he returned. For the next two years he worked on a succession of farm jobs in Brandel, Pennell, Norton, Scribner, Williamtown, and Starkie, Pennsylvania. Wherever he worked, he continued to feel himself discriminated against: "I often ate with the family, but I was never expected to sit with them in the evening. I'd sleep in the barn or the attic—I was always stuck off in a crack somewhere."

Early in 1928, while poking around in his attic quarters on a farm, he found a cache of ten ten-dollar gold pieces and stole them. He was arrested, spent thirty days in prison, returned to his circuit of farm jobs. Gradually he began to have friends around the countryside. Like the sharecroppers in Texarkana, his friends were poor people, with large, hungry families. William was always an important and welcome guest: he brought them gifts of chickens, fruits, and vegetables, filched from his employers.

While working on a farm in Starkie in the summer of 1929, William was in the habit of visiting a milkman's family a mile or so down the road. It was there he met Marianne Porter, the blue-eyed daughter of the proprietor of a small grocery store, who was vacationing with the family of her uncle, the milkman. Less than two weeks later, with sixty-five dollars he had saved, William and Marianne eloped. Afterwards William got a job at eleven dollars a week as a night dishwasher in a cafeteria. William was twenty-two, Marianne twenty-three. A year later their daughter, Carol, was born.

Their marriage had been a failure from the start, Miller said, but he had not acknowledged that until it was completely over. Never again had he been able to duplicate the bounty with which he had impressed Marianne during their brief courtship. Marianne's family had never accepted him, he said, and he had been unable to make a place for himself among her friends. In addition Marianne did not find him sexually desirable.

"My wife," he said, "was raised in the 'outside world.' She was a girl that liked friends, dancing and parties—things people are used to on the outside. I didn't have any experience in things like that. I only had one thing in my head, and I hung onto that like my whole life depended on it: I wanted a home, and I wanted somebody to love me."

When the baby was born, Miller said, he paid the hospital bill in weekly installments of three dollars and, keeping his night job, rang doorbells looking for additional work. In the daytime he scrubbed floors, washed windows, worked as a gardener and general handy man; but at best his earnings provided only the barest necessities. They lived in a series of furnished housekeeping rooms, heated by kerosene or coal, and usually with outside sanitary facilities. With the deepening of the depression, odd jobs became harder to find, and when he lost his dishwashing job, which he had grown to hate, the family went on the dole.

It seems strange to him now, Miller said, that though Marianne had grown cold and disdainful of him and, taking the baby, frequently returned to her parents, he was obsessed by a story-book image of happy family life, as if Marianne's love and the continuation of their marriage were a foregone conclusion. In his image they lived in a house, built by himself, somewhere in the country. In the spring of 1933, during one of their separations, he made a deal with two maiden ladies, the Page sisters, who owned considerable property in Rosehill and for whom he had been doing odd jobs from time to time. They gave him an acre of woodland, in return for which he contracted to work for them every Sunday for five years; in addition, he agreed to build a quarter-mile road from their property to the main highway, in exchange for two old barns, no longer in use, which he could tear down and use for lumber for his house. He prevailed on the owner of a small contracting company near by to sell him doors, windows, and roofing on credit, and weekends and every evening that spring he worked happily, clearing a piece of land, hauling his lumber, and building a three-room cabin.

When he had finished the house, he provided secondhand furniture, kerosene lamps for light, an oil stove for heat, and a wood-burning stove for cooking. He built "a neat little outhouse" at a convenient distance from the back door, whitewashed it, and cut "a nice little crescent moon" in the door. "I dug my own well—I was so lucky! I struck a spring at thirty-two feet—and I lined the whole well with a good stone wall, and then emptied it out two or three times till the water was clear and fresh."

In July, when everything was ready, he went to Marianne and, as he had done on previous occasions, persuaded her that this time "everything would be different." But Marianne was unhappy with William, hated the isolation of country life, hated the poverty and the primitive living, and in February of the next year took the baby and left him for good. She was to divorce him later.

William was in a raging depression one evening a few days later when, standing on a stepladder in his living-room and rummaging in the tiny attic he had built as a storage place for lumber, he knocked over a kerosene lamp he had set inside the trapdoor. The burning oil spilled through the cracks of the rough boards to the room below. The house burned down. He then went to the home of a former employer near by, committed a theft, and "hit the road." Three weeks later, when he returned, he was arrested and sentenced to ninety days. In prison he became seriously ill with pneumonia. Still sick and weak on his release from the prison hospital, he went to Marianne. The police had preceded him. He was not permitted to enter the house. He went to Angie, who was living in a neighboring community with her husband and children. The police had preceded him there, too. "They had no room for me." He hitchhiked to Strachey, about one hundred miles away, where Lucy, now married and also the mother of two children, was living. "She wouldn't have me either."

"Nobody would have me," he cried fiercely. "Not my wife. Not Angie or Lucy. Nobody. Lucy was in there sleeping with her husband and kids. I had to lay down under the stairs in the hall of the apartment house. I was crazy jealous, and for the first time in my life I hated everybody. I hated my sisters. I hated the farmers I had worked for—all *they* wanted me for was to work me from morning till night! I hated the people just passing on the street. I hated people so—all of them—that I wished I had the power to slaughter the whole civilization off the earth, because people were cruel and wicked, and nobody wanted me.

"In the morning, after Lucy's husband left for work, she let me in. When she went out to the store, I went all through that place. I took money. I took her husband's suit, a dress, some jewelry. I took an old hat, towels, napkins, anything—it didn't matter if I could use it or not; and I got on a bus, and I cried all the way to New York. I said: 'To hell with you all. I'll steal. I'll be as rotten as I want, and I'll have my home.' "

Miller didn't attempt to make a place for himself among other people again. His home that summer was a stone hut in the woods near Bethel, Vermont, much like the huts he had built for himself as a boy. He emerged only when the food with which he had supplied himself ran out; then he got a job on a farm, stayed long enough to commit a theft, and moved on to New Hampshire, where he replenished his supplies and settled in the woods again.

For the next four years, until spring 1938, that was his regime, with several states as his circuit. His childhood passion for ornamental stones revived, his thefts included jewelry as well as clothing and money. He looked on money and clothing as ordinary necessities. "Once in a while," he said—he spoke of this as of something shameful and forbidden—"the desire for a woman would get

so strong I'd buy a little loving." [1] But the jewelry he stole
retained an old and special meaning for him.

"I can't describe the thrill it used to give me when I'd
get a diamond or something precious like that," he said.
"At that time, to sell a pretty piece of jewelry, I'd have
to be starving! I know it's hard for somebody else to understand, but I got real love and companionship from
those beautiful things."

Miller looked on the periods spent with other people as
"evil times," to be borne only as a means to an end. He
was constantly afraid that he would be caught committing a theft. He was never free of the fear that the police,
tracing an earlier crime to him, would tap him on the
shoulder. He balanced that fear with hatred and a constant sense of injustice, which, though painful to live
with, stiffened his spine, making the accomplishment of
his ends easier. Only when he had finished a hitch on a
farm or in a city, had a pack on his back, a trinket or
two in his pockets, and was on his way to a spell of "living
with nature" did his "bad feelings" fall away.

His wardrobe for country living was sparse but practical: boots that laced high over his pants, a woolen shirt
or two, a mackinaw, a stocking cap, a hat to shed rain.
His pack consisted of a horse blanket, hatchet, hunting
knife, pocketknife with screwdriver, can- and bottle-
opener, matches, a handful of nails, a flashlight, a ball
of strong twine. For food he brought huge quantities of
dark bread, dried meats and fish, and canned sweet con-
densed milk.

He liked to settle in remote, "hard to find" places, and
he always looked for a water-supply first, "a good clear

[1] Miller didn't mention this, but medical records indicate he
was treated for gonorrhea in 1936.

brook or a spring. You have no idea how delicious water tastes when you get down on your belly and drink from a spring." Sometimes, enjoying it as a trick of wits, he liked finding an unsuspected cranny no more than a mile or two from a flourishing farm, and making camp there.

As soon as he made camp, if the weather was good, he sliced his bread, threaded it with string, and festooned the trees with it, leaving it until it was hard and dry. "That way it never got moldy. It would keep indefinitely and there was plenty for me *and* the birds."

He built his shelters with whatever materials were available. Best of all he liked a stone hut, but he also used tree branches and, if he happened to settle in the vicinity of an abandoned lumber camp, down-timber. Though he tried to use the coldest months of the year for the business of replenishing his supplies, occasionally, caught in the country in winter weather, he found shelter in the mouths of caves or built his shelter over a dugout, scooped out with a tin can or cooking utensil. "People don't know it, but in some places, if you know how to find them, the ground under the snow isn't frozen, even in below zero weather, and you can dig yourself a little place that's as cozy as a nest."

Often, making his bed of pine branches—"There's no sweeter bed in the world to lay on"—he slept in the open. "I loved to hear the wild little noises from the frogs and the crickets and the owls and katydids at night. Many nights I heard the whippoorwill. First thing in the morning, before it was even light, I'd hear the killdeer—they make a loud, sad noise and they're about the first to start looking for food in the morning. Then, little by little, I'd hear all the other birds joining in till they were all talking and singing at once."

He supplemented the food he brought with the meat of trapped game, mainly rabbits and squirrels. If there was a farm in the vicinity, he went on occasional foraging trips, drinking fresh milk on the spot, and carrying back chickens and fresh fruit and vegetables. He kept razor blades, soap, and a clean shirt for just such excursions: "so if I was seen walking along a road in the early morning, I wouldn't look suspicious." He also supplemented his diet with wild things growing around the countryside.

"Many times in the spring I'd tap the sugar maple and drink the sap. I'd bore a hole in the tree; then I'd punch the soft pith out of an elderberry twig and blow an air hole into it, and drive it into the tree and put a tin can under. The sugar maple isn't as pretty as the swamp or red maple," he said, "but I love that tree best of all in New England because the syrup is so good. I just love sweet things."

He ate walnuts, hickory nuts, and hazelnuts. The bark of certain trees, though not actually edible, was fine to chew while on long hikes and diminished the feeling of hunger. "The sassafras has a wonderful aromatic taste," he said. "It makes the saliva act up. Once you know that taste, you always look for it. You just crave it. The elm," he continued, "is bitter, but that's an interesting taste, too. Nature is just full of variety. The black birch has a lovely, sweet taste," and nibbling the young shoots of the Southern sourwood tree "is just great for quenching thirst."

He ate wild cherries, plums, crabapples, and berries. "May and June, I had wild strawberries, blackberries, dewberries, red raspberries, and June berries; in July and August, blueberries, thimbleberries—that's the black-capped raspberry—black elderberries, nannyberries, high-bush cranberries." With the help of a Boy Scout book and plant and tree encyclopedias, which he later began to carry, he discovered certain root foods. His leafy vege-tables were marsh marigold, watercress, chickweed, poke-weed, and milkweed, squirrel brier, sorrel grass, Russian thistle, and the young leaves of dandelion and clover.

His new life, haphazard at first, became gradually in-fused with a purpose. The childhood fascination with things that come from the earth—plants, odd stones, worms, and insects—returned, and with it the old drive to pry into hidden corners. Other things, seemingly un-related, which had gripped his interest in the past—the birth of a calf, the emergence of a chick from an egg, the daily progress of decay of a dead horse in a ditch, the "peaceful, beautiful" face of a boy suicide he saw once— "I wanted to lift up his eyelids and try to read what he saw in his eyes"—all converged and became articulated into what Miller described as a need "to find out the secret of life and death."

He busied himself with various woodland explora-tions, climbing trees to look into the nests of birds, exam-ining the contents of hollow logs and the nests of insects and small animals. He explored caves and abandoned mines—"in those that were flooded, I'd go just as far as I could." He crawled on his belly into crevices in the earth and in the sides of mountains. He retained his friendly feeling for cemeteries, visiting the family plot in Woodgreen when he could and, in other parts of the country, seeking out old, obscurely situated graveyards where he could pass the time undisturbed.

He never missed an opportunity to prowl through a house that was said to be haunted. He broke into shacks, abandoned farmhouses, and "gorgeous old mansions, just sitting there with the brush growing up all around, rotting away." He examined their construction and contents minutely; he admired the taste and the craftsmanship of the dead. He described furniture he had seen, now fallen into ruin, but which was "hand-made, without a single nail"; huge, musty interiors, their walls intricately carved panels of oak, mahogany, black walnut, and cherry; broad curving staircases, layered with dust; gigantic rococo-framed mirrors, now cracked and dingy; the skeletons of what had once been glittering crystal chandeliers.

The musty old mansions with their huge echoing chambers, carved walls, and chandeliers were not unlike some of the beautiful and mysterious mineral-encrusted caves he had explored, William said. They gave him an awe-inspiring sense of "going way, way back in time." He also loved the modest places where "ordinary people like you and me" had lived and died. As in the dream of his childhood, in which he found the beautiful and loving Clara, sitting in a remote woods-cabin, he often peopled these abandoned houses, too.

"Sometimes when I'd be tinkering with something, or just sitting around, I would get to thinking," he said. "I'd think about people that used to live there. I'd try to see the way they used to be, what they looked like, everything—even their expressions, and the color of their hair and eyes. I'd try to go through all the steps of their life, from before they were even born, till they died and were buried."

His preoccupation with the "secret of life and death" perhaps reached proportions of climax when the unaggressive but animal-loving Miller, who had once dared to pick up a pitchfork and threaten to "run it through the guts" of a farmer who struck a cow with a milking stool, began to kill rabbits and guinea pigs at various stages of pregnancy in order to "see for myself how life forms."

"I never did it so an animal would suffer. That's wicked!" he protested vehemently. He had placed each animal in a burlap sack, working its head into a corner, then given it quick death with a powerful blow on the head. Even if he had not hated cruelty, he went on, it had been necessary, for the sake of his investigations, to act quickly: he had wanted to "open them up quick, before there were changes inside," to snatch his observations in the split second between life and death, the beginning and the end.

And whether factual or the product of luxuriant fantasy, Miller also said that on many occasions, where early settlers or farmers in isolated areas had been buried in back yards, in ancient cemeteries, or in crypts along old roads, he had opened those final resting-places and literally followed the dead into their graves.

In April 1938, four years after he embarked on his new life, Miller was arrested outside a pawnship where he had sold two stolen watches. He was convicted on a grand-larceny charge and sentenced to from two to five years in prison. At the prison, a medium-security institution for youthful offenders, he found books through which to continue his researches. He labored through texts on geology, botany, horticulture, dendrology. Though much of what he read was too technical to be fully understood by him, of one thing he became certain: the source of all good things was the earth.

"All the comfort and riches in the world, food for us and for animals we eat, trees to build houses, iron to make steel for machinery, wood and coal to keep warm, even money, gold and silver and copper, and luxuries—beautiful things like diamonds, come from the earth."

He read voraciously on forestry and soil conservation, translating much of this new-found knowledge into practical experience in assigned work in the garden and wooded areas surrounding the institution. He had developed a tremendous concern for the welfare of the earth, that source of supply which was being plundered by "rotten, greedy people, thinking only of the dollar bill."

He read on archæology and it also became clear to him, he said, that in the end all things, "from the tiniest little ant to whole civilizations," returned to the earth who was "the mother of us all. Only death," he added vehemently, was "a privilege," and "mean, selfish people don't deserve to go back."

In about November 1940, three months after his release from prison, Miller broke parole and, as if racing against time, began a personal tour of inspection of soil and forest conditions in the United States. He had no patience now for the pretense of holding jobs. He would move into a rooming-house, rob it, and move on. (He also became expert at breaking and entering.) In the twenty-five months from November 1940 to January 1943 he crossed the United States from Maine to Oregon, from Utah to the Carolinas, and from Oklahoma to North Dakota "at least three times." All that he had read of soil and forest conditions, he said, "was true, and more besides."

Conditions in Maine, Vermont, New Hampshire, and northern Massachusetts were not too bad, but in Connecticut, Rhode Island, and southern Massachusetts they were "plain disgraceful.

"I found soil erosion; second and third growth of trees; no virgin timber except in patches; dead and dying rivers and streams. . . .

"New York State"—he made a gesture of disgust— "there's no virgin timber to speak of. The trees in lots of places have been hacked down and burned over two and three times. . . ."

In the middle Southern states "where trees have been planted and the government has enough sense to keep them under protection, conditions were pretty good, but that's just a drop in the bucket," he said. "Sixty-five per cent of the forests around there need reforestation, and the condition of the soil is just awful."

The "middle strip" from Tennessee and Kentucky across Oklahoma to California needed reforestation.

In Minnesota, Iowa, North and South Dakota, the earth had been so overfarmed "it's vicious," and forest conditions were "heartbreaking to see. I found second, third, and fourth growth of trees, almost no virgin timber, and lots of places just breaking into deserts."

As for the devastation caused by forest fires—he had seen for himself forests recently ravaged by fire. He had made it his business, whenever he heard of a fire, to get to the scene quickly, before the "evidence" was gone. What he saw made him so furious "I'd just have to sit down and cry—deer suffocated, lying dead on the ground, their fur scorched; trees, their leaves and limbs burned away, their 'stumps' black; dead birds, their broken eggs and half-formed young—

"It's murder, wholesale murder and nothing else," he

cried. "Those are the real criminals, the ones that start the fires. *They* should be caught and punished." He re-called a childhood poem:

> *Clouds of grey are in the sky,*
> *Flocks of birds are winging by,*
> *Trees are dressed in red and brown,*
> *Send their leaves a-tumbling down,*
> *Little flowers are slumbering deep—*"

He broke off, said earnestly: "A fire in late April or May, when birds are nesting and eggs are being laid, will kill millions. When I was a kid, you could look up in the sky and for fifteen, twenty solid minutes watch flocks, thou-sands and thousands of birds, flying by. The sky isn't black with flocks of birds any more.

"Without birds," he continued urgently, "the insects destroy the trees and young plants. Without trees, there is no natural mulch." Mulch, he explained, protected young plants from the cold and from the "heaving ac-tion" of the earth. It protected the earth, too. "It feeds her, and acts like a blanket when it's cold, and it absorbs water and lets it out nice and easy so the topsoil won't wash away, and the young plants will have something to grip onto.

"When you think that the average in this country was once between eighteen and thirty inches of good topsoil, and today it's only from six to nine inches, you can see how rotten people have treated the earth that gives them everything." He spoke in angry staccato bursts: "They kill the wild life. They tear the earth open for gold. They work her to death with their money crops. They go in there with fire and ax and they take her food right out of the air. If we don't watch out," he said warningly, "the earth will starve. All the good soil will wash away. The whole world will be a desert."

Miller became profoundly depressed during the latter part of those twenty-five months. "It got so I wasn't even stealing for things I could love any more," he said. "I only stole for cash or things I could turn into cash. My heart was so full of hate, I couldn't find love in anything —not even a diamond."

Only in his continued explorations of caves, mines abandoned houses, and cemeteries did he find some comfort. Often, after committing a theft, he went straight to a graveyard for refuge. "I know some people would think I was morbid. I wasn't—I loved the dead," he protested. "They gave me protection. A cemetery is the safest place in the world! I felt nothing but peace and love all around me."

In the fall of 1942, when Miller was thirty-four, he visited his last cemetery. It was an ancient graveyard at the site of a vanished settlement on top of a mountain, south of Oregon City. He had stumbled on it one night after a long climb along a road "that was more like a cow-path than a road." Underbrush had all but hidden the old tombstones. "The moonlight was so bright I could read back the dates and the names on the stones. The last death had taken place in about 1872." At the edge of the old graveyard, where the earth sloped downward, "nature had washed the soil away for me," and he found a skull, weeds pushing up through the eye sockets. He had held it in his palms and "scrutinized it a long time." Then he'd scooped out a place in the earth and covered it. "I thought: 'You poor soul, go back to sleep. How lucky you are to be sleeping in the earth!'"

Miller stayed on top of the mountain for about three

weeks. In November 1942 he returned to a Middle Western city. He lived in a rooming-house for a week, committed a burglary, hitchhiked to a neighboring city, committed another, set up housekeeping in a shack across the
state line. On January 3, 1943 he hitchhiked to town,
walked deliberately into a police station, and made a full
confession of his thefts. Turned over to the authorities
in the state where he had committed his last two crimes,
he was tried and sentenced to from two to ten years.

He entered the state prison on January 21. Several
months later, after recovering from an attack of influ-
enza, he began to suffer from difficulty in breathing, difficulty in hearing; and he began to go blind. The breathing and hearing difficulties cleared up after a time, Miller
said, but loss of vision continued progressively.

The first thing he noticed about his failing vision,
Miller continued, was that he "lost color. Everything
began to look milky. Then I could see dark shapes, like
shadows, but I couldn't see light any more. Then I lost
shapes, too. It was like—you know how night settles
down? Only this took a long time. Every day it got
darker and darker. Then everything got still and dark.
I couldn't see movements or shapes or shadows or anything else any more."

Miller was taken "out of the population" when his
eyesight became seriously affected, and served the remainder of his term in a private cell in the hospital ward.
On July 29, 1946 he was delivered to a prison in the state
in which he had broken parole. An examination at that
time showed his general physical condition to be good.
His eardrums were normal, but the right ear showed one-
quarter normal hearing. His vision at that time was O.D.,

20/200, and O.S., 20/200. He was examined again a few months later. The prison doctor wrote: "I found that the right eye showed total blindness and the left eye showed 5/200 vision which could be improved (with glasses) to 10/200. On retinoscopy, he showed a minus 3 in each eye in all meridians. Ophthalmoscopic examination showed the media clear, the pupils equal and reacting to light sluggishly, the optic disks very pale, the vessels being prominent by comparison and showing generalized retinitis. . . ."

On January 28, 1947, about two years before the return of his vision, Miller was examined by an outside specialist. His findings: ". . . Pupils react to light but more slowly in right eye. Media clear but marked pallor of disks, more exaggerated in right; ocular movements good in all directions. Vision, O.D.—counts fingers at one foot; O.S., two feet. Visual fields restricted in all meridians. Has marked myopic error of refraction. This is a rather advanced optic atrophy of unknown origin. No treatment is of any value and prognosis of improvement hopeless."

Miller, confined to the hospital ward of the prison, was provided with a Braille teacher. Later, when Miller recovered his vision, the prison doctor was to write that during the time Miller was in the ward, "I had opportunity to observe him closely. I had a feeling that this inmate was putting one over and many times tried to trap him to expose himself but without success."

On December 7, 1948, the term of his parole completed, Miller was taken to a neighboring city by a detective and there turned over to a representative of the Department of Welfare. He took Miller to the institute, a model agency not only devoted to the training and re-habilitation of the blind, but operating a group of successful factories for their employment.

Miller entered a strange and frightening world when he emerged from prison. It was a world of fluid and constantly shifting sounds, smells, and impressions, without landmarks or boundaries, and charged with invisible dangers. At the huge railroad station where his detective guide turned him over to the Department of Welfare representative, what he knew to be human din and voices flowed over and all around him, now momentarily familiar, now meaningless, now dissolved into an angry, persistent droning, "like billions of hives of bees." Terror had gripped him during the subway trip to another part of the city, the close, crammed atmosphere of the underground station giving him a sense of suffocation, and the aggressive roar of trains setting up alarms of ringing in his ears. "Even the bus trip to the institute, after we got off the subway, scared me," Miller declared. "I was scared of everything. I was defenseless—I was helpless as a newborn baby."

The successful training of the blind entails more than the mechanical teaching of skills. It involves the alleviation of anxiety through patience, tact, and kindly understanding, the building of confidence and self-esteem. With the recently blind, who are faced with relearning the most rudimentary of skills—tricks of eating, shaving, dressing, how to distinguish one coin from another, how to walk alone—it also requires a degree of kindly personal attention normally accorded only to a child. The circumstances of Miller's blindness and the recognition of these precepts in the program of the institute contrived to give Miller something that extended beyond his blindness

into the deepest reaches of his personality, and for which
he had been searching all his life.

In an initial interview with one of the directors, a
thoughtful, soft-spoken man, for many years a leader in
his field and, like all key personnel at this agency, himself
a blind man, Miller's worst fears were immediately
allayed. He would not be permitted to go hungry: an
allowance with which to pay for his room and board
would be provided. No physical harm would come to
him: he would be escorted to and from his room, or
driven in a station wagon, until he had learned to make
his way alone. His prison record, which he feared would
be held against him, would be kept confidential, and he
was to consider himself free to discuss with members of
the staff any matter that was troubling him.

"Nobody ever talked to me like that before," Miller,
describing that conversation, exclaimed. "I never
had anybody to really take care of me, even when I
was a little kid. I felt so good—I felt, for the first time
in my life, like I had friends, people that cared for
me."

During the next few days Miller, launched on a course
of training in "orientation and travel technique," was
taught the location of "reference points" and took his
first halting steps, from one part of the building to another, alone. He was also entered in the Vocational Section, where, as a training in simple manual dexterity, he
was put to work at shaping brooms and weaving rubber
mats. He was rapidly promoted to more complex tasks—
the operation of simple machines involving rhythm and
hand-foot co-ordination; the cutting of lengths of string
for mops, involving tactual and spatial perception, and
the use of the hands in free motion; the centering of

diamond-shaped inlays in rubber mats, involving spatial concepts as well as mental imagery.

Miller's progress in orientation and travel was equally rapid, according to his instructor, a bluff, ruddy-faced man, who specialized in the teaching of travel techniques to soldiers blinded during the war. On December 16, still working indoors, he had his first lesson in cane technique. Six days later he had picked up speed in walking; was able to make his way around the dining- and locker-rooms, picking out obstacles with his cane; could locate the mop shop by its characteristic linty smell, and was able to direct his instructor from the lounge to the stairway by use of distinctive sound.

On December 27 he took his first trip around the block, and the next day was able to recognize street corners by sound and change in wind direction.

On January 3, after several reviews of past lessons, he was taken for a walk along Washington Avenue. He was drilled in cane rhythm, taught to "square himself" at street corners and how to hold his cane, while crossing, so as to pick up the curb on the opposite side.

On January 4, though visibly disturbed by the experience, he crossed a street alone. (The blind are not encouraged to cross streets without the help of a guide, but crossing is taught for use in emergencies, and for the building of confidence.)

On January 7 he made his way to Palmer Square, a small park a few blocks from the institute, without the knowledge that his travel instructor was close by. Joined by the instructor at the park, he was taught how to use building "shore lines" and curbs to make sure he was walking in a straight line.

Miller's rapid advancement had not come easily. "He

was a very curious blind man," an executive at the institute told me. "He was so very excessive in his efforts—so *studiedly* conscientious. He did things we wouldn't expect of any of the men, like putting into Braille everything he had learned during the day, memorizing it, and reciting it back the next day."

The travel instructor's reports are peppered with observations that Miller suffered conspicuously from tension. In one of them he wrote: "William concentrates so hard through his lessons, his forehead is drawn into a frown . . . he breaks into a sweat."

Miller, discussing that learning period, said: "I just *had* to make good. I loved those people. I just couldn't stand the thought that they might get disappointed in me."

In his last few reports, before Miller regained his vision, the instructor noted a marked decrease in tension. At one point he noted that "William was quite pleased with himself today." In the days before his sight returned, Miller said: "I could just feel happiness opening up inside me. They were all so nice. I was like a little child and they were patient with me, and taught me. They never lost their tempers. When I was out with my 'travel' teacher, he always bought me a little treat. When I'd see the director, he always wanted to know how I was getting along. Christmas time, the institute gave me a Braille watch—I just gloried in that thing. I don't know what word I could use to describe it."

On Sunday morning, January 16, Miller, feeling well-disposed toward the world, ventured beyond the life of the institute. He attended services at the Lutheran church, about a block from his residence. The next day he rejected the usual ride home in the station wagon and announced that he was going to make the trip alone, by bus. That day he had noticed the first of a series of "sharp little headaches," each lasting about twenty seconds, and returning at three- or four-hour intervals, but he had been "too happy to pay much attention to them." On Tuesday evening Miller again went to church, where a financial meeting was being held. He admitted he had been bored at the prospect of sitting through the reading of a financial report, but "I knew they were going to have a little social afterwards. They served coffee and cake." That night, when he went to bed, he felt a "tight feeling, like an iron band," around his head. It was the next morning at about one o'clock that he was awakened by that splitting headache and found that he could see.

Miller's position is reversed, but his case is not yet closed. He is earning his own living. He is living in a housekeeping room where he cooks his own meals and does his own housework. His relations with the personnel at the institute have necessarily become more casual, and in his work situation new demands are being made on him every day. Many questions remain, not least among them this one: will Miller, no longer in the receiving position of "a little child," accept the world as he finds it?

Spring 1949

WILLIAM MILLER

FOLLOW–UP: *November* 1951

WITH the return of his vision in January 1949, the attentions so valued by Miller were, for a time, increased. The complete medical checkup went into swing. Although the dynamics of his recovery were still a mystery, a program of dental work and of vitamin therapy was instituted in the hope of consolidating gains. In addition Miller became a celebrity. Word of his "miracle" had spread. Strangers who heard of it sent gifts of money and letters of encouragement. Wherever he went, at the institute and in his rooming-house, in church and on the streets of his neighborhood, he was greeted with handshakes and congratulations. He made new friends, and now that he could return to them a personage, he located his sisters and paid them a series of week-end visits. He never tired of relating the details of his miracle: how, making him feel valued, this had made him whole. "They tell me, the way my optic nerve is, they still don't understand how I can see. It's those people!" he would exclaim. "It's their love for me! Everybody is so good to me! I'll never disappoint my friends!" At this time Miller's vision was amazingly 20/40, only twenty per cent short of normal vision, despite a diagnosis of "primary optic atrophy of each nerve."

But even miracles become absorbed in the minutiæ of everyday life. Within three weeks after his recovery, excitement had begun to die down: Miller's miracle was swiftly becoming an accepted fact. It was the desire of busy institute personnel to continue guidance and medical attention, at the same time easing Miller into a more normal self-sufficient role. Miller was given a job behind the lunch counter in one of the factories for blind workers operated by the institute and began earning his own living. And though institute executives continued to watch over him, and Miller was welcome to bring matters that troubled him to their interested attention, the quality of intimacy entailed in their former relations—the instructions, the gentle reassurances, the solicitous hand at elbow, and the "special little treats," which had meant so much to Miller, were gone. The attentions he now received, though friendly and sympathetic, were of a highly different nature from those he had received when he had come to the institute frightened, helpless, and blind.

There is no doubt that Miller exerted great effort in his desire to continue to please, and that the obstacles which arose were beyond control by will. Miller met the challenge of self-sufficiency with excitement and pride, each day, eager and childlike, presenting little evidences of achievement for the approbation of his friends. But almost simultaneously he also became aware of a restlessness, a diffuse dissatisfaction, and a seeping of anxiety into his paradise.

On about February 13, about a month after recovery of his vision, Miller confided that the Canzoneris, the warmhearted, simple people with whom he roomed and in whose house his vision had returned, were somehow "not so nice as they used to be." They seemed "nosy" and less respectful. He suspected them of "snooping" among his personal effects. In addition it seemed to him

they were being unduly proprietary about his miracle—
"You'd think, the way they act, that *they* had done something," he remarked irritably. "Anyway," he hurriedly
added, "I want a nice little home of my own. I want a
little home where I can invite my friends and have beautiful things around me. Is that," he asked imploringly, "too
much for me to want?"

He confided worriedly that he was not very happy with
his work, either, but did not want to speak of this at the
institute. He was afraid of "disappointing my friends."
The clatter of dishes disturbed him, and he was exces-
sively fatigued from "standing on my feet all day." His
relations with his sisters were unsatisfactory, too. They
were not so enthusiastic as at their first reunion, he observed. Something—he didn't know what it was—was
lacking. He had visited them twice and already, he felt,
"I'm not really welcome. They keep asking me about my
plans as if I was a stranger. I hate to say this," he added
confidentially, "but I think they don't like having me
around with their kids." It was evident, certainly, that he
would not be permitted to look on their homes as his
own. "Sometimes I think it would be better if I went
away some place," he said, "and raised things from the
earth. I know I could find my happiness if I could work
the earth."

Whenever Miller discussed his problems with me or
with executives at the institute, he alternated between
apologetic demeanor, abject deference, and lavish declarations of good intent. At this time Miller was being
encouraged to remain among "friends," at least until the
condition of his eyes was assured. In the meantime, it
was pointed out to him, possibly he would find a niche
in the institute's large organization where he would be

content. If, later, he still wished to live and work in the country, then practical arrangements must be made. To Miller, whose grasp of practical considerations was flimsy, his melting desire for the earth in the face of bids to remain apparently carried other connotations. He wanted to please: "I'm going to stick it out! I'm going to make good! You'll see," he would declare. "I want my friends —more than anything I want my friends to be proud of me." Yet he was drawn irresistibly to that other desire, especially in times of stress. He spoke, as he painted increasingly glowing pictures, as of something forbidden and for which he must make an impassioned plea. "But *some* day," he would plead—"when my money is saved I want to have a piece of land. I wouldn't be leaving my friends," he would protest. "I'd have it near a highway where my friends could find it."

Having assured himself of approval and continued support in one quarter, Miller would hasten to the other as if to cement a relationship, as well as the "gains" of an interview. Frequently such meetings were followed by a letter such as the following, written in ink in a large, childlike, and very careful hand, often with the aid of a magnifying glass and a writing frame, designed for the partially blind:

I am so glad there are people in the world like yourself . . . I am taking your advice. . . . I intend to stay with the Institute. But please have faith in me. I shall never go on the wrong side of life again. I do need advice from my friends. . . . I must have a talk with you soon again . . . I'm sure after I have a talk with you I shall feel better about some things that are worrying me. They are personal problems. This time I'm going to win them all. . . . Thanks a million for being my friend. Just knowing your my friend is a uplift in itself. As Ever Your Friend,

William Miller

P.S. I have 24 dollars and 75¢ in the bank. I went without a lot of things to get it there, but I'm so proud. I have it.

Late in February Miller reported jubilantly that he had been transferred from the lunchroom where he had been so unhappy to the broom-making department of the factory. "Those people are so nice to me," he commented, "they are so understanding." He had found the "nice little home" he had wanted, too—a small housekeeping apartment with kitchenette, and he had bought pots and pans and some "beautiful dishes." The dishes provided with the apartment, he explained, had been ugly, "and I just love to have beautiful things around me." He had also started "a little indoor garden—I bought a few potted plants."

Something else had happened, he continued, which seemed "a gorgeous omen"; while cleaning his new house —he had overlooked no nook or cranny—"I stuck my hand down between the cushions of the old sofa they have in my place, and what do you think I found? An agate! One of those lovely old-fashioned ones—it's rose and pink and white. I haven't seen an agate like that since I was a kid," he exclaimed. "I took it right in there and washed it up and polished it, and put it in a cup on my table."

That wasn't all: "It looks like my dreams will come true!" Miller exclaimed. He was corresponding with "a lovely woman," who had written to congratulate him on his recovery. She lived, of all places, in the state of his birth. He had not yet met her, but he intended to ask her to marry him. Yes, he knew such a plan seemed premature, "but I know she's a lovely person, and miracles *do* happen. I'm so lonely," he implored. "I need a partner in life. I need somebody to love me, that I can talk to—somebody to make a home for me. When I find my partner in life, half the battle will be over."

During the month of March, Miller visited his correspondent in Steinbeck, proposed marriage, and was refused. He moved again—back to a furnished room—and in an angry, renunciatory gesture gave away his plants, his new dishes, pots, and pans. He complained of nervousness. His eyes were troubling him. He was suffering from headaches and fatigue, and there was again a ringing in his ears. In April, work in the broom department having become intolerable, he was transferred to a third job, this time to the stock desk in the rubber-mat department, and, gratified by this demonstration of interest, he felt better for a time. But in a few days the old symptoms had returned. A diffuse, over-all anxiety was encompassing him. He was determined to "stick it out," he repeated again and again, and pleaded: "Have faith in me." At the same time he was talking with renewed ardor of returning to the land "where I belong." He talked of setting up a nursery business, "but that takes money," he said, "and I can't stand the thought of disappointing my friends." He talked of going "up in the mountains near Oregon City where the mountains are so beautiful, and there is so much greenery and so many varieties of trees," but he was afraid his eyes would fail and he would be stranded. He talked again of wanting to "stick it out" where he had friends and where he was receiving medical attention, "but I can't stand the city. This day and age—this city!" he cried, "to me is very cruel!"

At work he was tormented by the thud of the stamping machines, with the radio blaring over it. "Baseball! Baseball! That's all you hear!" he exclaimed. "It reminds me of the workshop in the pen. In the penitentiary all you ever heard—starting with the spring it was baseball! In the fall it was football!"

The demands of the men—he was distributing materials to the workers—made him nervous. They groused. "They're always pulling at you! They're so fussy! They're always cracking wise!" They complained that he was not providing them with materials fast enough, Miller said angrily. They complained that the materials were faulty. One man, he said shrilly, had accused him of keeping the best materials for himself. He had been stabbed by panic. "What did he mean?" Miller asked. "The ringing in my ears is so bad it feels like my head is breaking! All they have to do is accuse me of being a thief! This city!" he cried. "With my record! With two convictions here, nobody would believe me! The third time I would get life! I'm so afraid something will happen. I'm afraid somebody will accuse me of something. I'm afraid I'll run into somebody that knows my record—I would be disgraced."

Money was a source of great anxiety, too. He had started that savings account. He was *trying*, he pointed out. If ever he was to have that piece of land he wanted, he *had* to have money, he said. "I can't seem to make ends meet."

The gift money he had received had gone for basic necessities: he had needed clothing, shoes, a suit, shirts, and neckties—"When I got my sight back and saw my neckties," he said fastidiously, "the colors were so terrible I threw them all away." The cost of living was high; he had spent good money "to outfit my little home, but I couldn't keep that up either," he said aggrievedly. And food—he had such a hankering as wouldn't be satisfied:

"I don't know what it is—I don't know what I want out of life! I feel so nervous. I'm so hungry all the time. I know I eat five and six times more than other people. I just feel like I need something in my stomach. I get up at night and go out and get something to eat because I know I won't sleep if I don't put something in my stomach.

"I'm so unhappy here," he burst out, "I'm losing my sight again. What I see from my right eye is milky; the flowers don't take on the colors I know they should. I know what the colors should be, and when I look at them I *know* they aren't right. The other day at a friend's house I admired a plant. I said: 'What a beautiful forsythia you've got!' I went over to admire it," he continued miserably, "and I saw it was a weigela! I just didn't see it right—I saw it as a blur. They tell me: 'Stay here where you can be treated.'" The only treatment, he declared, "would be to get the happiness out of life I want."

Later in April Miller paid a visit to a psychiatrist. He went, he later confided, because Mr. Hutchins and Mr. Smith of the institute had suggested it, "and I couldn't refuse those men, but a psychiatrist could never help me. I know what I need. A psychiatrist would never understand."

In the offices of the institute hope of helping Miller was becoming increasingly dim. "Miller isn't getting along," Hutchins stated late in April. "He needs a tremendous amount of attention and he can't seem to meet any of the demands of ordinary life. We have been doing all that is humanly possible, but we have a great many men in our care. We are simply not equipped to mother Miller further."

In the meantime the following notations had appeared on Miller's medical record:

"March 25, 1949: Field studies show a contracture of peripheral vision to 15° each eye.

"April 1: Patient complains of general weakness, backache, vision failing. Wants lighter work.

"April 12: Patient unhappy, emotionally unstable. . . .

"April 19: General condition improved. . . .

"April 22: Patient's fields have become constricted to pinpoint degree. . . .

"April 26: Patient complains of progressive loss of vision. Since January 19 [2] progressive loss of vision to O.D. 2/200; O.S. 10/200. Ocular picture is essentially the same. . . ."

On May 3 another notation was made in Miller's record: "Vision improving. Patient feels more at ease since making decision to leave city and go to the country."

That afternoon Miller, energetic, and looking spruce in shades of tan and brown, paid me a farewell visit. He had made his decision, he said, was happy; and his eyes were "much better." His good friends at the institute were not condemning him for his decision; they were actually helping him. They had presented him with a small sum of money in addition to two weeks' salary. They had introduced him to an employment service

[2] Uncorrected vision on January 19 had been O.D. 20/100, O.S. 20/70; corrected with lenses to 20/40.

where he had been given a job. He was going to be a gardener in a summer resort in Hartville. He would leave the city in a few days.

And that evening Miller wrote me a letter, urgent, propitiatory, full of high resolve. He repeated his reasons for wanting to live in the country, "and I hope and pray God will give me His speed and help." Now he would not be unhappy; lacking "a partner in life," he would find "love and comfort in the wild life, trees and wild flowers." In the country, too, he said, he was certain that his eyes would "clear up." He would write often to Mr. Smith, Mr. Hutchins, and me; and, he promised, never, never, never would he disappoint his friends. "How proud I'll be when I have made success and can show you same," he concluded.

There were more letters on May 10, May 23, and June 8: "It's heaven here in Hartville. . . . The old days are gone. New ones are here. I shall end it all if ever I find myself slipping in the gutter. I love life so much. . . ." Already, he wanted me to know, he had started "a little bank account." He was important in the quality and scope of his work: "I have to grow enough vegetables for at least two hundred people, and take care of all the flower beds." Mr. Bing, his employer, he said, had not seen a garden "as nice as mine for twenty years on this place," and when the season ended would surely give him "the best reference letter a person could have. Oh, if only you could see my beautiful gardens. . . ."

On June 20, Miller wrote: "Please don't be shoked [sic] when you hear what I have to say. I am going to the city again . . . I have lost all color vision with the exception of things black or white. I have sun blindness now. . . ."

He was going to the famous eye clinic in Foley, but, please, wanted nothing said of this new development to Mr. Hutchins or Mr. Smith "until I can get a doctor to send them explaining the condition." He wanted it known that "Mr. Bing is very fond of me—he knows the handicap I've been working under. . . ." He added: "Now I am being straightforward with you. . . . I want so much for you to have faith in me."

Three days later Miller wrote: ". . . I am back in the city, living at this address . . . I expect to go back to Hartville if I can get my eyes fixed up a little. . . . Please don't get any wild doubts. . . . I would like to have a talk with you. . . ." Unlike his earlier communications, all of which had been written with obvious care, this scrawl in pencil reflected anxiety, haste. An appointment was made for an interview, but Miller could not contain himself: two more letters followed in rapid succession.

He repeated: ". . . I hated to leave my beautiful gardens . . . I had to get out of the sun for my own protection." He said: ". . . I am very much concerned on letting you know every move I make, as your opinion and judgment on me I know will be fair. . . ." He reported that his eyes had been checked by Dr. Garrison, chief of the eye clinic at the institute, and that he was getting new glasses, and that "Mr. Bing will be glad to have me do the gardening next Spring again," but a few lines farther down the page, placating, and as if not to minimize the eye condition which had wrested him from that position: "My gardening days are over for good. . . . Now I have a nice job in a hospital—it is year around. . . . I must find my . . . happiness in helping others. I know I'll like this job. I have a lovely new home. . . . I painted my room and it looks beautiful. . . ."

Miller had saved the following momentous news for the very last. Prefacing it with further assurances about his liking for his new home and work—"I'm just a common porter, but it's an honest job"—and as if paving the way for favorable reception of his news, he announced boyishly: "Gosh, it's awful to live alone . . . but I hope to be married. . . . Does that surprise you? The girl I have in mind is my own age. . . . That will be a happy day. . . ."

Interview, July 9, 1949: Miller was meticulously scrubbed and combed, and was wearing his favorite crisp brown and tan summer cottons with harmonizing necktie. His face opened with pleasure when I commented on his appearance, and he spoke with pride and eagerness of his pleasure in "blended colors." He brought intelligence of the land: the country was beautiful, but the untended sections were "a disgrace: I had to try very hard to find a tree or a shrub that hadn't been attacked by some insect or some fungus attack. And the birds! I hardly saw a bluebird, not even one—and I was there at the beginning of the nesting season! And the robins were very scarce!" He didn't tarry long on this subject, however. He plunged into a zealous account of events since his departure from the city early in May.

"I was so happy! I tried so hard! I was so disappointed!" In this effusion of pleading and protestation was contained all Miller's need for sympathy, forbearance, and absolution. "I couldn't help myself," he protested. "Everything will be different from now on." [8]

[8] It is to be borne in mind by the reader that the censure against which Miller constantly pleaded existed solely in his mind. Although I was genuinely interested and sympathetic, my

"I tried so hard," Miller repeated. "And Mr. Bing, my boss—that man loved me, I worked so hard." The job had called for only eight hours daily, "but I worked fourteen and sixteen hours—I worked from early morning till late at night." He had designed gardens, Miller said with pride. He had hauled plants and earth—"I didn't have a truck; it was back-breaking! I did it all with a wheelbarrow." And he had "planted enough vegetables for two big buildings, and for marketing, too. We were suffering from drought," he continued, "so I stayed up late at night watering the lawns and plants. I planted the greenhouse full of beautiful roses, and I stayed up late at night taking care of them, too.

"One thing I proved to myself," he remarked importantly. "I *am* a gardener! It would have taken six men six months to do what I did in the 40 days I was there. It was so amazing Mr. Bing told the employment office he would be happy to have me back any time. He told me I could make my home there forever as far as he was concerned. I was going to buy a piece of land right on the property, and Mr. Bing—he had this old cabin—he was going to give it to me to move on my land. It broke my heart to have to go away."

He had naturally been exhausted, Miller continued. Even Mr. Bing had pointed out that " 'Rome wasn't built in a day.' " But Miller had an image of gardens restored to opulence, and himself forever honored among his vegetables and flowers. It was the "dry spell" which began at the end of his third week in Hartville that blasted all his hopes. "The sun was glaring! The sun on

primary relationship to my subjects is that of "historian," and not of counselor; in so far as humanly possible, my attitude was one of friendly neutrality.

the earth was blinding me! I couldn't look at it! In the greenhouse every time I turned, the sun on the glass would shoot into my eyes. Things began to get milky. I could just barely see. I couldn't see the flowers or anything."

In the glowing days before leaving the city for Hartville, Miller had made hurried preparations, not for a few months in the country, and in a spirit of experiment, but as if for the rest of his days in the Elysian fields. He had bought overalls, work shirts, and gardening gloves. For cold weather, heavy boots, a sweater, a cap, and a heavy jacket. For long winter nights he had gathered together his gardening books, cherished even in blindness, and purchased a small radio. Now in equally precipitous fashion Miller proceeded to strip himself of all he had so eagerly gained.

"I gave a woman who worked in the office my second suit of clothes. I told her, 'Give it to your husband!' I gave her my ties and my new jacket." To a family down the road he gave his overalls, work shirts, his beloved boots and gardening gloves. "I gave away everything," Miller said. "I gave Mr. Bing my gardening books—I thought I would never use them again! My little radio I sold because I needed the cash. I was disgusted," he said. "I wanted to get out of there as fast as I could. I threw up everything!"

Mr. Bing had remonstrated. Stay, he had said. There was no need to run away. Miller could work in the early hours of the morning before the sun was strong, and in the evenings after sundown. In the meantime, Bing pointed out, there was the famous eye clinic in Foley, less than sixty miles away, where Miller could get help. Miller, in panic, had been unable to accept this advice.

Miller had not wanted to return to his friends in the city "a failure." In addition there was that old apprehension which tugged at his consciousness, that in this place where he had already been twice convicted and was surely under suspicion, "something might happen"; that through some mistake, accident, peculiar mesh of circumstances, he would again be confronted with a crime. Divested of all but what he could carry in a small canvas handbag, Miller had set out, a stranger, to throw himself on the mercy of strangers, in a place where he was totally unknown. At the eye clinic in Foley, Miller was interviewed, examined, and told to return to the city, where he had established welfare status, and his case was known. Back in the city, he rented a small room, where he awaited his appointment with Dr. Garrison. In the meantime he bathed, ate, rested, and when he had slept, walked in the open air. What he had feared did not happen: panic died away. By the time he reached Dr. Garrison, he said delightedly: "My eyes must have been rested from the sun. Dr. Garrison said they were better than before I went away. Of course," he added, "I'll probably never be able to work the earth again."

(Medical record, June 1949: "Patient complains of sensitivity to light, blurred vision, general weakness, nervousness. O.D. 6/200, improved to 20/200 with lenses. O.S. 10/200, improved to 20/70. . . .")

Miller had hoped to return to his old position in the institute. This, he was told, was no longer possible, but it was with the help of institute personnel that he obtained the hospital job with which he was so pleased. He was earning ninety dollars a month, plus two meals daily, he reported. And should his eyes fail again, he remarked, in what better place could he be than in a hospital?

As for the contemplated marriage, as on the previous occasion, Miller had not yet met the lady; he was corresponding with her. This correspondence, he explained, had begun while he was in Hartville, when a staff member, seeing him writing to Mr. Hutchins in Braille, told him about Norma, "a good, Christian woman," whose hobby it was to translate material into Braille for the blind. The subject had only to be mentioned: Miller's eyes were already full of dreams. Forgotten were the experiences of the past, forgotten the statements of only a moment before. Miller's tone was that of a man needing only sanction to convert fantasy into reality.

"She's a good, kind, charitable woman," he argued. "She loves nature like I do, and she's interested in the blind. We have a whole lot in common." She was also comfortably fixed, he went on, her family having a winter home in Buck Falls and, in an attractive resort community, a pleasant guest house, which Norma managed in summer. "We would make a lovely couple!" Miller exclaimed. "In winter we could live in Buck Falls—that's a beautiful place! In summer she could manage the guest house, and I would do all the gardening. I'll make her happy! I know it! I will turn that place of hers into a gorgeous garden spot!"

On August 5 Miller announced that in a few days he would see Norma for the first time. He had already proposed by mail. "She said I would like to say yes, but I guess I'd better say I hope so until I've seen you and know you better. Those were her words," he wrote. On August 10, after his meeting with Norma, he reported that they liked each other "an awful lot," and added: "I think we will get married within a year." He had placed a deposit on an engagement and wedding-ring set: "Just think, I have someone to love and really want me." He still liked his hospital job, and he was "very well liked by all. Even though the pay is small, I am sticking it out here until Spring."

In an interview on August 14 Miller described his visit with Norma more fully. She was "a wonderful girl," but, he felt, "too much under the thumb of her family." Conceivably his original plans for their future would have to be altered—"I'm not sure her people like me enough." He was doing some week-end gardening and handy work around the neighborhood to supplement his income, and he described the set of rings that he was buying for Norma on the installment plan: ". . . it's a set of three rings. I got her a little cocktail ring with five little rubies and a tiny diamond in the center, an engagement ring that has five little diamond chips, too, and a wedding band." The set, he said impressively, was costing him one hundred and sixty dollars.

On September 5 Miller announced that he was returning to Hartville. He had already given his notice to the hospital. "You probably think this is strange after me telling you only two weeks ago how well I liked it at the hospital," he wrote. "Well, I hope to marry Norma on my next birthday. And Norma will not live in the city anywhere." Nor would Norma live in any summer resort, "but she will live on a farm." He was going to Hartville to rent a small farm. He planned also, he said, "to buy . . . equipment for pruning trees, shrubs and vines. This sort of work can be done all winter long, the winter months being the best for pruning trees." At the same time, he said, "I shall be getting my name established in

a township. By Spring I hope to go into landscape gardening very strong."

Norma's wedding and engagement rings were paid for
in full. (Where he had got the money to complete the
payments he did not, at this time, say.) On Christmas
Day, he said, he hoped to become officially engaged.
Only one thing stood in the way of all these plans, "and
that is the problem of money; I only have about sixty
dollars to start with. This isn't near enough, but if I
have to do with that amount, I will try it."

Miller's next communication told of astonishing happenings. He was in Hillbrook, not in Hartville as he
had intended. Shortly before leaving the city he had
received a special-delivery letter from a Mrs. Smythe-
Whitmore, "a grand person," summoning him to an interview at the exclusive Eidelweiss Arms Hotel. She had
heard his story and wanted to help him. "She decided
to bring me to Hillbrook to landscape her place. . . . It
looks now I may have my farm before Spring. . . . I am
engaged to Norma. . . . All my dreams come true. . . ."

On September 28 he wrote: ". . . Mrs. Smythe-Whitmore has turned out to be a flop. . . . She expects me to
landscape her place for nothing. I told her no good. One
of these sob sisters with more money than brains. I don't
know what to do. I've spent all my money getting here
and settled. Now I wish to hell I never seen this place.
Why is it I can't get a decent wage wherever I go . . . ?"

In a subsequent interview Miller sketched in the details of this adventure. Mrs. Smythe-Whitmore's letter,
which Miller had received as he was preparing to leave
the city to rent a farm with only sixty dollars in his
pocket, had struck him not merely as a special delivery
but as a special deliverance. His visit with Mrs. Smythe-

Whitmore at the elegant Eidelweiss Arms Hotel had fortified that impression. It didn't occur to the rapt Miller to discuss salary as Mrs. Smythe-Whitmore told him how she had heard of him, described her estate, and told him "that I was just the one to make it into a dream place." Nor did he mention the matter of transportation: "She looked like a nice woman. I assumed," he replied irritably, "that she had means." He had talked of more elevated things—how the earth should be nurtured, forests restocked, and constant war be waged against the earth's despoilers, and how working in this cause was his only joy. When Mrs. Smythe-Whitmore set a date for his arrival, Miller, at last found worthy, had rushed into his usual feverish preparations.

Miller's first misgivings occurred on arrival in Hillbrook when he was met at the station, not by his patroness, but by Mr. Smythe-Whitmore. His misgivings mounted when he learned that "my place wasn't ready for me. She had told me there would be a nice little place for me over the garage near their house. He parked me in a tourist camp. It seemed strange they didn't let me right in." In addition, he pointed out, though the Smythe-Whitmores paid his rent at the camp, "I had to buy my own food."

For several days, until his quarters were ready, Miller went to work from the camp. He reconnoitered the grounds. What he found, he said vehemently, was "a beautiful, big place," which had been "shamefully neglected. The shrubbery wasn't pruned. There were weeds all over the place, and they had only one measly little garden in the back. They wanted me to landscape the whole thing."

Miller made his plans, brought them to Mrs. Smythe-

Whitmore for discussion, then set to work. For more than a week he had pruned, weeded, and burned brush. He hauled rocks, earth, and shrubs, again not in a truck, but by his own power—in a wheelbarrow. That he did not ask the Smythe-Whitmores to hire a truck for this work was a design to demonstrate good faith. As when working for Mr. Bing in Hartville (and earlier, during his first weeks at the institute), Miller's efforts to please and impress had been Herculean. He was soon to learn that the gratitude, the tender attentions, the enthusiastic approbation he craved, were not forthcoming. Indeed, the more he expended himself, the more, it seemed to him, his efforts were taken for granted, and as resentment gathered there was in his design, perhaps, also something of intent to embarrass, even to accuse.

Miller's first talk with Mrs. Smythe-Whitmore in Hillbrook, while he was still at the tourist camp, had brought no specific understanding about salary. With good money going out, and suspicion seeping in, he had been uneasy, yet had been able only to hint at that question—and only apologetically. His eager heart had leaped when Mrs. Smythe-Whitmore remarked: "Don't worry about that. We'll take care of things." Now he was settled on the estate, and getting his food from the kitchen, but he was still dissatisfied. Not only did he feel unloved and unappreciated—where was the kudos he craved?—but the conviction was growing in him that he was actually being exploited. It was with resentment, yet with extreme difficulty that Miller, whose soaring hopes had surpassed mere business arrangements, finally blurted out: What *was* his salary to be? What, Mrs. Smythe-Whitmore wanted to know, had his previous salaries been? "I told her what Mr. Bing gave me—one hundred and fifty dollars a month and living quarters. She agreed to that," he said, "but at the same time," he added furiously, "she told me plenty of men would be glad to have a place to live and ten dollars a month during the winter months."

He would have settled for even that "for the sake of the flowers," he exclaimed, "but I could see that woman would never be satisfied. She agreed to my plans; then she kept asking me to change things around. The work I was doing for her—it was backbreaking! I would have to turn around and do it all over again!" In addition, he pointed out, "she didn't care what was good for the plants. Plants have their own environment, just like people!" he cried. "She was just plain dumb-ignorant! She wanted me to put sun plants in the shade, shade plants in the sun. Those plants would never thrive if they couldn't have what they need. After ten or twelve days like that," he said, "she got me so upset I quit in the middle of the day. I went to my room and I wrote her a letter, and I told her I came up there in good faith, with the intention of making her a dream place, and that nothing was the way she said it would be. I left the note in her house and went back to my quarters, and then her husband come over and he said, 'You'd better leave right now,' and he took me into town."

Miller had already communicated with Mr. Bing, asking to come back to Hartville. Mr. Bing had declined—"and that was supposed to be a life-time job," Miller commented bitterly. His intentions were good, he cried, yet it seemed to him no one, no one he cared for, loved or wanted him. He had returned to the city profoundly depressed, and again haunted by the fear of being accused of a theft. He was worried about Norma too, he confided. He was afraid she would hear of his record. Would she reject him, too?

City
October 17, 1949

. . . *I am afraid and worried and have worried myself sick thinking my past might back fire on me. How can I be happy when I have such a worry on my mind? However I have taken some of the worry out of the picture by going direct to Norma and laying the cards on the table and telling her the truth about myself. . . . And believe me it took a lot of courage to tell her. I realized I could never marry Norma unless she heard the truth from me. To show you the kind of girl Norma is she said she would still marry me. The only thing Norma and I have to worry about now is that Norma's family doesn't hear of it, because if they did the whole thing would be off. And I'm sure if I can't have Norma I'd want to meet my maker pretty quick. . . . I am doing handy man work at Excelsior. It is an office building. I work 10 a.m. to 7 p.m. . . .*

City
October 30, 1949

. . . *Please do not repeat this to anyone as this is strickly between you and I. This I do know. Nobody can do anything about it. I have lost the sight in my right eye completely. I can see only light and shadows with it, although my left eye is constantly getting stronger. Getting around at night is a difficult problem for me, as any kind of light at all blinds me. . . . I do have some problem with my work because of the eye condition, but I do . . . the best*

I know how. They all like me here. . . . Starting from this week I will be working six days a week instead of five days, making my pay larger. I am trying to save for when Norma and I will get married. I am working on a plan where by I can get a job on a estate as caretaker and gardener. Norma said she would go along with me on that. She's a lovely girl. I'm writing letters to wherever I can on that subject, as I must get out of the city as soon as possible. The city is making me very nervous. . . .

On November 25 Miller wrote briefly: He was doing well. His employer at the Excelsior had invited him to Thanksgiving dinner: "I had a grand time at his home. . . . I hope this little note finds you well and happy." I did not hear from Miller again for more than two months.

Interview, February 4, 1950: Miller was dressed in a navy-blue suit with spotless white shirt and deep-blue tie. His broad, blunt-featured face shone with beatitude. He had been through some bad times, terrible times, he said, but he had weathered them. Just before Christmas Norma had changed her mind: she had returned his rings, breaking their engagement, and though she did this kindly, he said, she denied him even the solace of friendship. In January, the city again having become intolerable, he had fled to a job in Hartville. The job, entailing care of a group of greenhouses, was to pay one hundred and sixty-five dollars a month and living-quarters. But once more Miller had made grandiose assumptions and was bitterly disillusioned.

"The job was misrepresented," he said. "The greenhouses were neglected and run down—and they were thirteen miles from where I was staying, and I didn't have a car. And when I got there," he added angrily, "I found out it [his quarters] was two rooms over a garage, and I would have to buy and cook my own food." He had returned immediately to the city, where, contrary to his fears, he was welcomed back to work at the Excelsior. "Everybody was so glad to have me back! They are all so good to me! I wish you could meet my boss, and all the lovely people I work for!" Now he had really learned his lesson: "This time I'm really settling down."

He was being given extra work around the building to supplement his income, and one of the tenants in the building who had a country house had promised week-end gardening in the spring. He was replenishing his wardrobe—a source of great satisfaction: now he had two good suits again, more than a half dozen shirts, three pairs of shoes, and a collection of handsome neckties. On Sunday mornings, he continued, he frequently went to church, not, he wanted it known, because he believed what was taught about God and death and the after life. The Church, he said tolerantly, was "just trying to give people peace in a way they can understand," but he knew better. He went to church because he liked the music and the people. Evenings, at about nine o'clock, at a certain table at the Bright Light Cafeteria, he nearly always found four or five acquaintances, one or two people who worked in the neighborhood, and the "regulars" like himself who lived in near-by rooming-houses and dropped in for a bedtime chat and "a little bite to eat."

Half apologetically Miller displayed a large and gleaming wrist watch. "I knew you would understand," he said happily when the watch had been duly admired. "I just couldn't resist it! I get so much comfort out of a beautiful thing like that." Next he showed a pen-and-pencil set. He had had a ring, too, he confessed, but that had been "a terrible disappointment." When Norma returned her rings, he said, he had turned them back to the dealer at a third of the cost to him. Shortly afterwards walking along Shore Avenue, a desultory street of pawnshops, second-hand book and magazine stores, souvenir, novelty and jewelry shops, his attention was caught by "a beautiful man's ring. It had a good-sized diamond and three little rubies. It was for the little finger," Miller recalled. "I was so miserable I just needed something like that to comfort me. It looked so pretty I went right in and bought it. It cost me sixty dollars."

He had gone straight home, where he could admire his ring under a magnifying glass, "but when I looked—it was so disappointing! I was so disappointed, it was terrible! I should have known it was too beautiful!" Miller exclaimed. "That stone was too big at such a low price not to have something wrong! The stone had a crack in it!"

Miller had lost his pleasure in the ring immediately. "I put it away; I just lost interest. If it wasn't perfect I didn't want it." Later, when he had needed money, he said, he sold it to his friend Buck Toledano, a cab-driver who frequently joined Miller and his new cronies at the Bright Light Cafeteria, where they met for bedtime snacks. In the meantime, he said, "I've got this watch. This seems to satisfy me for now. I don't have such a craving for jewelry any more."

Perhaps it was Miller's most important news that lay behind his present beatitude: for the third time he had great expectations. Throughout the interview Miller's manner had been that of one demonstrating virtues—industry, patience, humility, self-restraint. "I'm being a *good* boy," his manner seemed to say. "I'm doing all the proper things. Surely when the sweets are passed, I too will be found worthy." This time Miller's expectations concerned Hattie McBride, "a lovely, quiet girl about thirty-nine," a file clerk who lived with her father on a small farm within commuting distance of the city. They were "grand people," Miller said. He was especially pleased that Mr. McBride, a retired policeman, seemed to accept him. In Mr. McBride's acceptance, paradoxically, lay a special security.

Oh, he was crossing no bridges, Miller opined. "I've learned my lesson! I wouldn't leave my job for anything! But I *would* leave," he said in the old imploring tone, "for a nice little place in the country. I could be a big help to him. I could sell milk and flowers and vegetables. I would make money, and I would add to the land—just ten acres is all that I would need. I could keep two cows, about three hundred chickens, and a few pigs. I would do all the work myself—I don't even need a horse. I would eat from what I raised, and I would sell the rest, and I'd take that cash and turn it back into seed and put it right back in the earth where it belongs. . . ."

Interview, February 16, 1950: This was an unseasonably warm day. The interview took place on a bench in a large public park. Miller, though still in comparatively good spirits, was in a somewhat reflective mood. He spoke of his sisters: "I've seen them a few times," he said, "but once you've been in trouble some people will always watch their step. They gave people a very bad impression while I was in jail," he said resentfully, "and now they can't even face me when I'm making good. I guess they keep looking for me to get in trouble even when I'm making good."

He spoke glowingly of Hattie, but confessed anxiety, too. He was worried about the condition of his eyes. Should he tell Hattie? And should he tell her of his prison record? Would he lose her as he lost Norma? Did he dare *not* to tell her? "I get so worried about my record backfiring on me. I get scared at night. I'm nervous about Hattie's father," he added confidentially. "A man like that—he likes me, but he used to be a policeman! Suppose he hears about me! Those cops—they can be brutal.

"It's a feeling," Miller continued, as he tried to explain. "I wouldn't steal," he protested. "I'll *never* steal again. Even when I know that's true, sometimes I feel like the police are watching me. It makes me so nervous! That's why I'm always thinking about going to live in the country. Conscience," he remarked, "is an awful thing sometimes."

And he spoke long and eloquently of his old preoccupation with the "secret of life and death."

"I think about it," he said, "but I'll never go back to the graves. I think about my whole life," he continued. "I was always lonely for Clara—she was the one love of my life. Even today I still think about her. I always remember that dream when I was a little kid and I found her in the woods. Even when I was a little kid in the orphanage—when I found that place where my father and mother and Clara were buried—I wanted to get right down and scratch the dirt away. I wanted to rip that thing [the stone] out and just get in there—I was always trying to figure out what death was. I was always hearing about the end of the world, but I found out there is no end. I don't believe in heaven or hell. I don't believe in God the way they teach you in church either. It's different from that. . . . Instead of wearing black to a funeral people ought to be happy when a person dies," he exclaimed. "Because he's going back into the earth where he came from.

"I know the truth now," Miller continued. "I *studied* death. When I used to go into those crypts, or in the graveyard—I'd concentrate so hard it was like my body didn't even exist. I went right *into* death. . . ."

Miller warmed to his subject. "I used to think I wanted to be buried, but when I die I want to be cremated," he declared. "It takes too long for the flesh to decay and be taken into the earth. When you're buried," he explained, "there's so much useless stuff. There's cloth, metals, decorations—it's just a waste of earth space! Even the flesh doesn't benefit the earth till it's decayed. In fact it sours the earth! And it takes a body about ten years to get decayed. It's the potash from the bones that's left after the body decays that benefits the earth. That's the part the earth takes back. When I die," he said, "I want to be cremated and have the potash that's left thrown in a field where the earth and the wild flowers can get the benefit right away."

Miller looked around. The air was balmy, the trees showing green. I commented that spring had come early this year. "No," he said, still scanning the landscape. "I look for another snowstorm before winter is really over." How did he know? "I've been watching the birds and squirrels," he said. "I had a squirrel in my lap last week. By springtime," he explained, "they should be ready to shed, but their fur is still thick and tight. The buds on the trees—they're still tight, too. The frogs should be starting to croak. Instead," he said, "they're still snug as a bug in the mud."

He paused. Then, with mounting lyricism: "Nature! If I could be with nature. I like to get right down to the earth. I did it as a kid, and I still like to sit on the warm dirt and get fascinated watching a little bug. . . . I pick the leaves of different trees and look at them. I hold them up to the light and see all their little veins, and the perfect pattern they make; the backs of some of them are silvery, and bright on the other side. . . . If I could paint the picture that is in my mind on the earth! If I could put my *mind* on a piece of earth! I would make such a beautiful garden! *I* would show them where God is."

On March 12 Miller wrote that in two or three weeks he was leaving the city again. ". . . As I told you, I've already lost the sight in my right eye, and during the last two weeks I have had trouble with the other eye." He had seen Dr. Garrison twice in the past week, the first time in his office, the second time in a hospital where Dr. Garrison had invited another eye specialist to take a look at him. "I guess," Miller commented, "Dr. Garrison knows how serious it all is."

Miller outlined his plans. This time he was going to Newclark, where he would "settle down the rest of my life." If he was to become completely blind again he did not wish to be in the city. He had chosen Newclark "because there is an agricultural school for the blind in that state. By going there," he pointed out, "I will have established myself as a resident . . . and will become a citizen. Thereby . . . I can apply for state aid and work at the farm school for the blind. So you see I am working on a long range program. . . ."

On the face of it this seemed a realistic plan, though I was to learn later that, characteristically, mere knowledge that such a school existed had been enough for

Miller. So desirable had been his plan, it was compelling; the need to make inquiries had seemed superfluous to him. And as the letter progressed, ingratiating, mounting in longing, and then flaring into ardor, Miller jumped the track; and here again was that blatant quality of disjuncture, of unreality. It was as if at one moment the limitations imposed on him by the condition of his eyes were grasped realistically enough. At the next moment Miller was displaying a supreme disregard, not only for the condition of his eyes, but for *all* the realities of life. It was, mysteriously, as if his sliding scale of vision were, after all, subservient to some higher strategy, with the unquenchable compulsion of his desire, his only necessary magic.

"There is plenty of work for a gardener in Newclark," the letter continued. ". . . This summer I am going to study plant therapy . . . by feel.[4] I hope before fall to build a one-room little house on a piece of land where I can grow my own food and be independent. . . . That's what I want more than anything else in the world, and that is to have a tiny piece of my own, and I'll never get it in the city, that's for sure." The letter concluded with the old vehement cry: "all the money in the world will not make me happy in the city. I hate it here in the city. . . ."

I received the foregoing letter on March 13. That evening, in a condition bordering on hysteria, Miller telephoned. Could I see him immediately? Something terrible had happened. We arranged to meet in my office an hour later.

Miller arrived, tense, perspiring profusely, and in a

[4] The practice of plant therapy by a blind man is an impossibility.

highly nervous state. His speech was explosive and disjoined. "This city!" he burst out. "I'm getting away from here! I'm going so far—I'll never come back.

"I'll have two hundred dollars when I get my next salary. I don't want to get married. I don't want anything. I just want to be alone. I want to get back to the country. If I go to Newclark—I have no record there! That's what has me so nervous all the time! I know I can make a go of it," he continued. "Even if I go completely blind—I'm a *good* gardener," he argued. "I'll study—I'll know the colors by the species of the plants. I'll grow my own food. A blind man can milk a cow."

Miller talked on, a frantic outpouring. Out of the disconnected mass, bit by bit, the following information emerged. Friendship with Hattie had been progressing nicely. He had been seeing her in the city, visiting her in the country, and making ambitious plans. But as hope mounted, so did apprehension until, about two weeks before, unable to endure the tension any longer, Miller had confessed his prison record. "She was shocked. She broke the engagement," he said. "She said if her father ever found out he would kill me. It made me sick to my stomach."

In the following week Miller had been ill, depressed, afraid. What if Hattie told her father? He managed to keep on with his work, but, feeling unloved, unwanted, and lacking the prestige of plans, he had no heart for chitchat at the Bright Light Cafeteria. "I just stayed to myself."

On Monday, March 6, vision failing, suffering from headache and from that alarming clangor in his ears, he had paid his visit to Dr. Garrison. A day or two later he went the second time. On the evening of March 11, somewhat comforted, he had dropped in at the cafeteria. His cronies were buzzing with excitement. Had he heard about Buck, they asked. They were taking up a collection, two dollars from each, for Buck's family. Did he want to contribute? Two evenings before, they told him, Buck had been found sitting slumped over the wheel of his cab, the motor still running. He had been struck on the back of the head. He was dead.

Miller had been fond of Buck, cab-driver, philosopher, man about town, who brought to the cafeteria a continuous store of anecdotes and comments about the foibles of human nature. Miller had given Buck one of his suits to pass on to his growing son, and some ties, and a shirt, which had been given him by one of the businessmen at the Excelsior. Buck had died in this terrible way, but there was no room for grief in Miller's constricted heart.

Now it had happened, that conspiracy of circumstances which pointed the finger at him. "This is the thing I was afraid of all the time," he cried. "It lays there in my mind—I can't get it out of my mind!" Suppose, he asked, Hattie's ex-policeman father had become suspicious. He had only to consult the police records, so accessible to him. Suppose, in addition, police were wondering where Buck got that diamond ring. Surely that, too, led inevitably to him. Suppose it was a stolen ring. That was entirely possible of a ring bought on shabby Shore Avenue. "Even if I didn't steal it, they would never believe me! What will I do if detectives come and question me? What would they say to my boss? Those people think the world of me! I don't want to be a thief. I don't want to fall in the gutter!"

Miller said that he had rushed home from the cafeteria to search for the receipt, his proof that he had bought the ring, but that he had not been able to find it. Nor could he return to the dealer for a copy of the receipt: he was afraid that if inquiries were being made, "I would attract attention." He was still searching. He was getting out of town. But before he went, there was something else, he said, that he wanted me to know. "After I'm gone you might hear a lot of things. I want to protect my good name."

In the fine days, just after the return of his vision, and while he was still a celebrity, Miller had among his friends one named Harriet Blivens. Mrs. Blivens, a widow, was a woman in her sixties, "but looks to be about forty." They had become friends after she stopped him on the street near church one day saying: " 'You are Mr. Miller. Mrs. Hansen told me about you. She said you were a wonderful man, and I should know you.' She invited me to Sunday dinner," he said. He had become a frequent visitor in Mrs. Blivens's home.

In September, just after his talk with Mrs. Smythe-Whitmore at the Eidelweiss Arms, Miller continued, he had paid a visit to Mrs. Blivens. "This looked like my big opportunity. I was so happy," he said. "But I was worried. I needed money to get there, and I needed work clothes and something in my pocket—I just hated to go up to those people looking like a pauper. I was telling Mrs. Blivens about my big opportunity," he went on, "and the next time I came she handed me this envelope. She said: 'Mr. Miller, I want to help you.' Those were her words," he said. "It was a gift—it was a gift and nothing else." The envelope contained ninety dollars. That, combined with his savings, had paid for Norma's rings, for his country wardrobe and equipment, and his fare to Hillbrook. After the fiasco in Hillbrook and his igno-

minious return, he had taken a room in another neighborhood and had not seen Mrs. Blivens again. It was not
until late in November when, working at the Excelsior,
having weathered the loss of Norma, and once more
thinking of marriage, this time to Hattie, Miller in expansive mood ventured back to the old neighborhood.

"When I got there," Miller said, "I heard the rumor
was going around that 'Miller got her for a hundred
dollars!' In the hardware store I heard the same thing
again! That woman!" he exclaimed. "She was ruining my
good reputation! She was going around saying I misled
her and got a hundred dollars from her. A thing like that
going around—it was terrible!

"I didn't mislead her," Miller continued indignantly.
"*She* had ideas in her *own* mind. I never even liked her.
She used to invite me for meals and for tea. Tea!" he exclaimed. "Beer is more what it was! She stank to high
heaven with booze! Once she invited me to room in her
house, but I would never do that. I saw," he said sancti-
moniously, "that there was sex in it. I wasn't interested.
I used to visit her because I was lonesome," he said appeal-
ingly. "I liked her as a friend. I never said anything else."

He had been furious, Miller went on. "That was when
I took out the diamond ring and sold it to Buck Toledano. I sold it for thirty-eight dollars! I took that thirty-
eight dollars and a whole week's salary, and I went over
there and I knocked on her door. When that woman
saw me she went white as snow. She said: 'I thought
you were never coming back.' I said: 'It's evident you
never expected me back! You smeared my name all over
the neighborhood.' Then I asked her: 'Do you want your
money back?' She said: 'Yes.' I said: 'You can have
your money back, but you can't have it till you sign a

receipt,' and I wrote out the receipt and read it to her, and I held that money tight in my hand till she signed it. Then I took it and went around to everybody! I went all around the neighborhood. I went to the hardware store where my name had been plastered around, and I saw to a couple of other old gossipers, too. I even went to the pastor and to Mrs. Hansen—she's a lovely person! I showed it to everyone, and I have it right here to prove it." With a proud and angry gesture Miller produced a carefully folded piece of paper. Miller's large, meticulously drawn oval letters filled the square.

I received from Mr. William Miller 90 dollars [it said]. This is the 90 dollars I gave Mr. William Miller as a gift. He is returning the gift 90 dollars, on this day November 27, 1949.

Ignobly crowded into the small space beneath this flourishing statement, and written in a cramped, Victorian hand was the signature: "Harriet Blivens."

At the close of the interview I helped Miller to his bus. Even with my arm, as well as his cane to guide him, he seemed fearful, uncertain, giving almost an impression of tottering.

Medical record, March 1950:

"Weakness; sensitivity to light; blurred vision; patient complains of old symptoms, including ringing in ears. O.D. light perception, corrected to 5/200 with lenses. O.S. vision down to 5/200, corrected to 6/200."

In an interview some time later Dr. Garrison pointed out that the degree of Miller's vision and the actual physical findings had been "definitely at odds." The doctor noted that "fluctuations in Miller's vision certainly seem to coincide with emotional changes, but whether for better or for worse the original diagnosis has always remained the same." That Miller should have been blind or nearly blind was not incommensurate with medical findings, although, the doctor pointed out, in cases of early optic atrophy the presence of some vision is not unusual. But how Miller had regained his sight after so long a period of blindness, and how, in the face of his "optic picture," he was able to see as well as he had— these remain the provocative questions.

Newclark
March 21, 1950

. . . *I have now taken a positive step toward a happier life. With my handicap I will try very hard to build up a small trade in the landscaping line. I am just a few miles from the agricultural school although just at present the school isn't operating. . . . I have very little money, and none coming in . . . but hoping some will soon. I hope by fall to have a small piece of land and try to build a small cabin. . . . The first night I came here I was very lucky to find a room with a private family and they want me to make it my home and don't want me to just stay in my room. They . . . are lovely to me. So maybe that's a lucky sign for me.*

Steinbeck, Pa.
May 11, 1950

. . . *I thought I would settle down and find a permanent home before I wrote you. I secured work at a large nursery here just a twenty minute ride from my home. I have been working at this nursery for three weeks and so far as I know I will try to stick this one out. I have a lovely*

*little apartment which I painted and fixed up myself. . . .
I work six days one week and 7 days every other
week. . . . I visit my sister quite often. . . . She has
been very helpful to me. . . . I earn about fifty dollars a
week. . . . I feel as though I may find . . . happiness
in my life. . . . I shall drop you a letter from time to
time. . . .*

Montgomery
September 16, 1950

. . . This will I know be news to you. I got married a
few weeks ago. . . . We have a farm that Mrs. Miller
bought with her own money using every penny she had,
which was four thousand. The farm cost 9 thousand and
five hundred dollars. When we bought this place it was
asoomed I would get a job in Jensen and finish paying off
the . . . morgage. . . . I agreed to pay the morgage
. . . forty dollars per month, and the interest twice an-
nually. The first interest, one hundred and thirty seven
dollars, is due in February 1951. The taxes are one hundred and fifteen dollars per year and due in April 1951.
Electric lights cost us three per month.

We have just a few dollars between Mrs. Miller and I,
enough to keep us alive a month. . . . I haven't been
able to secure work in the mill in Jensen. Unemployment
is a serious thing as far as we are concern. Two weeks
from now our first [mortgage] payment of forty dollars
is due, but we only have five dollars toward it. Where do
we go from here? . . . Our only salvation now is to stock
our farm with laying hens and horse and wagon. . . . I
have been all over the state trying to raise about two
thousand dollars to stock this farm. If that can be done
we have hope we can save this farm, but if we cannot

stock this farm it will be a total loss to both of us. But I
couldn't raise a dime anywhere. . . . Can you give me
any advice on this problem . . . ? I sincerely hope to
hear from you soon.

Interview, November 26, 1950:   Miller, back in the city,
had telephoned for an appointment. Normally a husky,
barrel-chested fellow with a bland, ingratiating expression, Miller was extremely tense and jumpy, and was
much thinner than when I had last seen him, nine
months before. His eyes, magnified by thick-lensed
glasses, seemed to have undergone a subtle change in
color, and the areas beneath them were dark and deeply
indented. His forehead was drawn. On his face was the
intent expression of a man engaged in dogged effort to
keep a dissolving world in focus. He was volatile, irritable,
and scattered in his speech. His cane, as he approached
me, had beaten an angry rhythm. This was to be our
final interview.

Newclark, like all the other places to which he had
rushed in flight and search, had been a disappointment—
the agricultural home for the blind to which he had
looked as a haven closed; the small piece of land and the
small cabin, so available in fantasy, not to be had; the
demands of work, great; pay, small; the cost of living,
high. And he had so many crying needs. He had no
sooner settled in Newclark than that remorseless objective again beckoned. He began thinking of family and
birthplace, and returned to Steinbeck. But here, too,
something he craved, needed—he was "weak," "blind,"
"lost," a newborn puppy shoved from the hutch—was
not forthcoming. There was only one strain of hope:
Mrs. Elvira Webster, a woman several years his senior,

who ran a rooming-house in Steinbeck. It was not clear to me whether Miller met her at this time or they had come to know each other in the course of his previous visits. "I was lonesome and she was lonesome, so I used to visit her," Miller said. "She liked to hear me talk about nature. She was so nice to me. I wanted to marry her."

His plans were no sooner budding, and dreams enfolding him, than Mrs. Webster made a decision she had long been considering. She closed up the rooming-house. Taking her life's savings, she moved to Columbus, where she had relatives, and where she had been offered a wage and living-quarters in return for looking after a country store. Miller was desolate. Within ten days of Mrs. Webster's departure he had written telling her of his great love, asking if there was work to be had in Columbus where he could be close to her; and before he could receive her negative reply, he had presented himself at her door. He made an impassioned plea. Mrs. Webster took him in.

Their first two or three weeks were idyllic, he said. They lived in an apartment above the store. Characteristically, for a time Miller worked long and hard and ostentatiously, scrubbing floors, arranging the stock, and endearing himself to the customers. He and Elvira decided to be married. But before long the old restiveness, the gnawing dissatisfaction, again assailed him.

Miller was irritable as he tried, fumblingly, to describe that state of mind. Elvira's relatives had liked him in the beginning, but developed "a prejudice against me: I could tell they wanted her to get rid of me." Elvira, too, was somehow disappointing. "I wanted love," he cried. "I wanted a peaceful home and someone to love me!"

Elvira, as it turned out, was self-preoccupied, critical, demanding. "She wasn't well—she couldn't work much—she complained about her stomach. It was all mental," Miller snapped. "She was a very nervous person! I wasn't well myself, and I was doing all that work, and it didn't seem like it was appreciated by anybody."

As the wedding day approached, Miller himself became increasingly nervous. His eyes were poor. His head ached. He was worried, tired. One evening while Elvira was in the store downstairs, "I threw a pair of overalls out of the window. Then I took three hundred dollars in cash that she had in the house, and I climbed down the back of the house, and I just lit out.

"I don't know what's the matter with me," Miller cried. "I don't want to steal."

He had gone about two miles "but I couldn't stand it. I felt—what I felt—it was suffering! I turned around and went back—nobody will ever know the pain I felt. I went past Elvira—she was sitting in the store—and I went upstairs, and I called her to come up. The darn fool!" he sputtered. "Why did she have to keep money like that in the house? I handed her the money and I said: 'Elvira, here's your money! For God's sake, hide it away.' I told her: 'I had this impulse to take it, but I didn't! I brought it back!'

"She was very upset. I don't blame her," he continued wretchedly. "She wasn't going to marry me, even if her reputation was ruined. I pleaded with her for days—I wanted to explain it to her: I *had* this impulse, but if I could bring it back—I was getting over it. If I could only be where I was happy—I loved that woman," he declared. "It was those relations of hers—it was that store. I told her if we could only get away by ourselves—if we could have a little farm—if she would only stick with me, I knew I could lick it."

He had pleaded his case, but at the same time, Miller told me: "I was scared. I *wanted* to make good, but I was scared something would happen. I wanted everything to be nice, but I was too upset. The night before we got married I told her all about my prison record. I told her if she wanted, I would go away. She decided to take a chance."

About two weeks after their marriage Miller took another sum of money, fled to another city, returned. "I brought back everything except about forty dollars that I had spent for room, and buses, and things like that." Again he had pleaded—"I got in so deep with lies—I don't know what got into me: I didn't want her to leave me. I told her I had a little property in Cliff City. I said I went to see about selling it to raise a little money for a farm. I told her, if we could only get away—if we could put down a payment on a farm, I would get a job to pay the mortgage payments, and I could raise chickens and grow flowers and vegetables in my spare time. . . ."

Miller must have been persuasive: Mrs. Miller put her life's savings into the purchase of a farm, chosen for its proximity to a factory. The money from Miller's imaginary property, of course, never materialized. Neither did the job in a factory. "I took the word of the farm-owner that I could get a job in the factory," Miller said aggrievedly. That his fluctuating vision might have been a deterrent in factory work was apparently never a consideration. And whether Mrs. Miller was fully aware of her husband's handicap remains a mystery. Now Miller had his farm at last, but no job, no money, no equipment with which to run a farm. Bills mounted. Mrs. Miller's reserves dwindled and with them her hope, her confidence, and forbearance. She was "sick," "cried," "nagged." Miller, wretched and half blind, worked for his neighbors in the harvesting of their crops.

From this point onward Miller's account became increasingly garbled. On at least two more occasions he took money, ran away, returned. Each time he ran a little farther, stayed a little longer, and brought back less. He spoke of jewelry he had taken, too. "By that time my eyes were so bad it was like so much junk to me—I just pawned it. But I got it back! I got it back for her! I borrowed money, and I worked—I worked like a dog picking apples—you can write to the man and ask him. I got every bit of it back."

On some days he fought for his marriage. "If I brought things back," he said he told his wife, "I *must* be making an improvement. At other times," he said, "I felt everything was hopeless. I couldn't do anything right, and I was sorry for Elvira—that woman felt so ashamed, but at the same time I couldn't stand her pecking at me. She was always pecking, so I would tell her if she wanted to get rid of me, maybe that would be best. And then I would want her back."

At summer's end the Millers went together to a lawyer. They told him of Miller's thefts and restitutions. Neither wanted trouble or publicity: they wanted a discreet divorce. Miller agreed to pay the legal fees at the rate of five dollars a week and left town immediately.

Since that time, Miller said, he had been in several cities and had worked at several jobs. He had also attempted a reconciliation with Mrs. Miller. At this time he was working as janitor and night watchman in an animal hospital in the city.

"I'm here now," he said, "but I don't know where I'm going to be. I know I can't stay here. I can't seem to settle down anywhere. I'm paying for the divorce, but I don't know how long I can keep it up. I don't know what's going to happen to me. I'm sick and I'm worried. I'm worried, and I'm looking for something. I don't want to fall in the gutter. I'm just living in a suitcase. It looks like it will never be different. I've got to live in a suitcase all the rest of my life—I'll be that way till I die."

Miller emptied his pockets on the desk, fumbling and peering as he sifted the documents of his life, and then shoved them across the desk to me. "I don't know where I'm going," he repeated. "I don't know where I'm going to be." It seemed to please him that somewhere was a repository for the stuff of his life. Would I, he wanted to know, take it for safekeeping?

There were two money-order receipts, each for the sum of five dollars, made out to his wife's lawyer. There was the receipt signed by Harriet Blivens; the business card of the veterinarian, his present employer; the card of an eye doctor residing in another city. There were two plain white filing cards. On each of these Miller had printed: "IN CASE OF DEATH PLEASE GET IN TOUCH WITH"— and had added the name and address of a sister. There was Buck's memorial card; on one side were the dates of his birth and death, and a prayer; on the other side was a glowing colored picture of the Holy Mother and Child. Finally there was a letter from Mrs. Miller's lawyer acknowledging receipt of a money order, telling Miller that his wife had been ill, that she was hard put to raise cash due on the mortgage, and that there was no hope whatever for a reconciliation.

I did not hear from Miller again until February 1951,

when within a space of five days I received two letters from him. Neither bore a return address. Only the post-marks, San Simele and Desmond, indicated his where-abouts. Both were high-keyed and somewhat garbled. Gone was the old meticulous penmanship.

"This is the last letter you'll ever receive from me," the first began. "I expect to be back in prison shortly." He had been unable to find work anywhere, he said, "and if I did find it I couldn't heled it as I now have little better than light perception."

He had "borrowed five hundred dollars from a person in Bellhope with the promis to pay it back with five days. I intended to give it back just as I said I would do. . . ." He had "borrowed large sums of money several times during the year and each time I gave it back. . . . The money seemed to be my only friend. But this time I failed to give it back. . . . But this time I lied to get the money as I did all the other times. . . . But this time I let the money get away from me. . . . I wanted companionship. . . . I went to Sharktown . . . and from there I went from one city to another. . . . Within three weeks the five hundred is gone. . . ."

He wished himself dead. He could stand the strain no longer. ". . . I wanted to make a life a good one." He supposed "after you read this letter you will hate me like the rest will. . . . I hope you won't hate me. . . . You were a friend. . . ." The letter closed with the following postscript: "I am mentally ill my head is bursting." The second communication was more or less a repetition of this one.

About four months later, in June, came another com-munication, and on July 10 another. These, too, were without return address. Each envelope bore the postmark of a different state. "I have never been able to give myself up to the police. . . . I am very sick. . . . I don't know where it will end for me . . ." but he had found "some of the answers to the things I'm searching for. . . . I know the only God that exist is within our inner soul's thinking power. . . . Last night I knocked out a church window so I could be in the church alone and think. . . . Yes, I have study the dead again. . . ."

He was making his living by stealing. ". . . I never stay more than six or seven days in one town. . . . I cannot help myself. Please don't hate me, and please forgive me for writing to you, but your the only person I can write to. . . . I find it very hard to get money to live on, so may get picked up any day now. You shall be notified when that time comes. . . ."

On July 23, from still another state, Miller wrote: "This is it. I can't stand the strain any longer. I must get back into an institution very soon. This Wednesday I will let the police have me. . . . As far as I know I will be sent to the state Prison in Arkinsant. I am in the city of Durant now and I have written the city police to pick me up down town in front of one large department store at noon Wednesday. . . ."

Shortly after receiving this letter I had a talk with Dr. Hertz, the veterinarian, who had been Miller's last employer. Miller had left that job within a day or two after our final interview. Dr. Hertz remembered Miller well. He spoke of him as "an odd character."

Had Miller worked well?

"Well? Well, yes and no. He worked very hard. There's no question about that. But the job didn't require that much work. And he made such a show of it." When Miller had taken the job, it was explained to him that he would begin at nine o'clock each evening. The next day he showed up at six thirty. It was pointed out to him that there was no necessity for such zeal. Miller protested that he "didn't mind," and the next day showed up at six thirty again. "We gave up," the doctor said. "After that he was a little more relaxed. His starting hours varied, but he was never late; he always arrived early."

Among Miller's duties was that of mopping the floors, and a pail and mops were provided for that purpose. Miller, the doctor said, wouldn't think of using the mops. "He insisted on scrubbing the floors on his hands and knees. He was so meticulous," the doctor smilingly added, "soap and water were not enough. He asked for Lysol and he insisted on using Lysol in the water."

A supply of crackers for personnel was kept in the hospital refrigerator. These were pointed out to Miller: should he get hungry during the night, he was told, he was to feel free to help himself. Miller had been very grateful. Every morning when staff members arrived they found the supply entirely gobbled up.

"He was an odd person," Dr. Hertz repeated. "He had everybody feeling so sorry for him. He was on duty here on Thanksgiving Day. Darned if some neighborhood woman didn't bring him Thanksgiving dinner! You can imagine what that meant to a man like him. He was so overjoyed he just couldn't stop talking about it."

Miller had stayed on this job for a total of only about ten days. One evening when the doctor arrived he found Miller's keys to the hospital, along with a note, in a conspicuous spot on his desk. He was quitting, Miller had said, because he could not endure the yelping of the dogs, and the odor of animal excrement. "Five minutes

later the phone rang. It was Miller," the doctor continued. "He wanted to make sure I had found the keys. He
seemed terribly afraid they would fall into the wrong
hands and that something might be stolen."

Following is the transcription of a letter, written in
Braille, to a staff member of the Institute for the Training and Rehabilitation of the Blind:

> *Arkinsant State Penitentiary*
> *Durant, Ark.*
> *November 20, 1951*

> *. . . I have suffered mentally terrible since short stay
> here. I am very unhappy man brokenhearted to say the
> least. I have been a thief since childhood and I tried
> desperately to control myself but failed. I knew I could
> never break the urge to steal. Therefore before I came
> to you, I destroyed my eyes first by burning them, and
> when that did not work I forced them out of my head
> with my thumbs several times until I killed the
> nerve. . . . . It was a sad day for me when my sight
> came back. . . . But what you didn't know was that
> instead of my sight coming back to stay it was only
> temporary. . . . I went blind the past year I have gone
> into total blindness. What I tried to do . . . years ago
> has now finally happened. But too late, now I am blind
> brokenhearted and in prison. . . . The only happiness
> in my life was at your school. . . .*

A check on the veracity of Miller's statement that he
was again totally blind brought the following responses.
One informant wrote:

With regard to William Miller's eye condition, he is blind as a bat, and was at the time he committed his last offense—stealing money from a church. He has never given out as to how he accomplished this deed. As to his adjustment, he is mean as hell. . . .

A second informant stated:

We have contacted the . . . opthalmologist who is a highly respected man in his field . . . and he has told us that William Miller is totally blind, and there is no possibility of his sight returning. . . . I might add that I have talked with Miller to some extent. . . . All of those of us who have had any contact with him are fully convinced that . . . his interests, as well as the interests of society in general, would probably be better served if it was possible for him to be hospitalized. It appears however that this state can't place him in a mental hospital at the present time because of lack of residence requirements, and it further appears that those who could claim him are reluctant to do so. For your additional information, Mr. Miller was . . . sentenced after making a very impassionate plea for a long term in the penitentiary, and it seems after he was sentenced . . . he begged for additional time. . . ."

Such self-mutilation as Miller claims, according to Dr. Garrison, would not account for the condition of optic atrophy. In addition, the doctor has pointed out, such a procedure as Miller described in his letter would have produced evidence such as scar tissue, indications of hemorrhage, and/or dislocation of the globes. "There was no evidence in the course of numerous examinations of any damage to Miller's eyes that could have been inflicted by his own hand."

Miller may well have willed himself blind to escape an unbearable situation. He may even have enacted, in fantasy, or by token deed, that awful ceremonial. And it may be that, having exploited his eye condition, Miller also came to have a sense of mastery over it. Only now, perhaps, "blind, brokenhearted and in prison," the enormity of that old, terrible wish has exploded into consciousness, and, the wish and deed being as one to him, Miller alone claims the ultimate responsibility.

CHORUS: ... *how couldst thou in such wise quench thy vision? What more than human power urged thee?*

ŒDIPUS: *Apollo, friends, Apollo was he that brought these my woes to pass ... but the hand that struck these eyes was none save mine. ...* [5]

[5] Sophocles: *Œdipus the King;* translation by R. C. Jebb.

THREE   MEN

MARTIN BEARDSON

Now that he has embarked on his "regime" again, twenty-five-year-old Martin Beardson gets up between eight and half past eight of a morning. If in the preceding days he has managed to maintain his "certain harmony of mind and body," then his sleep will have been deep and dreamless, and he is once more calm and refreshed. But this hard-won calm cannot be taken for granted. Not yet. Not until it has become firmly established, proof against the disturbances of everyday life.

As Martin moves about his room, setting water for his cereal to boil on his one-burner electric plate, pulling on his jeans, and the sponge-soled shoes he chose so carefully because "they bring a spring to my walk" he is aware of a certain "élan," but also of a touch of apprehension, a need to proceed with care. At any moment the sudden thing can happen. A door may slam, the insidious droning of a radio down the hall may penetrate his consciousness, a car may backfire. Even some clumsiness of his own can shatter that precarious "harmony" as a wrong note splinters fragile glass; then comes anger, anger, misery.

Any of a score of chance happenings, disturbing his sleep, interrupting his writing, painting, or listening to music, or interrupting "an important train of thought," Martin complains, can set him back three days, a week or more, in his slow, uphill climb toward the longed-for state of grace. Just one such wrench, if he is not watchful, can open him up to a whole series of "onslaughts," weakening his will and prodding his sleeping adversary within, until he is catapulted into the very direction from which he is attempting a return.

It is at such times, Martin says, that he is "betrayed" involuntarily in his sleep, or, alone in his room, that he is forced to commit what he terms "conscious self-betrayal." At such times, too, he is likely to take to the streets. One muddy, drizzling day, in the bushes of a public park, he came together with a drunken seaman. Afterwards the stranger railed, demanded money, and, threatening violence, spilled the contents of Martin's wallet on the ground. Martin scooped it back and fled to his room. Then he ran all the way back to the park, to the secret place in the bushes, and hunted frantically in the rain for something he had not been able to find on his return home—his mother's photograph. The picture, as it turned out, had been safe in a book on the dresser all the time. Another time, "after a series of debauches"—for, once released, Martin explains, the impulse has its own dreadful momentum—he was "enticed" by a man who turned out to be a detective, and he arrested Martin.

"After a siege like that—I was relieved of my money, too," Martin, referring to the fine he paid in court, puts in bitterly—"I'm completely debilitated, drained— I look it, too. Then I have to start on the regime all over again."

In Martin's tumble-down room papers litter the closet. They fill a dresser drawer. They spill out of dusty boxes, and over a table near his bed—newspaper clippings, snapshots, sketch pads, letters, receipts, pictures snipped from magazines, and pages upon pages of Martin's outpourings, typed, scrawled in crayon, pencil, or ink. Among these are a number of charts that he has kept for a while and discarded—artifacts of Martin's "lost regimes." Each is a rough scheduling of days, sometimes covering only two weeks, sometimes extending to five. Some of the dates are underscored. Some are crossed out, some are followed by heavily marked X's. Following some of the X's are comments like these: *"No more!"* *"This is absolutely and positively the last!"* *"No!!"* The comforting line: *"Only sixteen more days this month,"* may be written next to a fresh number halfway down a page. Against certain dates are written the names of books or recordings. "Those," Martin says, "are rewards—things I promise myself if I can be absolutely continent until that date."

Scattered through these papers, too, are a number of rough portrait sketches—as Martin sees himself at certain times. Self-pity and cruelty, love and loathing, anger and entreaty converge in these corrupt and mutilated renditions of reality. The shoulders of Martin's slim but well-formed figure are rendered as narrow and sloping dejectedly. The strawberry mark that stains Martin's left temple and the outer corner of that eye is set down as a grotesque, obliterating splash. The firm flesh of Martin's boyish cheeks, and his full, expressive mouth are depicted as flaccid. The thick, close-cropped hair is drawn in dead patches on the skull. The eyelids sag like empty pockets.

Many times, as if fleeing inevitable collision with this image of himself, Martin ranges the shabby rooming-house districts of the large city where he lives. Always his quest is for a "better" or a "quieter" room. But each room into which he moves, it usually turns out, is worse than the last one. If the house itself is quiet, his window gives on the street and he is caught unprepared, naked and vulnerable in the early morning, by the clanking of garbage trucks. Or, if the street is quiet, then the walls of his room are thin, he is plagued by wrangling or amorous neighbors, an old cage elevator groans its way from floor to floor, or footsteps in the uncarpeted hall outside his door send up flares of irresistible imaginings.

"Quiet! Quiet is so important. Terribly important," Martin cries. "I have enough to contend with without those shocks and disruptions all the time. The idea! The idea that I should have to live in these trashy, shoddy surroundings! It has always been that way. Everything— everything I have ever had has been second-rate!"

Martin has a job; he works as a messenger for four hours a day. He earns about sixty-five dollars a month. Gifts of clothing and of money from members of his family help to provide for his needs. But Martin resents having to hold a job at all. "The job," he says, "brings only a measly few dollars. It's only bearable because it takes care of part of my daily quota of exercise." Martin has other, more pressing matters on his mind. He has a sense of an ultimate commitment, a score to settle, an ancient wrong to right.

While his cereal is boiling, Martin gets out his cherished electric razor. He completes his shave with a minute examination of his face in the mirror. Though he is still far, far from "the peak," today he is not dissatisfied. His flesh, he sees, is "not so pasty," his hair "looks more alive." His mouth "is firmer, not so sensual." His eyes have "a clarity, a pleasant gaiety." On this day, it seems to Martin, he might be taken for "a young and famous artist," a little eccentric, perhaps, in his denims and worn jacket, but distinguished nevertheless. Or he might be "the interesting individualistic youngest son of an international financier, living incognito in this slum. . . ."

In the course of his day Martin looks into many mirrors. He will search mirrors on chewing-gum machines, on cigar counters, in window displays. Passing a plate-glass window, he will take his reflection by surprise as if to catch a fleeting impression of himself through the eyes of another seeing him in passing. The mirror fulfills an important function in Martin's regime. It measures and verifies, curbs and expounds, promises and rebukes. It tells him the score. Once Martin decided to stop looking in mirrors. "I thought if I stopped I would feel more candid; I wanted to feel more spontaneous. Like a damned fool," he says virulently, "I lost control of myself completely."

By half past nine Martin is ready to eat his breakfast—three oranges, milk, a bowl of cereal covered by a half pint of light cream and containing a good-sized pat of butter. That eaten, he makes a last quick survey in the mirror and starts for work. His day's work finished at about two thirty, Martin generally has a lunch of fruit and milk in his room. If he is especially hungry he walks to a cafeteria for "a heavy meal—two or three orders of mashed potatoes with plenty of butter; some vegetables; a glass of orange or tomato juice and a buttered roll." Except for the bus trip to work in the morning "because I'm usually late," Martin walks wherever he goes. The "regime," he explains, requires that he walk at least five miles a day. Sometimes it demands even more walking;

it depends on that important relationship of "inner stresses and balances." After lunch Martin must have about two hours of sleep.

"I'm usually so exhausted I fall asleep immediately, provided there are no noises and I'm not too upset. Four hours on the streets is a strain," Martin explains. "I get so stimulated, I get so depressed. I'm so conscious of people—the way they look at me. If they look at me with interest, that's upsetting, too. It makes me so nervous and excited. At this stage of the regime, with all that vitality gathering in my system again, there is so much tension. I'm so alert. My dreams are so vivid. . . ."

An undisturbed nap restores him to "harmony." It serves another purpose, too. "It clears away the monotony and drudgery of that stupid job. When I wake up it's like starting a separate little day of my own. Besides, if I didn't get that sleep I couldn't control myself later when I go to the gym for my swim. I couldn't go into the shower room, it would be too exciting. Even at best, I often tell myself"—and Martin is smiling now: " 'Well, here goes Daniel into the lions' den again!' "

Swimming is an important part of Martin's daily routine. "I have always loved the water." Occasionally, when he is feeling especially strong, he does a little weight-lifting, too. Afterwards, if nothing has disturbed his composure, he takes a leisurely route homeward, perhaps stopping at the library for books, or at a music shop to listen to records. But wherever he goes, whatever he does, Martin has a consciousness of an anarchic force within; rolled tight inside of him, yet stirring like a secret, it gives him a sense of pleasurable excitement, of suspense. He feels an omnipresence of danger, and something else besides—

Among the litter of Martin's scrambled writings, there is a passage that, perhaps, indicates something of this state of being. "I can fool all the people all the time," he had written. "The first thing to realize is that everyone else is a damn fool. Let's see— Who said that before? Some crackpot whom I consider a fool myself. . . . There might plausibly be some Super-being or immortal who thinks *me* a crazy ass. Well, *I* think I'm a crazy ass, which makes *me* the Super-being. . . ."

Then, as if referring to some ominous and ultimately annihilating force that is to be permitted a certain amount of play but must also be held inexorably in leash, he had continued: "The fact is I never let that Super-being loose for any longer than I am doing now. It runs most of my life, but it doesn't exactly run loose; just makes me shift my eyes to escape the looks around me. If it ran loose I would kill myself. Today it is nowhere near that, but for the past two weeks I shoved its cage door wide open—"

For supper Martin usually eats three eggs, bread, butter, and peanut butter or cheese, and for a drink takes either milk or grape juice. He abstains from meat and fish.

"I learned by experimentation that meat is too stimulating." Tea, coffee, alcohol, spices, and tobacco are "too stimulating, too." So is sugar, even the little contained in a slice of pound cake or a scoop of ice cream, though Martin has a craving for sweets. "Grape juice is the closest I ever let myself get to eating anything sweet. If I indulge a little," he explains, "I develop a terrific appetite for it. Then I overdo it."

The trick of his regime, Martin emphasizes again and again, is to bring "body and mind and spirit into a perfect balance." As the body stores vitality, he explains, rules of exercise and a bland but nourishing diet must be followed rigorously to keep his sexuality in check. At the same time mind and spirit must be carefully fostered so that they may become charged with comparable "vital forces." Otherwise, Martin says, harm will come of it; the Super-being will prevail. Indeed, at times Martin cannot refrain from a sidelong admiration for its stubborn, crafty ways.

After supper Martin begins "a leveling off" in preparation for proper sleep. Sometimes he goes to a movie. More often he reads. George Bernard Shaw is by far his favorite literary personality. In Bunyan's *Pilgrim's Progress* he finds much that is applicable to "my own travail." He draws comfort, instruction and courage from *Thus Spake Zarathustra* and other works of Nietzsche. Or, choosing from the disorderly stacks of records on the floor, he starts his phonograph and settles down to draw or write. "I try to shut everything out of my consciousness except the music. I like to write freely, without forethought. . . . I let the music inspire me. . . ."

If, in the course of the evening, despite all the disciplines of his regime, Martin grows restless, irritated, is assailed by fantasies and then driven to a sexual act, there are reasons, he says with bitter anger. That is because the good in the phonograph records he now possesses has long been assimilated—"I should have plenty of new ones, so the impact will be fresh, so the music will absorb me"; that is because of his "shoddy surroundings—I should have beautiful things around me, not these cheap reproductions I have to hang on the wall." It is because of "poverty," "lack of beauty," because he doesn't have the right book at the right time, the precise color for a painting at the moment when he wants it; because he doesn't have "money," "quiet," "space," "a good light."

"Have you ever noticed," Martin asks, "how rich people really feel they are born to the purple? They look it, too. You see poor people at the markets buying their fruits and vegetables—what they get isn't fresh! The bloom has worn off! It isn't at the peak! Wealthy people," he continues, "have always had the best of everything! They're so full of the best in life—they're so self-contained! You can see it in their looks, their bearing, the way they walk and talk. You notice it in the way they look at you. . . ."

It is as if Martin's Super-being reacts with rage and lust at any suggestion of a slight or deprivation. When the Super-being is aroused, Martin's fantasies are grandiose. The trouble is that Martin is deceived—the magnificent dream goes wrong. The actual encounter is somehow a repetition of another and another encounter, rooted in an ancient and bloody feud. The outcome, envisioned with banners, is "filthy and degrading." Martin's opponent rises, still contemptuous and strong, while Martin, who was "intended for the purple," finds himself again undone. "Wasted," "debilitated," "drained," sick with self-loathing, he assesses in mirrors the ravages of the fray.

Because he has been deceived so many times, because he is "poor" and cannot sustain the cost of war, Martin turns again and again to the promise of his regime. Vegetarianism, pacifism, continence—those are the precepts Martin preaches. In two months, three, perhaps a little longer, Martin promises himself—if he could only store up his forces—he would "pass the crisis" and finally achieve his objective—a distillation not unlike a disembodied state.

To Martin's way of thinking, Mahatma Gandhi's "greatness of mind," his "wonderful powers of endurance, and beautiful serenity of spirit" were the consummation of just such disciplines as Martin tries to follow, "and Gandhi," he remarks, "had a terrible time conquering the yammering of the flesh." That Gandhi was fragile and unprepossessing in appearance Martin attributes to "the wasting influences of his early marriage; it was years before Gandhi took a separate room."

The "sheer genius" of George Bernard Shaw is to Martin another such testament. "To Shaw," Martin says, "sex has always been extremely secondary. Shaw considers the act of sex ridiculous! [1] He didn't have his first affair until he was twenty-nine, and then he was virtually raped—he was seduced by his mother's singing pupil. I'm convinced that after those first few times Shaw has been continent.

"The thing about Shaw," Martin continues raptly, "he surpasses himself! He's completely independent of sex, as he is of everybody and everything else! Even his vegetarianism—aside from health and humanitarian reasons, and his ideas about the useless waste of labor in raising animals for food," Martin explains, "Shaw doesn't *need* meat. And yet he can look at another man and say, 'What you need is a good steak!'"

Shaw's marriage? Patiently, smilingly Martin explains: "That was a very spiritual relationship. Shaw wasn't in love with her sexually. He was in love with her eyes—her green eyes! They were healthy people, you know; if it

[1] Interviews began before Shaw's death.

had been anything but platonic there certainly would have been issue. Besides, everybody knows that Ellen Terry was the one great love of Shaw's life, and he wouldn't think of having sexual relations with her. . . ."

Shaw, Gandhi, Nietzsche—these are the examples to which Martin clings. But he knows better than by mere example what such self-surpassal could bring. Like the travailing Christian, in *Pilgrim's Progress*, Martin says, he, too, had had "intimations of the Celestial City." He has foreseen it in mirrors; daydreaming among skyscrapers, has caught glimpses of it in the admiring regard in faces floating by, and several times, when in following past regimes he *almost* achieved his objective, "I actually experienced it—

"My whole appearance changed! My face filled out in a very healthy manner. I could feel the blood flowing pleasantly throughout my whole body, but I wasn't conscious of any particular part of my body, like feverish forehead, clammy hands and feet, or that awful gnawing in my vital parts. Except for a tremendous feeling of well-being, and energy, I wasn't conscious of my body at all.

"I felt the most marvelous élan! I felt that the most far-reaching accomplishments were extremely possible! I was much, much more attractive. . . . I was so full of *present* enjoyment. Food tasted simply wonderful! Every object and color I saw struck me in a distinct, wonderful fashion! I felt I was experiencing everything in a new way, with innocence, like a child does, but with the added attraction of a much more complicated perception. . . ."

If he could maintain that state until he passed the "crisis," Martin believes he would surmount ugliness, weakness, poverty. With all manner of sustaining riches banked up within himself, all struggle would fall away. He would then be as in the third metamorphosis described by Zarathustra: " '. . . a new beginning, a game, a self-rolling wheel, a first movement, a holy Yea. . . .' " Then with what gaiety he would encounter the world! With what brilliance, clarity, and wit he would write! What pictures he would paint!

"I know I have talent," Martin cries. "When I was a child they used to say I was brilliant, a genius! If I weren't so— If I could—" Face working, and voice edged with tears, he stops. "If I could only get through that crisis! Then I could really let my imagination soar!"

Martin Beardson, the second of two children—his brother, Jonathan, was three years older than he—was born in Newkirk, Columbia, a large, callow city of great business and manufacturing interests, in a time of national hedonism, flamboyant installment buying, and flourishing country-club life. The year was 1924. Martin's father, the son of a small-town schoolmaster and a vigorous, hard-working woman who took in boarders to supplement the family income, was a "self-made man." He had helped to support himself while he was in high school. He worked his way through a famous university, becoming a star athlete and honor student. He rose to the rank of captain during World War I. At the time of Martin's birth he was well on his way to becoming a prosperous and influential businessman.

Martin's mother also had been reared in a small community, but her parents, Martin likes to point out, were "much more upper class" than those of his father, and her upbringing in "a much more genteel tradition."

There had been some wealth on his maternal grand-mother's side of the family. His grandfather was a comfortably well-to-do professional man. "My mother's people," Martin says, "always lived in a very fine neighborhood. They were the leading people in town!"

Except for brief periods, and then only in recent years, Martin has never known deprivation in terms of food, clothing, and comfortable shelter. By realistic standards, he also enjoyed many luxuries. The houses in which Martin lived when he was growing up never consisted of less than from four to seven rooms. The household was seldom without a full-time servant. When Martin and Jonathan were small, they summered in the pleasant, tree-shaded home of their maternal grandparents. When they were older, they were sent to fashionable camps. Each boy had plenty of toys, each was encouraged in his hobbies. Yet Martin has always had a sense of poverty no less poignant than if he had been a slum child, and a sense of grievance no less biting than if he had lived all his life on the periphery of want.

Martin has no recollections of his father during his earliest years. He was two when his parents separated. His father remained in Newkirk. His mother took the boys to live near the home of her people in Snow Falls, five hundred miles away. Shortly after this she moved her household to Mailer, a thriving city near by. It was not until Martin was about eight, following another visit in Snow Falls, that the family returned to Newkirk, and that Martin remembers beginning to see his father again on any regular basis. By that time Martin had already developed a conviction that all was not as it should be, that there had been a dreadful change in the family fortunes. He had also come to have an unpleasant sense of his own personal distinction, and this, too, it seemed to him, was somehow related to "poverty."

Of all those who were important in his childhood, only the memory of his mother evokes from Martin a warm response. His father, his brother—for that matter, most of the men he has known—are recalled chiefly with rancor. Of his mother Martin speaks with love and compassion, if sometimes also with resentment; mainly he speaks of her as of something he poignantly aspired to, but had never quite achieved.

The most pervasive memory of Martin's childhood is that of an acute sensitivity to his mother's attitudes. His mother had not been an easy person for him to fathom. For one thing, her social life kept her away from home a great deal. In addition Martin had felt in her demeanor a certain withheld quality which, even in their most intimate moments, made her seem remote. But very early in life it was borne in on Martin that his mother was "a very superior person.

"She was interested in going only with the best people. . . . When she got something it was important that it be the best quality. . . . She liked to vacation in the most exclusive places, to visit in the best houses. My mother," Martin exclaims, "had very high standards! She was extremely class-conscious! Her whole orientation was upper-class!"

Martin also became aware, early in life, that his mother was restless, discontented. Undoubtedly many problems occupied Mrs. Beardson, but of two things Martin was certain: the family's income was incommensurate with his mother's social standards, and for this his father was to blame.

Martin's recitals are studded with recollections of "my

mother's struggle against social oblivion." He commemorates her courage-in-adversity—"No matter what, she always kept up her contacts"—her obstinate charm in the face of humiliating want, and her unfailing efforts to "raise our social level."

He speaks of his mother's dissatisfaction with the family's physical setting. In the first ten years of his life they moved seven times. He remembers her disheartened shrug when, early in the depression, it became necessary to transfer her boys from private to public school. By the time he got back into private school Martin was in the eighth grade and had attended eight different schools. And he remembers her tone of bitter dryness whenever she spoke of money.

" 'Boys, don't marry for love. Marry for money,' " she had once remarked. " 'That's what counts.' " Another time, when opening an envelope containing a check from their father, Martin recalls, "she just looked at it for a minute and all she said was: 'Boys, your father is a Scotchman.' " His mother had not been one to make scenes—"she didn't care for emotional displays," Martin puts in. "She said it quietly, but you could tell—she meant every word of it."

Martin even discovered that his queenly mother could be unhappy enough to cry. He had walked into her room one afternoon, and "there she was on the bed, crying." This had been a dreadful revelation. "I turned and went right out." He never asked his mother the reason for those tears, "but," Martin says, "it must have been about money."

He knew how his mother felt, Martin exclaims. "She was sick of the struggle. . . . We were living in those paltry surroundings, and yet socially she had the highest ambitions. . . . Oh, my father gave us enough for the necessities of life, but he had such a vulgar, low-class idea of what life should be. A thing like maintaining a position—that was beyond him! He just had no conception of—of *noblesse oblige!*"

Martin, too, had found reason for tears in the family's "lack of money," a commodity so crucial to a high social position, and gradually he formulated certain equations.

The truly desirable people of this world, like those his mother followed, were "upper-class."

"Upper-class" people had "the best of everything"; they wore the best clothes, went with the best people, lived in fine houses, were attractive, admired, and sought after.

By inverse reasoning, to have less than the best—that was to be poor, unendowed, and unadmired.

These addled concepts, like faulty premises developed in syllogistic thinking, and perpetuated in an endless chain of metaphorical connections—wealth with position with worth with popularity, wit, strength, and later with other things—were to become the lodestone of Martin's existence—a "frame of reference" that would implement outlook and behavior in every area of his life.

That his mother was upper-class, despite the privations she suffered, Martin has never doubted. He knew by the company she kept; "She had a lot of very wealthy friends. She was extremely popular, with women and men. She always had a boy friend." He knew by the favors she enjoyed: "Every winter she went to Florida—her wealthy friends took her. She had a Steinway grand that one of her friends loaned her. . . ." He knew by her "taste," her "discrimination," her "standards. . . . And I always thought she was *extremely* good-looking," he adds admiringly.

He had taste, discrimination, and lofty standards, too, Martin cries. He repeats again and again: "I was class-conscious at a very early age." Even as a small boy, he says insistently, "I was obsessed with beautiful houses; I could tell in a minute if clothes were of the best quality; I craved soft, beautiful things. . . . The privations I suffered made my life a hell.

."The neighborhoods I was stuck in were common, ugly — They weren't lower-class neighborhoods, no," he acknowledges, "but they were a long way from the sort where the people my mother admired and went with lived. . . . Little kids I played with—I never felt I could introduce their mothers to mine. Oh, she would never snub them—my mother was a perfect lady. If they met on the street she always said hello, but they just weren't of her element. . . ."

He remembers his humiliation one day when the family servant "brought her little colored boy to work. I was playing with him. My mother called me in and asked me not to play in front of the house." Another time, when he was older, he continues unhappily, "my mother had to tell me: 'I wish you wouldn't go with Hank so much. His mother waits on tables at parties I go to. It's embarrassing to both of us.'" And he remembers the anxiety that gripped him in school one afternoon when the teacher asked the class: "'How many rooms are there in your house?'

"I was class-conscious at a very early age," Martin repeats again, that statement like the urgent declaration of some superior and innate personal characteristic, "but

my position was so untenable. I *always* felt that under-
current—that Jack wasn't as good as Susie because he
didn't have as much. If you played with Jack, well—birds
of a feather! If you played with Susie, her house was better, so you weren't as good." Martin solved that dilemma
by eliminating any possibility of the "superiority" of another. When the teacher called on him, he blurted out:
" 'Twenty-one rooms'—I counted every closet and cup-
board in our house." But then when another boy said *his*
house had only six rooms, Martin's agony was complete.
"I thought that by bragging I had shown him up; I was
afraid I had made him mad."

That it was his reasoning that was untenable doesn't
occur to Martin. As if lacking some ordinary bit of equipment essential to accurate navigation, Martin slants across
experience; he recounts such incidents to make quite another point. Martin stresses only the exigency of his feeling—an exigency that, he argues, could only be known
to the elect. And but for the money of which he feels his
father deprived him—money for the big house, the fine
school and neighborhood, for that high position which
his class-consciousness demanded, he would have been
spared such anxieties, "my whole life would have been
different," he declares.

Martin cannot remember any such actuality, but at
times it is "almost like I remember—I know that my
mother and I— We must have lived on a completely
different scale. . . . If we didn't," he says with irritation, "we should have! Not everybody has the capacity
for the best things in life."

Clearly injustice had been done. Sometimes he got so
depressed, Martin says, "I used to think about going into
my closet and hanging myself." Sometimes he had "aw-

ful tantrums." He had long, delicious daydreams, too—
he was "a prince or a king," "a handsome explorer," "a
famous naturalist," "a financial wizard. . . ." In these
daydreams "my father was nonexistent." His brother—
"I didn't bother with him, but my plans," Martin says,
"always included my mother.

"I used to think of schemes for making piles of
money. . . . I was going to be rich. Very rich. Richer
than all my mother's friends. We were going to live in a
beautiful mansion.

"My mother—I worshipped her! I thought she was the
most perfect woman, better than any other mother, rich
or poor. When she came to school I was tremendously
thrilled just to have her walk in the door! I wanted to put
my mother on top of the world!"

If riches and social position were the crown his mother
sought, Martin, as a young child, felt a lack of more
fundamental riches, not yet translated into symbols of
affluence and social position. And if his strivings got
caught up in that other, wider circle—at the heart of the
constellation, like the magnetic polestar, shimmered the
image of his mother.

Martin has never felt that he got enough of his mother's attention. Important though he believes her social
activities to have been, still he cannot refrain from complaining: "She was at home with us very seldom."

In winter there was her customary trip to Florida. She
often went her own way in summer, sending the boys to
camp or to stay with her parents. When they were all
living together, "she would come home at four or five
o'clock in the afternoon, and then rush off to some
dinner.

"She had important dates at least four times a week," Martin recalls, "it seemed like every night. I used to say to her: 'Stay home with us.' She would look at me in that calm, detached way and say: 'I do go out too much.' Whenever we saw her all dressed up—she would look so beautiful!—we would say: 'Oh, do you have to go out tonight?' "

His mother had not been a cold person; Martin is quick to make that clear. "She wasn't *un*affectionate. She would hug us. She always kissed us good-night if she was at home when we went to bed. And she was very considerate. If she was entertaining, she would always come upstairs and ask if the piano was keeping us awake. But she was formal in her affections—she didn't *show* her feelings the way a lot of people do. . . ."

Even her evenings alone with her boys, as Martin describes them, had a certain formality about them. For Martin those evenings are infused with nostalgia, though more often than not "they were ruined by my brother, Jon." Still Martin presents a picture, perfect as a tableau in some far-off pageantry, or like a scene arrested in memory from a cherished story book, of what he thought such evenings should be, and occasionally, he says, one of them turned out just as he had wanted.

"After dinner my mother would play the piano for an hour. Then we would have a big fire, and we would sit in front of the fire. I'd sit on her lap." Jon? Martin brushes over that question—"He would sit on the arm of the chair. And we would talk," he continues. "She would tell all about the big houses she had been to, and the parties and the people. . . ."

Martin was passionately eager to share his mother's interests. On week-end mornings, after she had been to a party, "I would climb into her bed and have her tell me all about the big houses again." Jonathan was seldom far behind, "but Jon," Martin says fiercely, "was a faker! He didn't have an appreciation for beautiful things like my mother and me."

If Jon followed him into their mother's bed on weekend mornings, "I was the only one who got into bed with her at night. I had nightmares. I used to wake up in a cold sweat," Martin explains. But those exclusive nighttime visits lost their luster, too. "She didn't pay much attention to me. When I was ten or eleven—it made me realize I was a big boy and she was a woman—she would turn her back to me."

It seemed to him he was constantly groping toward his mother, trying to reach her height. There was always a distance between them. But Martin clings to this thesis: if he had no other thing, he alone in the family was joined with his mother in an aristocracy of spirit. His father? Martin makes a glib disposal of him. "He had the cash, but to my mother's crowd my father's friends would have seemed vulgar, funny— Maybe, she was taken in by him for a while, but that could never last! My father was definitely not in the same class with my mother!"

Jon? Martin is superior, amused. When the family was living in Mailer, Mrs. Beardson had taken a course in interior decoration. Jon, Martin recalls, was busy with his own mundane concerns, "but even at that age I could sit for hours just watching my mother sketch!" When he and Jon were older and the family went for a drive, "my mother and I would be positively yelling: 'Slow down! Slow down!' We would be going through the most magnificent, exclusive sections. *We* wanted to look at the beautiful mansions! My brother! He wasn't even conscious!

"With my mother and me—we had an understanding," Martin continues urgently. "There was something between us that could never be with my father or Jon. It wasn't something you say with words; it was something you feel—it was an understanding when we looked at one another."

Yet Martin could not rest. That mystic bond, that tacit understanding, that ineluctable consciousness of class had somehow never been enough. Martin felt poor, weak, deprived—in workaday life, unable to compete. Life had been difficult enough, he cries, with his mother away with her wealthy friends so much. There was Jonathan to contend with, too. And like his father, who "had the cash," Jonathan, too, had resources that Martin did not possess.

Martin remembers himself in childhood as a thin, spindly-legged, garrulous little boy, intensely proud, but with a secret sense of personal deficiency, and an overweening wish for recognition. The birthmark which stains his left temple and the outer corner of that eye, and which is still a source of angry despair to him, loomed immense and conspicuous in his childhood consciousness of self.

The family saying: "Jonathan has the looks but Martin has the brains," still rankles. Try as he might, on whatever level, Martin never felt that he could hold his own against his brother.

Martin was small; his brother was older, bigger. Martin was volatile; Jonathan was "the steady one." Martin was frail, tense, demanding; Jonathan was robust, self-sufficient. Martin flinched from the rough-and-tumble of boys' games, was fearful of physical injury, and prey to shoves and jibes. Jonathan was physically brave, adaptable.

"My brother," Martin says coldly, "couldn't help but absorb some of my mother's values, but he wasn't in my mother's class. He was more my father's kind." His words pile up in a crescendo of anxiety. "He wasn't a *really* husky football-player type like my father, either. My father was six feet tall, with a football-player's build, and even in middle age he was a marvelous athlete . . . but Jon was good at baseball and tennis, things like that. . . . He was *coarse*," Martin continues. "He was *insensitive*— he had no *taste*." Martin emphasizes his words as if by dint of sheer perseverance he might actually banish Jon along with his "plebeian" father. "He was a gang boy, the kind that runs with a gang! He was a tyrant!" Martin, now almost in tears, exclaims. "He always bullied me."

If, by Martin's reasoning, he had been deprived and undermined by his father, he puts similar constructions on Jon's effect on him. When he was about six, Martin recalls resentfully, he and Jon attended a summer play school. Both boys knew how to play a little march tune on the piano. Both wanted the distinction of playing it as the class marched out for games. And, despite attempted mediations by the teacher, as the class prepared to leave the room, every day both boys would rush to the piano. "He would fight me! He would shove me off the bench! He always embarrassed me socially!

"At home," Martin continues, "I had all my collections. *He* knew how particular I was about my things. He would mess them up! He made me so nervous all the time!

"If I didn't want to give him something of mine, he

would take it. . . . He never asked permission to ride
my bike. . . . Once my grandfather gave me a beautiful
set of chrome-tipped arrows. Jon grabbed them and shot
them all off in the air. I had to run all over the neighborhood looking for them. . . ."

Worst of all, Martin continues furiously, his brother
was always interjecting himself "between my mother and
me. I always wanted to impress my mother. If I did
something Jon would belittle it; if something went
wrong, he would gloat. He didn't *have* to say anything!
I could see that smug, fat, superior look on his face. . . .
Once I traced a picture; I palmed it off as my own—
Good Lord! Wherever we went, in front of my mother,
in front of her friends—" Martin draws his face into an
angry imitation of Jonathan's nasty teasing—" 'Ooh, what
Martin did!' "

Martin's health was a particular source of friction between the brothers. "I was always delicate. I was thin. I
vomited at least once a week for the first ten years of my
life. I was very constipated; sometimes I went a whole
week without being able to have a bowel movement.
After meals—it was usually right after breakfast—we
would be sitting at the table, and I would get those severe
pains in my stomach. I would tell my mother: 'I've got
a stomach ache.' My brother," Martin says furiously,
"would say: 'Oh, Martin is faking!' "

Martin had been taken to doctors and dosed with laxa-
tives. He was lectured repeatedly on the importance of
establishing "regular habits." His mother had given him
enemas. But as time went by, it seemed to Martin that
Jon's malignant influence had prevailed—that his stomach
trouble was taken for granted in the household. "Nobody

seemed particularly concerned. My brother—he would tell my mother I was faking! My mother? She would say: 'Go and lie down for a while'; she wasn't very solicitous. I came to the conclusion she believed him." (Yet Martin cherishes the following memory: He was playing in his room one afternoon while Mrs. Beardson entertained a visitor downstairs. Perhaps to test her, he uttered a little cry. "It wasn't very loud, but my mother heard it immediately! She was up those stairs in no time! But then," he continues ruefully, "she only looked in for a minute— she just smiled and chatted for a minute and then went back.")

Martin's complicity in that vicious circle of wrangling with Jon—his fierce competitiveness, his finicky possessiveness, his provocative tendency to "brag," to "put on airs," and perhaps to lift his ego further, his need to elicit evidence that Jon was, indeed, made of crasser stuff than he—this remains beyond his consideration. It is as if in his wish to identify more closely with his mother (and to impress upon her how much they had in common), Martin was constantly enacting a crude travesty of what he saw to be her struggle. If she longed for position, he, too, longed for position. If she was obstructed, he was doubly obstructed. And if Mr. Beardson was her evil genius, it behooved Martin to demonstrate, to himself as well as to his mother, that Jon was his counterpart. Even his stomach trouble is attributed by Martin to that hateful combination—his father who deprived him of money, and Jon's further "persecutions." The validity of that conclusion is self-evident to Martin. "At home I would sit in the bathroom for hours, and I couldn't have a movement . . . but in summer," he points out, "away from home, away from all those social pressures and from my brother's persecutions, my health was always better—my stomach trouble always improved."

And here Martin gives a remarkable demonstration of virtuosity of logic. The whole world parenthesized by the periphery of his vision, Martin can wander widely, dance up garden paths, and yet never cross the frontiers of his personal frame of reference.

By Martin's elaborate schema,[2] no personal deficiency —no flaw in health, grace, stamina, or achievement (those appurtenances of position)—and no rebuff that he has suffered, but has its genesis in the initial privation of wealth, and hence of the position he craved. By the very nature of his being, he explains with animation, these were urgent necessities if he was to "realize myself." His needs being great, he was constantly undersupplied. "I suffered—my health—my appearance—my whole personality was weakened."

If Jon, living in identical economic circumstances, did not suffer, that only proved that Jon had lesser needs— that he was *lower*-class. And yet, by Martin's labyrinthine logic, that gave Jon gross advantages over him. Being of a lower order, Jon could thrive, expand, gather dividends even in "paltry surroundings."

Martin's attitudes toward his brother were, for the most part, carried into his relations with other boys. At times he looked on them as on cunningly constructed infernal machines—mindless, sans sensibility, all steam

[2] "In Kant: Any one of certain forms or rules of the 'productive imagination' through which the understanding is able to apply its 'categories' to the manifold of sense-perception in the process of realizing knowledge or experience." (Oxford Dictionary.)

and thrust of powerful pistons, their mere existence a design to show him up. At other times he saw in their physical prowess, their aggressiveness and careless, roistering ways, a calculated cruelty. Either way they were injurious to him. Yet what was injurious to him, he noted with envy and resentment, was to those short-trousered gladiators merely vigorous play. And though Martin assured himself repeatedly that their pleasures were not his pleasures, and their social standing far below his, still he saw that they, too, had an exclusiveness, were quick to recognize a "non-belonger," and were cruel and contemptuous to those who didn't measure up.

"At home," he says bleakly, "it was Jon; at school it was the other boys. In the third grade—my first day in that school, a boy took a dislike for me. He would shove me every time he saw me in the hall."

He recounts this incident with hallucinatory immediacy: "There was a game we had to play. I hated it. I wasn't any good at rough games," he cries, "and I was always conscious of my skinny body and that strawberry mark on my face! The kids would stand in a circle, and you had to run around the circle, and they would flip you with towels till you got back to your place! They snapped them hard! It was like a whip crack! It was painful! One day a boy hit me on my privates."

To Martin, already burdened with that sense of conspicuous inadequacy, and to whom every crack of the towel seemed a comment of contempt, this had been more than a painful physical injury. Only an obstinate pride kept him running.

"I thought I was going to drop, but I didn't dare. . . . I was practically fainting when I got back to my place, but

I wouldn't. . . . I stood there. I had to stand there with a silly grin on my face," he adds in rage and self-contempt, "until the whistle blew and the period was over.

"Physical training! In school I used to worry about it all day. After school I used to run home to avoid the embarrassment of not wanting to play. I was always so constrained with boys! All they ever wanted to play was baseball, and when I would try I would hurt my hands. . . ."

Martin preferred playing with girls, or with children younger than himself. "They weren't so violent. Besides," he declares, "I liked to be the leader. And they liked imaginative games like I did."

He frequently played alone, "though often I was lonely." He had his collections of rocks, butterflies, bird nests. He had pets—tropical fish, a turtle ("People were naming all their animals Prince so I named him Track Prints for the markings on his back"). He had a dog he had found on a street and, at various times, cats. "I was always bringing home stray animals."

And he spent long afternoons visiting with older people—when he was in Snow Falls, with one or another of three elderly widows who were his grandmother's friends and neighbors; when he was at home, with the maid in his mother's kitchen. But whatever he did, Martin was caught in a burst of divergent emotions.

Martin had a need for motherly attention, and this was provided by those elderly women he knew. "I would go and admire their flower gardens; they would give me some flowers. They would talk to me and give me milk and cookies."

Sometimes he saw in them a wistfulness so reminiscent of his own that he was moved to a tender compassion—

"They seemed so all alone. . . . Nobody seemed to care what happened to them."

Then there was that social arbiter which constantly sat on his shoulder. Jon, being "a gang boy, could always find friends his own age; I was more particular." Yet Martin could not win. There was always that dismaying moment when he saw himself as identified with the socially cast-off.

"I was peculiar that way," he exclaims with angry exasperation. "Strays, servants, old ladies—I was always sorry for them! With some old ladies I knew, lots of times I was bored to death," he defends himself, "but I sat with them for hours because I was sorry for them!"

This dilemma was immensely magnified in Martin's relations with the successive servants his mother employed, who fed him, applauded him, comforted him, and generally tucked him into bed. Because they filled an important need, it was his tendency to become profoundly attached to them. "I didn't care if a maid smoked, or left the breakfast dishes, or kept the radio on all day," he cries defiantly. "I liked coming home from school and finding somebody I knew. . . ."

Because they were servants, and black—beyond the "social pale"—he was especially sorry for them. "I used to try to entertain them. I would play records. . . . I would bring them my animals to pet. . . ."

Because he identified with them, "I had a fit whenever a maid was fired; I was always defending the servants, even against my mother, who could do no wrong. . . . I know I was peculiar," he cries. "Whenever a maid was fired—I would come home from school—I would know immediately that something was wrong! I would get so depressed. I would picture her walking the streets, helpless, with no money— Maybe that was because I often thought about leaving home myself."

And because he suffered, displayed "bad manners," made "scenes," while Jon remained "ostentatious," seemingly impervious to such storms of feeling, Martin felt that Jon was "showing me up."

If Martin feels that his mother was insensitive to his needs, he does not like to blame her. It is as if, even today, his need for her still acute, and his position too precarious to risk her displeasure, Martin must keep such resentments diverted. Time and again in childhood he had exploded into anger as today, recounting those childhood woes, anger erupts again. But almost in the same moment Martin propitiates, veers— No, it was not his mother who was to blame. It was Jon with his sly advantages of insensitivity, looks, and brawn— It was poverty, that struggle to maintain position, that kept his mother abstracted—

"I used to think of my mother as looking at me, but in a very detached way. I *know* my mother loved me," he says insistently, "but I always thought she had so many important worries on her mind that she couldn't bother with me."

When he was in a play at school, he continues, and told his mother about it, "she would just smile and say: 'That's nice.'" When he complained about the boys on the street, "she would just nod sympathetically and say: 'Don't get hurt.'" When he complained about Jon, "she wouldn't interfere! She wouldn't do anything! She wouldn't take sides!" When he was particularly insistent, his mother would say: "'Jonathan, you mustn't annoy Martin,'" but in the same breath would add: "'Martin, you are a crybaby!' Then Jon would repeat it.

He would repeat it when my mother wasn't at home. 'Martin is a crybaby!' "

That Jon was three years older was, by Martin's peculiar emphasis, merely another of Jon's affronts. When Mrs. Beardson introduced her boys to friends, she would refer to Jon as "the man of the house." When she set out for Florida, it was Jon she addressed when she said: " 'Look after things. You are the man of the house.' " As Jon grew into adolescence, Martin observed achingly an increasing rapport between them. "My mother would talk to Jon on mature subjects. . . . I would see them enjoying a cartoon in *Esquire*. . . . I wanted to impress my mother! I wanted to be on my mother's level!"

Ultimately it was his mother's "detachment" that Martin wanted to crack. That his great competitiveness and his voracious need for attention, his complaints, demands, and tendency to find in the most casual incident the sign of subtle disdain, may have increased the distance between them is barely fathomed by Martin. He knows only that he was thwarted, wretched, deprived—"too poor to be able to reach my mother's level" —and to the degree that he suffered he wanted to make himself felt. He flung himself against his mother's "detachment" as if trying to storm a castle.

He was miserable in school, had nightmares, was nervous, ill—he wanted some extravagant response from his mother. Jon bullied him, had taken his bike, embarrassed him—Martin demanded redress; he wanted to witness his mother's fury. He was "weak," "pale," "funny-looking," felt outstripped and outclassed—*do* something, he wanted his mother to do something! Whether because he believed that this was something she would surely understand, or because he himself had come to fully believe it—that in wealth and social position all inadequacies are absorbed—he invoked their "spiritual bond": he complained bitterly and incessantly about the neighborhood, the lowliness of his playfellows, about the house, its furnishings; and, in effect, "Lift me up," he implored. Jon's "superior sneer" hovered in his consciousness like the grin of the Cheshire cat.

For all his suffering, Martin could not achieve his objective. Then frustration would reach a climax. There were those "awful tantrums. . . . I would yell and smash things. A couple of times I threw knives. . . . When I lost control, everybody ran for cover. Jon would lock himself up in the bathroom. My mother? Once or twice she slapped me. Usually she didn't do anything— she just went in her room and closed the door. A couple of times," Martin says sorrowfully, "I made my mother cry. . . . I would tell her she was a terrible mother, that I hated her, that she didn't love me enough— I would suffer for weeks afterwards; I would follow her like a dog. I always had to tell her how beautiful she was, how much I really loved her."

There were those thoughts about suicide. "I guess I was thinking about all the sympathy I would get, how terrible everybody would feel. . . ."

Perhaps as a training in endurance against the "onslaughts" of rough-and-tumble boys, Martin took pleasure in grueling daydreams in which he rose above all manner of terrible tortures. "I had fantasies about husky boys all the time. I would have them tie me up in a sack and hang me up in the garage and torture me. Oh, they were complete daydreams, with all the sufferings," Martin says with a kind of gaiety, "but their torture never killed me!"

He had other impulses, too, the thought of which still distresses him. He had loved his animals. "I took wonderful care of them—people used to comment on it." Yet sometimes while playing with his dog, "I would get those mixed feelings—I would spank him till he yelped. Then I would feel so terrible I would cry and have to beg his forgiveness."

And, "helpless, with no money," Martin would "leave home—

"There would be one of those arguments with Jon, and my mother wouldn't take sides. I would say, 'I'm leaving forever.' My mother wouldn't say anything, and I would rush out of the house. . . . Once when it started to rain I came back and crawled in the doghouse —it was a barrel with straw in it. My mother must have seen me through the window because she came to the back door. She just stood there looking through the screen—she didn't say anything in particular—I think she said, 'You're going to get very dirty in the doghouse,' something like that— She was so calm! She was always so calm and aloof! I crawled out of the barrel and slunk into the house, and there was Jon, sitting there and looking very manly and knowing—

"He was a faker! A vulgar, pompous faker!" Martin cries. "I wrestled him lots of times, and plenty of times I beat him, but he would never admit it. . . . Even when I pinned him down to the floor, he would never admit I could do it. . . . I often look at those husky, self-assured men," Martin continues with a quiet emphasis. "I admire strong men. I guess that's because I have always felt the uncertainty of life so much, and strong men seemingly have a mastery over life— That attracts me even if I know it's an illusion. Because if it comes to

final blows," Martin says, "you *know* the brainy one—
you *know* in the end the skinny little scientist can harm
power! That's the final word!"

With brief exceptions Martin's school career was also
full of trouble. The fears, anxieties, ambitions, and frustrations that typified his life at home were carried into
the classroom. In addition life for Martin was so full of
change—change to the new neighborhood, the new school
—and with each change came the moment when, seeing
himself as if through the eyes of the onlookers—"pale,"
"frail," "conspicuous"—he must pass in review before a
brand-new teacher and a brand-new set of schoolmates.

This was always a wretched moment, but it was a moment of promise, too. For Martin harbored a dream that
also brought an excitement to these occasions and helped
him to carry himself with an exaggerated insouciance.
Martin dreamed of impressing the girls—"I always
wanted to make a big impression on the girls"; of sur-
passing the boys—"as far as boys went," he states, "to be
good at all, for me—I had to be the *best*"; and of winning from the teacher an astonished admiration such as
no other child could evoke.

But there was always the telltale incident, the devastat-
ing comparison, the real or fancied rebuff. There was the
inevitable accumulation of anxiety, which lay like a fog
between himself and his books. There were the decline
in grades and the increased compulsion to wrest recognition, the decline in health and the increased demands
for special considerations. Frustrations piled on frustrations, and whatever his difficulties or dissatisfactions with
self, there was that rescuing projection of blame. Boys!
Boys! That was the crux of his trouble! And there was

the inevitable outcry for the better house, neighborhood, school—for that rarefied atmosphere where, above the common crowd, he would be one with prestige and riches all around, and the tastes, standards, and demands in that Shangri-La would be one with him.

For many children, going to school for the first time is a happy challenge. If there is a dread of leaving the comfortable familiarity of home, there is also pride in growth, and pleasure in the enlargement of experience. To Martin, beginning his school career perhaps denoted more than that—a step away from his mother's "poor" house, and a step toward that life outside where, it seemed to him, his mother's heart lived.

This is suggested by the tack of Martin's animated dialogues as he conjures up memories of that period in his life. He describes with an almost gustatory pleasure his eagerness to begin going to kindergarten. That this was to be a *private* school, he remarks, was of vast importance to him, and that Jon had preceded him only increased his impatience.

He recalls his delight when, on being assigned to a class, he saw the son of one of his mother's friends. "I walked right up to him; I said: 'I know you—you're Michael—my mother visits at your house.'" He had played with a number of children, he says with unveiled snobbery, "but Michael was my one close friend."

At Whitman, where he entered first grade, he was "one of the most active, gregarious children. Even at that age, I wanted to make a big impression—I was itching to make my mark. . . ." And then Martin suffered a "terrible social setback." Because of a decrease in income, Mrs. Beardson was faced with transferring one of the boys to public school, and perhaps because Jon was older, and already established in his work, the choice fell on Martin. (This, and another similar incident occurring several years later, are presented by Martin as exemplifications of his claim that by his very inferiority Jon triumphed at his expense. "Because *I* was the brilliant one, the family was always telling my mother Jon needed better schools!") Martin had raised such a clamor that within a few weeks he was back at Whitman.

Late in 1931 Mrs. Beardson and the children returned to Snow Falls to live near the home of her parents, and this time both boys were enrolled in public school. Martin's recollection is that this was a comparatively happy period for him, and he gives some seemingly realistic reasons for this. The school was small. It was situated in an attractive community. The atmosphere was leisurely, the teachers pleasant. But as Martin talks on, it becomes increasingly clear that, in his mind his mother being inseparable from whatever was good and desirable, all that was good and desirable in this environment had somehow emanated from her. The burden of all his comments—that he was within his mother's bailiwick! His mother was known in this school; she herself, he points out, had once been a student there. And as if by her radiant presence, even the onus that this was a *public* school seems purged from Martin's mind.

When Martin was eight the family returned to Newkirk, the place of his birth, and both boys were enrolled in Hubbard, a bustling, big city public school. Martin was in the third grade. He was to remain in this school for nearly two years.

This was a period marked by a heightening of all Martin's difficulties. The lines of his life struggle had by this time been drawn. Now reinforcements came into the conflict. His father, whom he scarcely remembered, and about whom he says he had "thought . . . as little as possible," appeared on the scene; he became a regular visitor in the household. Martin's sense of physical vulnerability in the face of his father's vigor, and his acute feelings of economic dependency, compelled him to propitiatory behavior, but inwardly he was resentful. "I always knew that men control the purse strings, that they had the power to give or take away. . . . I could *never* forget that life for me was different than for the people my mother admired."

He felt, in addition, a further unnamed danger. Paternal advances were suspiciously received. Paternal gifts were persistently found wanting. With any spontaneous surge of pleasure or admiration came signal flares of warning.

It is with difficulty, and then only in response to persistent questioning, that Martin is able to grant his father any appreciable virtues. "Yes, he was good-looking," Martin admits, "but he wasn't really attractive—he went bald early." (Affection?) "Oh, he would kiss us when he arrived. When he said good-night," Martin remarks disdainfully, "he would hold out his cheek and say: 'Give your Daddy a buss!'" (Candy?) Martin is deprecatory. "Oh, he always brought candy." (Presents?) "He bought us bikes," Martin recalls. "Yes, they were good ones; he got us presents so seldom that when he did bring something, it *had* to be pretty good. . . . He did bring me an electric train," Martin volunteers, "but he didn't do it until a long time after I asked for it; by that time I wasn't interested. . . . He was so common," Martin exclaims. "He had such vulgar ideas about money. 'Now take care of that,' " he mimics his father, " 'that cost your daddy a lot of dough.' "

It is as if any acknowledgment that his father was good, generous, attractive, worthy of his or his mother's notice, was tantamount to enemy infiltration behind his lines. Martin had a position to defend, and he continues to defend it, even to this day. "I remember a dinner once when my father was there. . . . My parents were talking. I said: 'God damn you, Mother!' " He doesn't remember quite why he said that—"I think," he remarks, "it had something to do with Jon." But if it was his wish to drive a wedge into that conversation, he succeeded admirably. "My mother said nothing as usual, but my father jumped up and took me by the ear. It didn't hurt," he says contemptuously, "but I did think he was overstepping his bounds."

Martin became aware of his mother's relations with other men as well—her "dates," the deference with which they treated her, the atmosphere of courtship, sensed rather than observed. Nor was the economic depression without effect on him. There had been revisions in family plans, if not in wishes; economies, if not serious denials. For a short time Mrs. Beardson even went to work. To Martin, for whom the word "poverty" had such sweeping connotations, the atmosphere in his own home of cynical resignation and, more amorphous, of the depression all around, was like a baleful influence hanging over him. Resentment of his father, Jon (those instrumentalities of ill), and, by extension, "all their bullying kind," raged on, the initial conflict projected on an ever widening screen. It was in this frame of mind that Martin became a student at Hubbard, where "on my first day . . . a boy took a dislike for me; he would shove me every time he saw me in the hall."

Martin's spirits, his health, and his school work dwindled to an unprecedented low while he was a student at Hubbard. During his first two or three months there he had found a modicum of reassurance in the select atmosphere of the "fresh-air class . . . for frail children." Then he was transferred to a regular class, and gone were even the "little naps," the comfort of special nourishments, the beneficent atmosphere of motherly steward-ship in which he could feel he was still among the privi-leged. If ever he experienced the contumely that he equated with being "poor," if ever his "whole personal-ity was weakened," that happened now. He despised the crowded classroom. He felt shunned by the busy, imper-sonal teacher. He feared the jostling boys who fattened on dross, having none of his delicate need for the ameni-ties of rank. Even the sharpness of his mind for which his relatives always praised him, he says, was blunted. "The teacher would put a problem on the board. I felt like a fool; I didn't know what she was talking about! She would give me that look—'Good Lord,'" he interprets, "'that boy is so stupid.'"

When Martin was ten years old and about to enter the fifth grade, the family prepared to move again, this time into a house on the outskirts of Brunswick, the most ex-clusive residential section in town. Martin was to go to Whitney. This was also a public school, but, like the one in Snow Falls, a public school with a difference. In addition Martin looked to another happy prospect. Al-though Mrs. Beardson was not a member of the Bruns-wick Country Club, she had friends who were. Arrange-ments were to be made for Jon and Martin to have the run of the club, along with the children of her friends.

There had been considerable family discussion about these plans, and Martin had bloomed into ever more sumptuous fantasies. When he finally saw the house in which they were going to live, "I had a fit; it was nothing like what I expected. . . . How," he had cried, "can I invite my wealthy friends?" But he had been mollified by the other aspects of this change.

With entrance at Whitney, Martin experienced an upsurge of his oldest, fondest hopes. What he had always dreamed now seemed within the realm of possibility. The move to Brunswick had brought him into the periphery of his mother's world at last. He began to come into contact with children whose family names his mother mentioned, to enter houses his mother entered, to frequent the Brunswick Country Club, the social center of his mother's set. Martin was a boy with an urgent appointment. Time was short. There were innumerable preparations to be made, and obstacles to overcome. Martin made a supreme effort.

For a time Martin's school work improved markedly. "Before, my grades had been awful; I barely got by. Now I began getting A's and B's." He gained a reputation for being "brilliant but erratic," designations that were to become interchangeable in his mind, and to which he was to cling tenaciously in years to come. But Martin had neither energy nor staying power for all his concerns. He wanted to excel in all things, but, most important, he wanted to be "socially prominent," like the people his mother followed. From the time he entered the seventh grade in Brunswick Junior High School, through the eighth, ninth, and tenth grades at Coates, a private school, and through the eleventh and twelfth in a boys' boarding school, though he managed to keep up with his class, his work was to deteriorate steadily.

In his social relations there was change, if not improvement. The stakes were dazzlingly high, and his foot on the threshold at last, but "the cards," as it had always seemed to him, "were stacked against me." The more lofty his aspirations, the more puny Martin felt beside them, and the more exorbitant, he felt, were the demands on his poor resources. As the first flush of optimism faded and anxiety mounted, Martin's efforts became increasingly frenetic. The onset of a precocious adolescence was to bring another dimension to the struggle, the search for solution shifting to a new level of complexity.

The disparity between the house in which he lived and the aristocratic impression he wanted to make continued to agitate him. Martin dreamed. As if to force dream and reality into convergence, he took to scouring the neighborhood for a house or apartment more in keeping with his visions; he assailed his mother with charming descriptions of houses that were too large, too expensive, or otherwise unsuitable; he brooded. He was temporarily appeased, about a year after they went to Brunswick, when the family moved again.

He became increasingly fastidious about the appearance of things around him. "If a chair was wrong in the living-room I would move it. . . . When I went to bed the blinds had to be exactly even with the window sill or it annoyed me. . . . I used to spend hours fixing up the yard. . . . I had a picture in my mind of just how everything should be. I knew just how the lawn should look, how far the garage door should be open, everything—I wanted everything to be perfect."

He attended religiously the weekly classes in dancing and social behavior which were held at the country club, and the parties that followed them. He took infinite pains preparing himself for these engagements. And, as had always been his tendency, he chattered. Martin chattered to wrest attention, to hide discomfiture, and to overleap the lurking rebuff that he saw everywhere—to present a glittering extension of self which dazzled, yet distracted.

"I would start getting ready for a party hours ahead of time. I liked to take a shower or a long, hot tub—in the tub I would start dreaming my dreams. I used to make up a different fantasy for every party. I would be a mountaineer or a fabulous hermit, or the secret heir to a throne, and I would keep it up more or less all evening. . . . I was always late," Martin adds reminiscently. "I would get so busy thinking about how I would act, and all the things I would say, I would forget all about the time. I would be so witty, I'd get amused myself. . . . People were always saying: 'That boy is so interesting!' They would say: 'Martin is so amusing!' They'd say: 'That boy is either crazy or a genius!'"

In preparing for a social engagement not only was it necessary to prime himself to a conviction of the desired concept of self; it was also essential, before he would leave his room, that the image he saw in the mirror correspond with that concept. This was a delicate and time-consuming process.

"I would start picking out my tie, and look in the mirror, and go and put on another one. It would take me half an hour just to pick the right tie, and all the time I would be thinking about all the things I would say and do. I would change my shirt a half dozen times. . . ."

Although fastidious about his surroundings, Martin reserved certain privileges for himself: "My clothes," he puts in grandly, "just lay on the floor where I dropped them." One day while he was getting ready for a party, "the maid barged in while I was jitterbugging naked in front of the mirror to some of my brother's jazz records." Martin had been so startled, he was furious. "I was so engrossed, I was in another world. It broke the spell." He had also been hugely embarrassed. "I felt like she had unveiled my innermost secrets."

The schoolroom, too, became a social arena. "When I first came to Brunswick I was so starved for attention I would be positively thrilled whenever a teacher would draw me out. Then I would say things in class and make people laugh, and that encouraged me. . . . I could be very witty! I would interrupt the teacher in class all the time, but I was so funny she would burst out laughing. She *couldn't* get mad."

He went in for school theatricals. "In one play I appeared practically naked on the stage. I was an African King!" Being in plays, Martin confides, had been "a terrible strain; I used to swear I would never be in another one, but I loved the applause. . . . When the applause was good, I could live on that for weeks. . . .

"I became extremely popular," Martin exclaims with mounting self-intoxication. "In the eighth grade all the girls voted for me for class president. But not the boys," he adds with a jab of resentment. "The boys didn't like me; there were always one or two who hated me like poison. But the girls thought I was cute. I conducted the most hilarious class!" he runs on. "I had three secretaries, and I would have them all sit on my lap! I always had a flock of girls around me! I could be so entertaining! I would go into my act! I would start spinning out my line! *I* was the center! I was a brand-new personality every time!"

Martin whirled, ran, reeled. He was a will-o'-the-wisp, confounding with fugitive appearances: "I always kept them guessing! People never knew what to expect from me next!"

He was a fashionable young man about town: "At dinner parties I would bring the table down!"

He was a clown, a sorcerer, a prestidigitator. He produced pigeons from coat sleeves, pearls from his ears, rabbits from his pockets. "If somebody asked me where I lived I would say: 'Where Santa Claus lives!' If they wanted to know what my father did I would say: 'He runs the United States mint!' If they wanted to know my age—anything, I would go into my spiel. . . . I bragged about everything. I was very rich and famous."

What Martin envisioned was not mere social acceptance, but unprecedented triumph. "My brother," he points out, "was good at the ordinary things, but he could *never* be famous like me!" The hosannas that billowed the walls of his dreams—and himself brilliant yet effortless, provocative yet elusive, sought after but unconcerned—would some day burst their confines and carry to the farthermost reaches of his mother's lofty detachment. As it thrilled him to be recognized as his mother's son— " 'Oh, you are Priscilla Beardson's boy,' " he quotes; " 'you have the most wonderful mother' "—so he wished to be reconciled with her in commensurate praise.

The trouble was, there were snares—snares within himself and in an unco-operative reality. A thousand situations lurked in readiness to expose him as wanting. There was always the inopportune slip, the chair pulled out from under, the malicious foot stuck out to send him sprawling. "I had to be the *best*," Martin repeats with urgency, "and in that crowd, my Lord, you had to have an awful lot just to be on their level." He hadn't had the advantages the other children had; *they* "were loaded —things came easily for them. *I* was always poor . . . I was under so much strain all the time. . . . I had so much to overcome. . . . The only thing I had to depend on was my personality."

His falling grades embarrassed him. "I *wanted* to learn. I *had* the *ability*. I knew if I could concentrate, I could learn, but I couldn't concentrate. . . ." In a quick shift of mood, and calling on George Bernard Shaw to bear him out, Martin suddenly launches into a denunciation of "unimaginative teachers," "required subjects," and of "assembly-belt education that regiments minds and destroys the most precious possession a person can have— his individuality." As for examinations—to be measured, formulated, pinned down, that was ridiculous! Could the manifold qualities of, say, the mysterious, shifting sea be assessed in an examination, he asks. "Before an examination I used to go crazy with worry. I didn't believe in tests. I still don't. They are stupid!

". . . I have the utmost contempt for IQ's. *The utmost*," Martin was to write one day several years later as he brooded on this subject. "Someone said it was like measuring a big street with a small fish. Some brilliant people are so nervous and full of anxiety at being judged by 'pencil and paper' that on sitting down to an IQ their emotion entirely clouds their ability to work out the stupid puzzles which were thought up by a lot of highly egotistical longhairs. My moods are so varying, and the ability to concentrate on certain things so changeable, that an IQ is merely an inaccurate barometer of the way my passions are lying at the particular moment. At one of my IQ examinations I remember being shoved into a room full of people at a circular desk where others could look at me. I was enormously . . . worried for fear I would not get the highest mark in the country. For I felt so enormously thwarted in my relations with the rest of the school and with my classmates that only the highest mark would do. I had to have recognition, and was enormously embarrassed when I was only the 10th highest, with a putrid 129, and then I was told that they didn't even expect that of me. My voice weakened and I grew hot and tired and could have slept 15 hours at this last blow. As a child my IQ was much higher. I tell all my friends that it is still above 200."

Compulsory athletics continued to plague him. "Football! Baseball! Gym! You *had* to play! I would get out there on the field and those bruisers would hit me—I would ache in every bone. I think they liked knocking me down because I was so nervous. . . . I wasn't any good; I was embarrassed because the girls were watching. . . ."

Perhaps most difficult to endure was his position at the club. "At the country club," he says, "I was the loudest kid in the crowd, but I wasn't even a member." He didn't have his own locker. He couldn't change his clothes at the club. Even his cash was "worthless" in that exalted milieu—"I couldn't buy my own Cokes; at parties I would have to get somebody to put them on his check and then give him the money. If I had a date with a girl —my Lord! It was important to make an impression! I felt so conspicuous! I felt I was there on sufferance!"

And even here were those despoiling boys. Many times

as Martin whirled in flights of fancy, he was brought down by a blast from some irritated boy—" 'Look who's talking; you aren't even a member!' " It was always some man or boy who brought him down like a stone.

One of his bitterest memories involves the country-club dancing master. In dancing class one day a boy decided he wanted Martin's seat. "He just walked up and pulled me out of it and took it." This had been humiliating enough: "I couldn't fight him," Martin says, "and I couldn't just skulk away; there were too many people watching." He was trying ineffectually, and, he felt, with increasing loss of face, to recover his seat when the dancing master came over. "He got me back my seat all right," Martin exclaims. "He said: 'Patterson, you leave the room.' Then he looked at me and said: 'And Martin Beardson, you are a bum!'

"Bum! Bum! Any word but that one! Maybe *he* thought he was being funny. . . . I wasn't on their economic level as it was; he inferred I was some place where I didn't belong at all. . . . I despised him," Martin says virulently. "I hated him so much I used to watch him all the time; I used to lie awake at night thinking about him. . . . I wanted to know everything there was to know about him. I guess I wanted to find out that *he* was in a position to know a bum—that he was more of a bum than I was." What still rankles is that lesser people than himself were members of the club. Even Mr. Jamison, one of his mother's suitors who had lost his money in the crash, who tippled, and who, Martin says, "was a kind of family joke with us—he belonged! He belonged even though his name was always posted for non-payment of bills." His mother couldn't afford a membership. His father could afford it, "but *he* wasn't interested!

Anyway," Martin adds vehemently, "he wouldn't have fitted in! This was my mother's world! My mother's crowd was *extremely* exclusive. One black ball and you were out!"

Finally there were his own accidents—the involuntary assaults, the dreaded self-revelations; the insistency of emotions denied, and his own loose controls, the very momentum of his flights carrying him into areas best left unexplored and unexposed.

Rancor, envy, the impulse toward malice which often rose in him—these were not to be revealed. To offend those whose favor was so important to him was to court disaster. And was not the very existence of emotions of want incompatible with the roles he played—proof positive of inadequacy, that, after all, he did *not* qualify? Above all, Martin came to wish to avoid that subject which concerned him most, money; for Martin had become a student of modes and manners, in all their subtlest variations, that characterized "true aristocracy"; he could "spot in a second . . . the fake or the pretender.

"What is the better criterion of quality," he once catechized Jon, "a big car or a fine house?"

" 'A big car, I guess,' " Jon had replied carelessly.

"I told him: 'You're wrong. Stop and *think! Think* of the people we know who drive conservative cars, but live in the great houses! And who are the people with the showy cars?' " In matters such as this, Martin says with superiority, Jon was forced to defer to him.

There were those, Martin expounds, who lost their money in the crash, lived in comparatively modest quarters, and yet were people of quality. Perhaps they could not always pay their bills, but they were never remiss in their obligations to station. "One of my mother's friends lived in a small apartment," he points out, "but he wouldn't think of giving a dinner party without hiring a butler and a maid. . . . I still didn't approve of him, but he *did* have *noblesse oblige*."

There were those who had a great deal of money but vied with one another in talk and show, wearing flashy clothes and driving Cadillacs with white-walled tires— "a dead giveaway!" One was not to be taken in or to be identified with them. They were the "vulgar," the merely amusing *nouveaux riches*.

And there were those who lived in the *great* houses, dressed in rich yet conservative clothes, drove expensive but conservative cars. . . . Sure, serene, unassailable, these were the true aristocrats, wearing their mantles of privilege as naturally as skin. "People like that," Martin remarks, "have had the best so long they don't have to talk about wealth and position; it's written all over them. They just take it all for granted."

This was Martin himself, sure, serene, unassailable, speaking in an immaculate role; more than aristocrat, he was a *connoisseur* of aristocracy. A more comprehensive picture of his divided and stratified emotions is perhaps contained in the following discussion about books that he has enjoyed. During Martin's teens Thackeray was his favorite novelist, and one of his favorite characters was Henry Esmond, who "was bilked of his noble birthright . . . suffered, waited, and got justice in the end. . . . I always liked to think of myself as having lost my castle," Martin remarks with animation, "that I was living in decayed splendor, but I was going to get it back. . . ."

Becky Sharp, the heroine of Thackeray's *Vanity Fair*, was another of his favorites. "Cheap," "loud," "vulgar" she was. "She was an awful climber!" Yet Martin could not refrain from "a hilarious satisfaction whenever she pulled a fast one. . . . I guess I admired her ruthlessness. I didn't approve of her, but I could understand how she felt. . . . I have always loved those stories where a person has a cause, and will go to any lengths for it. Becky would stop at nothing. . . ."

Later, when he became a devotee of Bernard Shaw, Martin was to be "enormously impressed" by *Pygmalion*. "I was often suspicious of the rich myself," he comments contemptuously. "What made them so special . . . ? That was Shaw's point! The rich aren't so much! Shaw *proved* that you can take any flower girl and pass her off as a countess in a few months. If you take a person and surround him with good things, if you give him the best of everything— Believe me, it wouldn't take *me* long to soak it up!"

But such observations were socially dangerous. Besides, the consolations of literature were remote, his needs immediate. And where *did* he fit in? How could he be sure? Where, in all his soliloquies, among the contrapuntal thoughts, the chameleon feelings and turncoat truths, was that sure magical device by which to overleap the sum of all his confoundments? Martin knew only one—that simultaneous device of speech and fantasy— "I would go into my spiel . . . I would start spinning out my line. I would get so stimulated," Martin says wretchedly, "I'd be carried away myself. I would say the wrong thing."

Martin scarcely knows how it would come about. He would be at a dinner party, and the very thing he wished to avoid "would just come out among a lot of other things. I'd say the soup was awful, or I would criticize the furniture or tell the hostess she had too much money. Then there would be that dead silence. . . ." Or, primed to a princely impunity, at dancing parties sometimes Martin would find he had betrayed himself again. "I would get sorry for the wallflowers, and then I'd be stuck with them." This in turn would call for desperate reparative measures. "I would have to make a big joke out of it. I would get up and prance around. I would dance with three at a time."

Yes, it had been difficult, that struggle for social eminence. "I was always afraid that I had made myself ridiculous. But, I became extremely popular," Martin repeats. "I was the *center*. I was the only boy," he declares, "who didn't miss a single country-club dance in three years." As for those brawny boys who buffeted him on the football field, who embarrassed him before the girls, and who, though obviously his inferiors, displayed such "seeming mastery over life," somewhere along the way Martin also found himself engaged in a struggle to cut them down to size. If he could not best them on their level, then he must draw their fangs another way.

Two strong trends had run through Martin's childhood. He looked on men and boys as on enemies with power to degrade and deprive, and he turned to girls and women for affection, solace, and companionship. More than this, for the precedence that he had been unable to achieve at home, he sought multiple satisfactions. Many times while other boys played baseball or football, Martin was stealing goals; he was enacting dramas in which he was regal, expansive, and lavishly adored.

When he was about seven, he recalls, there was a little

girl named Susan with whom he liked to play. "We would lie in a hammock. We would talk and swing. I remember there was an awful lot of kissing." Another little girl he knew gave him tea parties in miniature dishes, and in these instances, too, there was "a lot of kissing.

"I was crazy about girls," Martin exclaims. "I still love girls. When I was in the fifth grade I had a club—they were all girls except me. I'd kiss all the girls. I would conduct the meetings . . . I was the boss! They each had to kiss me to get in."

Martin had repudiated rough-and-tumble boys, but he could never forget them. Boys sat like a judgment over his hours in the classroom. They crept into his consciousness when he was at play. They invaded his daydreams. They were the unresolved note, the sense of unfinished business, the circle that shut him out. They preyed on his concept of self, blighting much that might otherwise have given him comfort and pleasure, and drew him at the very moments in which he rejected them.

Sometimes, when he was a small boy, he recalls—such occasions made more auspicious with "a bunch of medals of my father's that I would pin on my chest"—he had made friendly overtures to a group of boys, and joined them in a game of war, or "kick-the-can." Then it would happen again—the inevitable controversy in which he could not hold his own, the undeferential remark, the demanding shove, and the ignominious retreat.

When he was about ten Martin was given a BB gun. He never really liked to shoot birds, he says bleakly. Hours after he had shot one, he would "cry and cry over it." But at the moment of the shooting, "I guess I liked the emotional experience. . . ." He "also wanted people to say: 'Martin is a marvelous marksman.' " His uncle had been a great hunter. "I guess I was imitating him. . . . I felt terrible when I saw a fish with a hook in its mouth," Martin continues resentfully, "but when my father took me and Jon away for week-ends I would fish, too. I knew if I said anything they would say: 'Oh, that's just Buck Fever! You'll get over that!' So I would feel I *ought* to get over it, or I would hide the way I felt."

Even the pastorals that he enacted were not inviolate. He was lying in the hammock with Susan one afternoon when her brother called him a sissy. "I was so humiliated," Martin says, "I never went back again." Occasionally boys had invaded his club. He had been irked, but made a pretense of acceptance. "What could I do?" he asks. But at the same time, perhaps by very reason of his sense of impotence, boys, especially "rough, crude self-sufficient boys," came to hold a peculiar fascination for him.

When he was in the fifth grade, he recalls, he was "in love with a girl named Joanie Lord. I would visit her all the time. I used to think of myself as her boy friend." One day he overheard Joan "talking about another boy as if I didn't even count. That was okay with me," he says aggrievedly, "though I did think she could at least have included me as a boy friend; at least the other girl could have said: 'What about Martin?' " Martin's interest in Joanie waned, but he "got sort of interested in that boy. Don't ask me why," he says with irritation. "He wasn't much! I never felt he was worthy to take my place! He just interested me!"

Martin continued to "love girls." He was to be "hard in love" a number of times. Indeed, it was his longing to be closer to certain girls that motivated, in large part, a persistent campaign, while he was in the seventh grade in public school, to be sent to Coates, an exclusive private school. Wanda Woods was one of those girls. "She seemed older than the other girls I knew, and she was closer to my mother. She was much more upper class than Joanie. I could tell because my mother went to their house *very* frequently."

Jennifer Carlson was another. "I used to ride past her school on my bike in the hope of seeing her. I used to ride past her house, too, because that was one of the big houses where my mother visited. Jennifer," Martin says, "was a beautiful brunette . . . very quiet, self-contained. She was much more sophisticated than the usual schoolgirl.

"I knew my mother would be extremely impressed if I went with her," Martin runs on. "My mother would have been just as impressed if I went with her sister. She was beautiful, too, but I preferred Jennifer, I guess because she was more like my mother. She didn't look like my mother, but her quietness was like my mother's. And she had the same subtle aloofness my mother had.

"I was crazy about her!" Martin exclaims. "She was the most beautiful thing. I used to get goose pimples just thinking about her. I used to think about marrying her. Later on, when I was having dates with her I was extremely proud. Because people would say: 'Who is that boy with that exquisite, beautiful girl?' They would say: 'If a girl that rich and lovely enjoys his company, he can't be such a bore! He must have something on the ball!' "

Still Martin was curiously divided. He adored girls, especially rich, beautiful, and seemingly inaccessible girls who were somehow reminiscent of his mother, but it was the indestructible boys from whom he could not withdraw his attention. When his crowd played kissing games, Martin played kissing games, but he found himself at all times sharply alert to the boys. When groups of boys sallied from the country club to spy on petting parties, or to hide behind bathhouse dressing-rooms where women changed for swimming, it was the manly hilarity of his companions that compelled his most watchful awareness. Here was the salient—his stormy petrel, those reckless, foraging boys with power to divert him from the profoundest of aims. Here was the conflict and the call, the trumpet among woodwinds, the spike on which, it seemed to him, he had always been impaled. Martin came to look on those brash, ubiquitous boys with a mixture of fear, loathing, and attraction amounting almost to idolatry.

Swaggering, hilarious boys had long dominated those rites of torture and survival which Martin enacted in fantasy. Somewhere along the way he introduced versions of these rites into his play with other children. When he was in the fifth grade he had "another girl friend, besides Joanie. She had a brother who was always hanging around. I used to have them tie me up with ropes."

As in his fantasies, this game involved struggle and suffering. Sometimes after a flurry of struggle he would give himself over to his bonds, enduring passively. At other times he would "strain and twist, trying to get free. It was no joke," he remarks. "I suffered." Sometimes the game took a deeply frightening turn. "They would go away together and leave me tied up, alone in the room. I would be scared to death. I think," he adds resentfully, "they would just forget about me."

Yet he had been drawn to this game and was prompted

again and again to bring about its playing. It was perhaps a symbolic re-enactment, like a trying again for assay, of what seemed to him the ever present circumstances of his life. Perhaps, too, it was a discipline, a test of craft, skill, and endurance—a banking, through ordeal, of powers. One thing is certain: if he suffered, there was also an excitement, a satisfaction in this game. It was as if, having tried himself in fantasy, Martin was ready now for the first tentative rehearsals for some ultimate encounter when all would be settled, known. Hog-tied, handicapped, tried by ordeal though he might be, he would burst his bonds and, like the fabled phœnix, rise in splendor from his pyre.

Yes, he had liked that game, Martin repeats. "Don't ask me why. I liked it," he says contemptuously, "even though I didn't think they were the ideal people to tie me up. I could have thought of others—some of those mature, husky, football boys; they would have been better. I didn't care to be tied up by girls at all," he explains, "and my girl friend's brother—he wasn't the type; he was the refined kind. There was another boy I used to watch, Harry Thatcher. I always wanted to be tied up by him. He had a strong, rough friend. . . . They weren't on my level socially—I didn't like them as friends," Martin says, "but they were so reckless and rough and rude, they interested me tremendously!"

And so another element had filtered into open behavior. Where in the past the stronger impulse had been to run away from men and boys, now it was not so. Distended with anger, frustrated in his ever more grandiose desires and, with the onset of adolescence the urgency of an exploding sexuality bringing not only an added impetus to his flights, but what seemed to him almost a sense of preternatural power, Martin flew in the teeth of what he feared and hated the most. It was perhaps at this time, among the angry forces which governed his life, that emergent sexuality was taken in—that Martin's "Super-being" was born.

If the "Super-being" this was, it was a cunning monster, employing craft for strength—harassment, excitation, diversion; inviting the unwary senses, and drawing the befuddled enemy as the mechanical rabbit draws hounds.

"I wasn't rich or strong or good-looking," Martin exclaims, "but I did have a magnetic personality! I could make them sit up and take notice!"

Martin had long known that wherever a flock of girls are gossiping, joking, and laughing, some boys are likely to appear. "The boys are bound to get curious," he says. "When they see the girls looking so entertained, they're bound to come over to see what's going on. . . ."

As a small boy when he was "entertaining the girls," the appearance of other boys had been like a threat to him. Now it had an additional and stimulating effect. Enfolded among laughing, responsive girls, Martin minimized the boys in his lordliest, most amusing manner. In the faces of the boys he flaunted his familiarity with the girls. He teased, ridiculed, baited. All eyes were on him. He was, indeed, "the center."

"I would taunt the boys. I would make fun of the things they did. I would laugh and make witty remarks, and the girls would laugh, too. I could be so provocative, they didn't know what it was all about. I would make them chase me.

"I used to hang around outside my house hoping some husky boys would come along so I could make them chase me. In physical education—as soon as the whistle would blow, they would chase me all over the field. When we had free play— It was certainly free! That gym floor was an inferno! There was one husky boy who always singled me out to wrestle with me.

"All the husky boys used to wrestle with me," Martin exclaims. "They would grab me in the home room and carry me outside. . . . They would take my pants off and dump me in the snow. If they didn't come after me in the home room, I would wait around outside the school and make remarks when they came out of the building."

The patronizing airiness and the curiously inappropriate urbanity with which he describes these maneuvers suggest that here were satisfactions for Martin of which the others could scarcely dream. Here were fantasies of such limitless lures and powers as transcended matter, as well as time and space. Something of Martin's unconscious processes and motivations may perhaps be gleaned from the following dialogue, supposedly overheard by him, which Martin, "just letting my thoughts flow," was to scribble down several years later.

"P: . . . That's the wondrous way about M, his way of causing . . . sensual emotion is so deft and seemingly unsensual, you go to bed with the idea of maybe having some hot time with a sexy red-head, and you discover that it was M who has really bound out your senses.

"S: Girls call such-and-so their boy friends and lovers, and they neck with such-and-so and exchange the usual phrases and admire each other's looks. But does such-and-so come into a sex dream? Not if [they] know and have been with M during a witty, comedy-filled evening. And why? M, consciously or unconsciously, knows what he does. I think that he discovered long ago how unprepossessing was his figure, with that large strawberry mark on his face and his skinny body. . . . He had to have plenty of what everyone likes—attention. . . . So he looked to the world with those deep eyes of his and felt his way in.

"He still isn't the Supreme Master of Inveigling. We see his mistakes popping out all the time, and he sees them at the same time, or sooner. . . . But he still packs us with emotion and we find it out in the never never world. I dream about him all the time, running around naked or kidding people and getting chased, or telling me everything that's wrong and laughing at all my errors . . . and getting extra friendly with the girls. . . . He is always leading from emotion to emotion and leaving us at the essential one—which we fill in later. . . ."

But such omnipotent aims have their price and take their toll. Martin, forever mobilized, forever running, could not come to rest. It was first to the girls to consolidate gains which, it seemed to him, dissolved at the turn of his back; then to the boys to draw, to circumvent, to interject his image. His motives being destructive, he was prey to fear; his aims grandiose, he was driven to ever increasing exertions. From time to time Martin wanted to stop.

"I was sick of everything! The whole social struggle! But I had such a compulsion to dominate! Socially I was the center, but being the center was wearing me out. . . . When they got disinterested I would have to start it all over again.

"It was terrible! It was terrible! It was better than being ignored. It was exciting but it was so exhausting. . . . The way those bruisers would go after me. . . . I was so nervous, I was hysterical. They called me Tillie," says Martin, wretched, resentful. "Tillie the Toiler! I despised that name, but I would never let them know it. I just laughed. I seemed witty and lighthearted, but basically I was miserable. I suffered. But in my social life I was always laughing."

Martin was twelve years old when after "a wrestle" in an open field one afternoon he mounted his bicycle to go home and "suddenly I couldn't steer; the whole world was reeling. . . . Afterwards I knew a great change had come over me. I knew because when I got home I couldn't look the maid in the face."

The provocations, the chases, the wrestles—these had always left Martin both overstimulated and exhausted, and it had been borne in on him, he says, long before the other boys seemed to realize it, that there was sexuality in this. And though they, too, came to half acknowledge it with that sly and ribald call, "No holds above the belt," often in the midst of a tussle, as if divining ill intent, Martin's opponent would grow suddenly uneasy, hostile, and "would stop immediately." But what happened that afternoon Martin had not reckoned on. That took him by surprise, bringing a startled recognition of explicit sexual knowledge. "The whole thing flashed into my mind! I knew how women were made, and I knew how men were made. It happened in a flash! Suddenly the whole thing was clear." It also presented him with what was to become the pivot of his present dilemma. He had had his first emission.

The following year was a highly charged, accelerated year for Martin. He continued his frenetic efforts to maintain his "social standing." He was "going with a girl I worshipped." He continued his campaign of harrassment and diversion of boys. He became involved in an overt but desultory sexual relationship with a schoolmate, Jake Branison, and a little later in another, this time with Jake's best friend, Harry, "a football type . . . a tough, lower-class boy, socially not on a level with my mother and me." It was at this time that Martin began to make his first coded notations, as if keeping a score. Every sexual encounter was carefully recorded. He was not fully clear then, Martin says, why he began keeping these records. He had been recording exploits—"that seemed very important"—but now he believes that he was also "trying to watch myself."

"It was all so new and remarkable. . . . It was a stunning experience! But even at that time," Martin declares, "I knew that I didn't want emissions. It wasn't clear in my mind, but I felt from the first time that this was something that *shouldn't* happen—not to me. It left me so drained, I would feel so weak and debilitated. . . . Even at that age I knew instinctively that I had to watch over my vital forces; because whenever it did happen, I would be depressed for days."

Martin was thirteen and a half when after a quiet illness, and with what seemed to him characteristic detachment, his mother was dead of an intestinal disorder. So fiercely involved had he been in his own struggle and quest that his mother's nine-month illness went seemingly unnoticed by him, and her death came as a surprise, which even today at times lacks reality for him.

Martin had long since turned his back on the belief that in his own house his dilemmas might be solved. It was not here that his hopes lay, but "in my mother's world." Besides, he points out, he was so accustomed to his mother's absences. "A couple of times," he says, "when the ambulance called for her, it shocked me, but then I got over it. I would forget about it." Even after her funeral, when he returned to school, "I was just as gay and witty as ever. People said: 'Martin is just the same!' They said: 'He hasn't changed a bit. Martin is so funny,'" he quotes, "'because he doesn't know what he is talking about.'"

Perhaps Martin had made a division in his mind between the "detached" mother he knew at home and the figure he pursued as apotheosized in "social success." In addition, Martin had become a past master at eluding unpleasant realities. Whatever his processes, he accomplished a prodigious feat.

Although Mrs. Beardson was in and out of the hospital several times during her illness, and Mr. Beardson took the boys to visit her regularly, Martin had asked few questions, overheard no worried conversations, and was peculiarly blind to the manifest anxiety in the faces all around. The word "hospital" seemed to have no more meaning for him than if it had been synonymous with "hotel." An ambulance called for his mother? He blocked that out of his mind. The possibility of death? That, too, was meaningless. It did not exist in his consciousness; it therefore could not occur. The only seeming reality to Martin had been his pressing social climb, and to that end he was heroically mobilized. His mother could not die. The entire design of his life was predicated on this. Even his last visit to the hospital, a day before her death, was approached as an ordinary call. Yet Martin could not quite escape the nudges of reality—those rude and jarring invasions which disturbed his dream, tipped his precarious equilibrium, frightened and angered him.

On that day, as was his custom, Mr. Beardson drove

the boys to the hospital. Martin had put some pictures he had taken into the glove compartment of the car. At the hospital, as his father parked the car, Martin began collecting his pictures. "My father looked at me and said: 'What have you there?' 'Pictures,' I said, 'to show Mother.' We were getting out of the car," Martin continues, "but he stopped right there. Jon and my father gave each other that look! They embarrassed me," he cries. "They looked at me as if I were an imbecile. 'She can't look at your pictures,' " his father had exclaimed. " 'She's too sick.' Nobody told me anything! *I* was supposed to *know!*"

In the course of an interview weeks later, the trigger tripped by an ostensibly unrelated event—the death of George Bernard Shaw—Martin was to be shaken with sobs as he recounted the details of his last visit with his mother, and mourned her death as if it had just occurred. But he did not, at the first telling, display any sorrow. His heart, rather, was filled with rancor and defiance—against Jon, against his father. On one hand, it seemed to Martin, they were always withholding something of vast importance from him—even information about his mother's illness. On the other hand, with their contemptuous irritation at his failure to acknowledge her illness, they seemed to demand a relinquishment of him.

"The next day," Martin says distantly, "I went to visit a friend. I wasn't changed. I went on just as usual." That evening when he received the news of her death, "I don't think I said anything, but I *did* want to be by myself. They followed me upstairs! My father and brother followed me upstairs! You would think," he says furiously, "that they could have seen I didn't want them!" Then Mr. Beardson moved in with the boys.

"Right away he began to make changes! He moved a nice maple chest out of my room and moved in some old modern white elephant that he wanted to store somewhere. It looked terrible! 'It looks nice,' *he* said. Of course, *I* knew he didn't think it looked nice," Martin says suspiciously. "I think he was using duplicity, but I couldn't say anything. He was the one in power. I guess I seemed to agree with him, but I think he knew I was using duplicity, too. . . .

"Next," Martin says, "he got rid of my mother's piano. The Steinway! The one my mother played! He took it away from me. . . . Yes, it was borrowed," he acknowledges with irritation, "but he could have bought it, couldn't he?"

Mr. Beardson also fired the maid. "I was attached to her, so he had to fire her!" And then they moved. That was another affront, another deprivation. "I didn't want to move, but *he* had to be close to his office!

"The way he acted!" Martin cries. "Everything my mother stood for, he was trying to wipe it out. He would drive into a gas station and say: 'Get out and wipe off the car!' My Lord, in a gas station, where there is a man for that purpose! And the way he changed things around. I guess he was trying to fix it so we wouldn't be constantly reminded of my mother, but, good God, *that* was a weird way of looking at things. I *wanted* to be reminded of my mother!"

Even more sinister: "My father took away my bank account!" Martin had seventy-five dollars. He had saved "systematically," avoiding withdrawals and watching over his gradually mounting wealth as he had begun to watch over those more private records of other losses and gains. "I had my own bankbook, and my own system. I didn't want anything to disturb my system. My father said: 'Let's make it into a hundred; let me invest it for you.' The idea! The idea, taking my money!" Martin cries. "I didn't feel they were my savings any more. Now he had control of my savings. . . . I think he wanted them to use in his own investments. . . ."

Sometimes Martin realizes that his father was not a boor, but a man of charm, ability, and prestige; that his father meant well, had been unstinting in matters of health and education, and not ungenerous with luxuries.

"I know I'm being hard on my father," Martin cries. "I'm sacrificing my father's feelings. I think you should know that he spent an awful lot of money on my health. He bought me a sailboat, another piano. . . ."

But such acknowledgments bring flashes of guilt, confusion, and self-doubt amounting almost to panic. It is as if, such facts crowding him, weakening the conviction of ill done him, Martin preferred that they were not so. Without the repeated evidence of affront—fire in the forge with which to temper steel, wind in his sails to give him impetus and speed, the "grounds more relative than this" to stiffen his spine and put iron in his arm—Martin felt himself in danger. For the deprivations, the affronts, the obstacles to his aim (no less than his "Holy Grail"), were integral to the configuration by which he steered his course. Without those Martin, off keel, hard-a-weather in unknown latitudes, and without bearings for reckoning, was like a pitched chip, careening, lost.

"Sure he got me a sailboat," Martin continues. "The piano, too. But it wasn't a Steinway like the one I lost. . . ." Even as he speaks, the protective gears begin to mesh. "If I wasn't ecstatic about something my father gave me, he would crab. If I didn't *hang* over it, I wasn't taking care of it! My Lord, economy! Utilitarianism! That boring low-class morality! I felt that money should be used to free me!

"Oh, I had this constant antagonism for him!" Martin continues. "I don't believe my mother could ever have loved him! Maybe she was taken in by that football prowess of his, but that could never last! She could never have loved somebody like him. I know most of the time when I was living with him, I felt like killing him. He knew it, too. Once when he was reading in the paper about a boy who killed his father, he said: 'Now don't you get any ideas!' He said it as a joke, but he meant it. And he knew I knew he meant it, too."

In the year or two before his mother's death Martin had managed to maintain about a C average in his school work. Following her death, Jon was enrolled at Studor, a boarding school for boys, and Martin remained in Newkirk with his father. Martin spent himself feverishly in the maintenance of his complex social affairs, but his work deteriorated further.

"In the tenth grade I barely got by. I failed completely in geometry." He took summer courses, failed in his first examination, and then, when he was given another, failed again. "I was passed anyway, but it was just a matter of indulgent teachers."

When Martin was fifteen and about to enter his junior year in high school, Jon went off to college, and Martin was sent to Studor. If, from the refracted angle by which he viewed experience, it was his father's purpose to pluck him from his orbit, disorienting him completely, this (though Martin set out willingly enough, Studor being a fashionable school) was an important step toward accomplishment of that aim. At Studor, an institution of high scholastic rating, Martin was unequipped, both in academic background and in capacity for application. The program was heavy—"a full day of school, with lots of athletics, and at least three hours of homework if you wanted to be any good." Martin hated the athletics, was unable to concentrate on his studies; and so acute was his consciousness of his economic dependency—"I was at my father's mercy"—that he lived in a constant state of acrimonious apprehension.

More urgent than all this, Martin's social arena—the particular conditions under which (Clown! Sorcerer! Arrogant *torero!*) he could escape his wretched identity and discharge his enmity had been disarranged. Set down in a world made up exclusively of boys, and without that flock of responsive, giggling girls against whom to play them off, Martin was immobilized. The provocative remarks, the fanciful and insinuating dialogues, the arabesques of light and laughter by which in the past he had dedicated the clumsy beast and nailed his barbs, preparing it for the kill—without the stimulus of feminine presence, and the gratification of feminine response, Martin was slow, blunt, his wit ill-timed and ill-turned, and the inferior, lumbering beast, denying him even the deference of notice, merely turned its back to him.

His first week at Studor, Martin complains, "one of the senior boys came over to me. I started to joke with him, and he got mad; he just turned around and walked away. He avoided me after that."

And: "Other people were strong! They had money and good looks and position. I only had my personality to depend on. In this place I was lost. I couldn't get going. I just couldn't let my personality soar. . . ."

And: "I didn't have a chance to be in plays. There were no girls—I always liked strutting around for the girls. Girls were very important! I was always much more extroverted with girls. Without girls, I was so flat and constrained and dull, I couldn't do anything. . . . I was lonely. I didn't have friends. I didn't know what would become of me."

The more angry, frustrated, and depressed, the more ravening was Martin's Super-being. In his solitary room Martin relieved his tensions. "It was horrible. It was like a drug. I wanted to stop, and I couldn't. I could see I was draining away all my vitality, and I couldn't help myself. . . . At night I couldn't sleep. In the morning I would look in the mirror. . . . My flesh was flabby, my skin was broken out. I felt so weak and depleted. . . . I was having emissions, and I didn't like it, and I couldn't help myself.

"I had this sex problem," Martin continues, "and I couldn't concentrate, and I was so worried about money. If I spent something—even a couple of dollars—it would worry me sick. My father kept my bank account up to forty or fifty dollars so if I needed something I could get it, but he was so peculiar about money; I could never be sure he was going to put it back. It made me so nervous. . . . I liked to keep up a big balance."

Only one thing gave him comfort. At one end of the school chapel was a music room where Martin would go to listen to records. Though he was familiar with classical music through his mother's interest in it, he had up to this time preferred listening to his brother's collection of jazz records. Now he turned to classical music.

"I found out," he explains, "that classical music inspired me. It stimulated me in a completely different way.

It reminded me of my mother." The records he played most were a Tchaikovsky piano concerto and *Tannhäuser*—especially *Tannhäuser*. "I would sit there gazing into the choir loft and thinking about my mother. . . . When I played *Tannhäuser*, that *was* my mother. It would change my mood completely." [3]

During his senior year Martin was more acclimated to his surroundings, and life, if not more relaxed, was at least somewhat more to his liking. Thackeray was the only novelist, at that time, who could hold his attention, but he read a great many short stories, and was especially fond of the magazines *Esquire* and *The New Yorker*. He got some good grades, despite his resentment of the masters, of "required study," and of "mechanical methods." In his senior year, too, he managed—though he felt himself always on shaky ground—to overcome the "social paralysis" that had gripped him in the beginning. In the absence of girls in the flesh Martin suffused the atmosphere with a quality of their presence: "I used to give hilarious lectures on how to make love to girls."

[3] Tannhäuser "escaped from the VENUSBERG with the help of Our Lady; but was refused the papal absolution until the miraculous budding of his staff indicated divine grace. . . ." In medieval German legend Venusberg was a mountain in which Venus, "perhaps a German goddess of death under a classical alias, lured mortal men, who gave themselves up to carnal delight and earned damnation for it. TANNHÄUSER was said to be the only man to escape." (*Columbia Encyclopedia*.)

Some weeks after Martin had given the above information, I asked him if he knew the story of Tannhäuser. He supposed that he had "read the blurbs in the albums, or heard it in my music appreciation classes," but seemed vague about it. "Anyway," he remarked, "when I listened, it was the *music*. . . . I would give myself over to the *music*." The above notes are offered for their general interest in relation to Martin's problem.

He became "popular" again. "Lots of times a whole gang of boys would come to my room to be entertained. . . . They called me the Count; they thought I was extremely wealthy and lighthearted. . . ." Martin also became involved in a sexual relationship, but, as earlier with Harry and Jake, there was no love lost here. All had been "definitely second-rate. We had nothing in common. I used to wish he would stay away from me."

There was only one boy, Jed Horton (a rare exception in Martin's life), for whom he had any genuine warmth of feeling, "but with him," Martin points out, "it wasn't sex—I wasn't interested in him sexually. He wasn't one of those mature, muscular boys."

Jed had been an honor student, president of the senior class and of the Studor student council. "He looked after us. He was always assuming responsibilities, and taking care of things for us. He was extremely well liked by everyone. . . . He was such a busy person, and yet when he talked to you, you knew you had all his attention. He used to kid me once in a while about where I lived," Martin, glowing, adds. "I always said I lived in a cave."

Jed had "every virtue," but no, they had not been friends. They hadn't been friends, Martin, now irritable, replies, "because the people in my life that I cared for were always so popular. There were always so many other people impinging on him. . . . I just worshipped him from a distance."

Yet so needy was Martin of a kind of attention that even from his distance he found comfort and pleasure in Jed. Jed's tone of personal concern when the class coats ordered for the senior boys were not up to snuff moved Martin as if in response to solicitude from another longed-for presence. "He was so disappointed. . . .

He had been in charge, and he wanted our coats to be perfect. . . ." And when Jed, in charge of evening roll call, made the rounds "to say good-night," Martin says with nostalgia, "I always used to think I detected something special in his voice when he said good-night to me."

Throughout his career at Studor, during week-ends and holidays at home, Martin continued to work at his social relations in Brunswick. It was during his first year in boarding school that he began dating Jennifer Carlson, that "beautiful, socially prominent girl," who was so reminiscent of his mother, and for a glimpse of whom, on his bicycle, he had once haunted Coates School.

Certain changes had long been taking place in Martin's set in Brunswick, but these, coming gradually in the natural course of events, were taken for granted by him. At some point along the way a brand-new set of "juniors" had sprung into place in the country-club dancing classes, and Martin's crowd were "young ladies and gentlemen." The club, with its tennis courts, skating pond, and other facilities, remained their meeting-ground. There was for a time an upsurge of prankishness, the "young gentlemen" running in packs through the lounges, disturbing the afternoon bridge tournaments, or engaging in water fights in the clubhouse bath- and dressing-rooms, but overlapping this, almost imperceptible at first, a more worldly state of affairs was coming into being.

On this island of privilege, in a world only now struggling out of economic depression and where, Martin says, "there was a great deal of idle drinking and gossip, and aping of our elders," pleasures had come easily and soon. At twelve and thirteen, girls blossomed out into long party dresses; at fourteen, boys into ownership of roadsters of their own. Dates were made on a more formal basis. New and exciting words sprang into use—a girl was "fast"; some of the boys "spiked" their Cokes from flasks only recently discarded by their parents at the close of Prohibition. Ostentatious speculations about the private peccadilloes of certain of their elders attested to the coming of man's estate.

Out of this splash of mobile individuals and alternating pairs, like the bursting of pods one by one, came a harvest of couples "going steady." The old helter-skelter community of pranks and kissing games had given way to something else. The day of the tender confidence, of kisses in the dark, and of the bold exploit in the rumble seat of the parked car had come.

All this, Martin, spinning in his separate orbit, had merely touched at the edges. He had continued in his accustomed way, "impressing" his girl with his entertainments of the crowd, "impressing" the crowd with his aristocratic girl, and living out dramas that the others could scarcely suspect. It was not until as a prep-school man returning home between semesters that Martin saw, as if for the first time, that something new had indeed been added. And it was borne in on him, with a kind of agony, that something new was expected.

It would be difficult to assess precisely by what complexes of factors Martin arrived at this juncture dancing, but like the hanged man who danced on air. Constitutional, environmental, educative, layer on layer interwoven, to the refractive defenses through which experience came to be sifted, little by little that particular architecture grew. On a sexual level, especially when speaking of girls and women, Martin is elusive, contradictory. Despite the comparatively worldly atmosphere in which he grew, and his own lavish accounts of childhood play (more than a little tinged with sexuality), Martin disclaims any sexual feeling, or even awareness of sexual matters in childhood. Yet in the course of interviews sufficient evidence emerged to suggest that Martin was not, in the deepest sense, unaware; that if he clung to what he suggestively calls "the happy bliss of innocence" while tracing the outlines of that disconcerting force, he had his reasons; and that if he had no conscious sexual feelings, he did at least have feelings about sexuality.

It is on the basis of spontaneously recounted experiences and reactions, rather than formulated declarations, that this much may be conjectured about Martin's sexual development: that sexuality, diffuse and amorphous or not, was (like his total feeling about himself) early a discomfiting possession; later, an uneasy secret to be concealed from even himself; finally—"poor," "rejected," daunted by a sense of taboo (his mother's subtle imprint on the faces of girls he "loved"), and outstripped by the "strong" and "brawny boys"—outraged sexuality became a weapon of hate.

To his best recollection, Martin states, he neither asked for nor was offered information about sexual matters when he was a little boy. What came to him, according to the impression he gives, came as if by default— almost against his wishes. "I just wasn't concerned with it," he says in much the same tone as when describing his early years; asked if he had wondered about his father, Martin stated shortly: "I thought about him as little as possible! Anyway," Martin adds, though his mother "wasn't a prig—she could enjoy a risqué joke like anybody else—in our house things like that were taken for granted; she didn't go in for those heavy, intimate discussions."

Oh, he may at one time have asked where babies come from, Martin grants. "I was probably told the stork brings them." And: "Oh, I guess I knew pretty early that there was *something* between men and women, and that babies grow in their mothers' stomachs, but I didn't know what it was, or what the details were. I wasn't interested! I was *very* innocent," Martin contends. "I was innocent until I was a big boy." It was not until that momentous wrestle when he was twelve and had his first emission, he claims, that he even thought about sexual intercourse, "and then," he points out, "it just happened! It just flooded in on me!"

Still, there had been incidents—the occasional admonition, the chance event, gesture, impression. Some of these had brought a formal constricted feeling, as when he was a little boy visiting one of his friends and he "barged into a room and saw her mother with her corset down. . . . She looked so shocked, I thought I had done something terrible."

Some had brought fits of hysterical laughter: "One of my little friends had a mother who was pregnant. She was so big! Nature's joke!" he comments. "We would go into hysterics every time we looked at her. We never talked about it, but we would get so hysterical we had to run away."

There had been some incidents that gave him pain— a sense of guilt and loss, or a feeling of having been snubbed. It was like that when, climbing into his mother's bed at night, she had begun to "turn her back to me. . . ." When he was ". . . seven or eight," one day his mother said: " 'Never play with your penis.' I was terribly embarrassed to have her say that. It was out of a clear sky! I felt as if she was accusing me of something. . . ." And there was the time when he was "an African King" in his school play and appeared "practically naked on the stage." The girls had helped him put on his body make-up. That evening after the show he was "prancing around the house," when his mother asked: " 'Who put all that make-up on your thighs?' I told her: 'The girls.' My mother never had to say much," he remarks. "She could get so much into a simple sentence! She said: 'Never let the girls touch you that way.' "

It is as if Martin wanted to deny sexuality in himself, in particular in relation to women. More than this, in his own personal interests, wanted to push sexuality entirely out of his mind. What was rejected in himself must be camouflaged. What was forbidden to him nobody else must have. What didn't exist in his mind did not exist at all. What he didn't know couldn't hurt him.

Of one thing Martin is positive: "My mother was all for continence herself! She had dates all the time, but nobody would ever suspect her of having an affair. Kissing—if I even thought of her as kissing, and it was an older man, it was ridiculous! I never observed any sensuality in her. . . . Even with my father," Martin continues, "I *know* she was on the continent side, and it was *very* easy for me to see through most women. . . . I know," he perseveres, "because when I was in that play —When she told me that"—and Martin presents his trump—"I have *always* felt that applied exactly to her as to me!"

• • •

There is a blatancy, a quality of cold, of heartlessness, despite the use of such words as "passion," "exhilaration," and "excitement," when Martin speaks of men who attract him sexually. The word "love," usually spoken with a salacious innuendo, is used in reference to physical characteristics that attract him—never to the men themselves, who are usually strangers. When speaking of girls he has known the words "love," "excitement," "exhilaration"—all are there, and though both vocabulary and atmosphere of feeling are suffused with voluptuousness, this is like the diffusion of light, as if "passion," a covert presence, must forever be nipped in the bud.

"One experience with a man," Martin says, "and I can't wait to get away. I'm sick of him. . . ." Love for a woman? "That's different. That's something that goes on all the time, but there is no sex in that."

Yet this is not quite true, and Martin is not quite disinterested. "There is a point of health, when I've been continent a long time and I'm looking strong and well," he says, "when even schoolgirls give me that Frank Sinatra giggle. . . ."

In fantasy Martin's "deft . . . witty, comedy-filled evenings," as he himself has testified, are designed to "bind out the senses" of girls as well as boys. "Girls may call so-and-so their boy friends and lovers, and . . . neck with such-and-so, and admire each other's looks," he has written, ". . . but does such-and-so come into a sex dream?"

And in a zestful description of a holiday with his mother "in an exclusive mountain retreat" about a year before her death, Martin again indicated something of sexual feeling for a girl. There he "got to know Lauren Williams better . . . a girl I always admired. . . .

"That whole vacation! Being with my mother! It was all so perfect! The whole atmosphere of that place—It was on such a lavish scale! I became quite a bit in love! I remember there was this waterfall and a pool where the water swirled and swirled around. It was a real erotic experience! This girl and I—we jumped off into that water for hours on end." But of all the girls he had known, Jennifer Carlson, with whom he began dating during his junior year at Studor, was "my one great love."

To be dating Jennifer Carlson was a considerable achievement, from Martin's point of view. She was "so beautiful," she had seemed "so out of reach," he had "worshipped her for years. I was tremendously thrilled to be going out with her. I wanted to marry her." And then, having come this far, Martin could not act.

"I felt under terrific pressure. We were practically pushed into each other's arms. I would put my arm around her and break into a cold sweat."

Martin could kiss Jennifer when they were in a crowd. "In the crowd, where everything was so stimulating, I was all right. I had my act! If something happened to embarrass me I could make some witty remark, or do something unexpected, and turn the whole thing! I had carte blanche," he says. "I could get away with the crudest manners in my crowd because of the character I had built up. But alone, alone with a girl, necking, that serious, heavy stuff—I couldn't do it!

"I had so much to contend with!" Martin bursts out. "I didn't have money. . . . When I took my girl to the club, I had to get somebody else to sign the check. . . . I was so embarrassed all the time. . . ."

Shortly after his sixteenth birthday, Martin and Jon set out, on New Year's Eve, to escort Jennifer and her cousin Rhoda to a party. Arriving early, the boys lolled in the living-room, making small talk with the girls. The conversation got around to birthdays. "Rhoda began needling me," Martin says angrily— "'Jen is *seventeen* and has never been kissed!' She was suggesting more than a kiss. I felt so conspicuous! Jen demurred," Martin says bleakly, "but I could tell she was acquiescent."

A few minutes later they started for their party, Rhoda with Jon, and Martin behind the wheel in Jennifer's car. "Jennifer," Martin recalls, "was wearing this beautiful fur coat." As they pulled away from the curb, Martin says, "I knew it—this time I knew we had to go and park.

"I put my arm around her," Martin continues—"I was so awkward, it was ridiculous. There she was, sitting there waiting for me to do my stuff, and there I was with my ridiculous, scrawny arm around that big fur coat. . . . She was stiff, but I could tell in that stiff way that she was acquiescent; I couldn't even move." He had remained "stalled, frozen," beside the still girl. "I felt so ridiculous," he repeats. "I thought: 'Good God, I have to do *something.*' I couldn't stand it any more. I said: 'Let's walk to the corner!' Did you ever hear of anything so ridiculous?"

They had got out of the car, walked arm in arm to the corner, back to the car, and then, between spatters of too casual conversation, had driven to their party. "At midnight," Martin says, "I kissed her. Then she kissed somebody else, and later she went home with someone else. I didn't date her again after that. I didn't bother. A couple of years later she married somebody else. That," he concludes wryly, "was millions down the drain."

Martin was seventeen and a graduate of Studor when he came home to Brunswick. For some time previous to his graduation his father had been asking what he would like to do. Martin was still smarting from the fiasco with Jennifer. His work at school had been undistinguished. He had no plans, felt pressed, resentful of pressure, and was frightened of the future. He ruminated. "I went back to a childhood dream—I was thinking of becoming a farmer."

Martin's dream of becoming a farmer was encouraged by his father. Martin decided to enroll in the agricultural college in Bartlett in the fall, and that summer Mr. Beardson purchased a farm. "But when my father drove me out to see this place—we passed *all* those lovely places, fine white farmhouses with beautiful barns and rolling land," Martin says—"when I saw this place—the house was painted an ugly gray color, and it had a blue roof— I thought: 'Och, how awful!'

"I was thinking of a great farm—a big, rambling old house, with lovely generous barns, with trees and gentle hills, and lots of dogs and animals around, where I could invite my friends. I was lonely. I wanted to invite my friend Jed Horton to come and stay on my farm."

He had restrained himself. "I only threw out a suggestion: 'It would be nicer if the house was white.' My father said: 'Oh no, you're wrong. This color is wonderful!' My mother," Martin says vehemently, "would never live in a house with a blue roof! A red roof, either! This was a place my mother wouldn't even remotely consider, and neither would I!"

As the summer wore on, Martin's enthusiasm for farming waned. "I guess my father sensed it. My father *did* adapt himself to my frame of mind," he concedes. "I was thinking about the theater. He offered me a chance to study for the theater." That fall, tuition paid and living-expenses provided, Martin, wearing two T-shirts under his regular clothing "to make me look huskier," traveled to another state, where he enrolled in an Academy of Theatre Arts.

At the academy Martin was "overstimulated," "feverish," "self-conscious." He had trouble sleeping. His skin was broken out. He dropped out of the academy, he says, "when they put me in a part where I had to make love to a woman. When I tried to do that, the whole class was in a case of inhibited hysterics. In the play *Out of the Frying Pan*," he continues, "some fellow comes out in his BVD's. They handed me that one, too. I felt ridiculous. The class was hysterical."

He had been very good in the first performance he gave, "but that was a monologue I made up myself. I was very funny, but not in that other way." He had got down on his knees and declaimed: " 'Oh, Hiram Burpo! Hiram Burpo, where are you? I cannot live without you!' I went through the business of a search—it was very funny, very burlesque—the instructor thought I was wonderful! At the end I said: 'Oh, there you are, Hiram Burpo,' and I whistled and snapped my fingers. It turned out to be a dog.

"I have always been successful when I could pick my own part, or write it myself," Martin continues. "But if I had to be told—if I was given too much direction, or I didn't like the part—I couldn't do it." But this was not his only complaint. Here, too, he had found "too many useless subjects." The course in acting would have been fine could he have chosen his roles. Voice, speech, and dancing were "all right—they allowed *some* spontaneous expression." But such studies as costuming, history of the theater, stage management, lighting—he felt no need for these. Anyway, he couldn't concentrate: he was "working on something more basic, far more important to me. I didn't study," he confesses, "but I did an awful lot of walking and thinking and reading. I needed time for myself. I had a lot on my mind."

Martin knew the word "homosexual." He had read some psychology books while at Studor. He knew some derogatory slang expressions for it, too. These he had heard from other boys and girls. He had permitted himself some far-off speculations, even at times surmise, but he had never actually given the name to his own orientation.

Other problems faced him—his father's demands: what are your plans, ambitions? What do you want to *be*? How will you make your living? What are you going to do with your life? Martin didn't know. "Everything was so inconclusive; I was up in the air about everything."

Martin searched for his identity, and for its place in the world, but committed himself to nothing, not even the fact of search. This was more like a watch than a search, less an admitted campaign than a feeling of his way. The pressures of reality he brushed away with exasperation, his only tribute to these, perhaps, in the dumb shows that rocked his sleep—the "night sweats," the "fevers," "gnawing in my vital parts," the "cold and clammy feet." Martin was trying for a vast detachment. "I just wanted to be neutral. I needed time to look around."

He observed his immediate environment. At the academy he had come into contact for the first time with overt homosexuals. He did not find them attractive. He made some acquaintanceships, but no friends. He walked in the woods. He walked about the city. He "spent an awful lot of time in the library reading, but it wasn't a systematic thing—I just followed my bent."

He dipped into countless psychology books—Freud, Menninger, and others whose names he has forgotten. He was not impressed.

He stumbled on Havelock Ellis. "In Ellis I found out that homosexuality is extremely prevalent. It goes with the artistic temperament. Some of the most famous people in the world were homosexuals."

He came upon discussions of "sexual energy as a life force"; upon words like "sublimation"; on "discussions about transformation of sexual energy into health and creative work." These ideas interested him profoundly, for, short-changed to begin with, had he himself not experienced that sense of "loss and ruin on emptying the fluid which makes us and creates us . . . and which ceases moulding the vessel when we decant it?" Then George Bernard Shaw, too, "came into my life."

Martin had missed the highly successful academy production of Shaw's *Pygmalion*, but, intrigued by the comments he heard, "went to the library to look for the play. I opened a book on a preface. It was on parents and children. The first thing I opened," Martin exclaims, "was an attack on education! It was an attack on the stupidities of conventional education, and on parents' ideas of bringing up children! I had no idea anyone else could feel so strongly, or put it into words so well. It was electrifying."

He read more Shaw—"I have been reading and re-reading him ever since"—the plays and prefaces, Shaw on religion, government, sex, diet, education; later Shaw's novels, biographies of Shaw, and Shaw's letters to Ellen Terry. "I was eager for everything! I agreed with him about so many things! I got so interested I was going to subscribe to a clipping service so I'd know everything about him. I found so much in common. . . ."

Shaw "denounced the teaching of Latin. 'A dead language!'" Martin quotes. Martin had felt "exactly the same about Latin." Shaw had described himself as "living in genteel poverty, although his family had distant claims to wealth. It was like that with me." Shaw's mother, too, had been a musician; his father had been "below him." "I remember Shaw joking about his father's drinking," Martin says. "He described him with a pig in his arms and butting his head against a stone wall that he thought was a gate. It was hilariously pathetic!" Shaw believed "everybody should have money and leisure." Was not that Martin's claim? Inspired by Shaw, Martin attended a number of Socialist Party meetings, "but I didn't care for the people." And there were Shaw's "vegetarianism and his views on sex"—these were "tremendously exciting!" Martin himself had given up meat for a while. "I did it for humanitarian reasons at the time, but later, when I read Shaw, and began to experiment with foods, I found out there were other reasons."

Wherever he looked Martin found nuggets of pure gold—between the lines in books, in Shaw's shipboard capers for newsreel cameramen, in quips for the morning papers. If there were contradictions, that was a mark of freedom! Most of all it was Shaw's spirit, that free-wheel-ing spontaneity and joyous self-acceptance, the wit, the uninhibited raillery at conventions and institutions, that delighted Martin. "I was overwhelmed by his personality." Here were no alligator tears, no pedestrian probings or humble apologies, no kindredship whatever with dismal earthbound sweat and moil. Shaw was above the fray, a Jovian tease, his elbow in the ribs of human frailty. In Shaw Martin found not only the embodiment of all that he wanted to become, but, by virtue of Shaw's fame and achievements, a vindication of what he was.

Martin set himself to ferret out the great man's secret. In the years to come, Shaw was to give him *Pilgrim's Progress* to succor him on his way: "In Pearson's biography," Martin says, "I read that Bunyan was a tremendous influence in Shaw's childhood."

He was to give Martin H. G. Wells to stimulate and entertain him: ". . . In *Tono-Bungay* I think it was— I remember this terrifically intellectual man, rather ugly, at a very wealthy house. The most beautiful woman there fell in love with him! They just wandered in the garden discussing the world in general—it was very platonic. . . ."

He was to give Martin Gandhi: "I never realized until recently that Shaw admired Gandhi. Of course Gandhi was a poor physical specimen compared to Shaw, but he was undermined by his early marriage. And he lived with his wife until he was well into his twenties before they finally took separate rooms."

And Nietzsche, the riddling Nietzsche: "Of all the philosophers, Shaw said: 'I am the most like Nietzsche.'"

" 'Eternal justice—' " Martin quotes. "That means that all things are equal, that if you make the grade—Nietzsche believed in *great* healthiness—then you can relax and still do anything! Nietzsche says *instinct* should be in the affirmative, then with no effort whatsoever you can accomplish anything. . . . He also believes in the 'eternal return.' That means you come back to exactly the same thing in the end. He speaks of it as a wheel. It's dynamite!

" 'Resist not temptation; reject that which is evil,' " Martin continues with his quotations. "*Both* Shaw and Nietzsche have said that. That's a tough one! It's a hard philosophy to explain in words!

"The mistake," Martin says, "is to try to follow it literally. I found out that *doesn't* work. It's so subtle! It's a combination of so many things—physical, mental, spiritual. You have to *reconcile* the whole thing, and then it has to become intuitive. It's a *very* delicate balance. Even eating a meal at the wrong time can throw you completely off the track because it's such a complex and delicate balance."

Shriven by Ellis and vindicated by Shaw, Martin had become "much more free in my thoughts and feelings." He began to announce himself, jokingly to be sure— "I used to say it in such a way you couldn't tell if it was true or not"—as a homosexual. With Shaw's example before him, he spoke his mind about other matters, too, and, it seems to him, with less ensuing anxiety. "I remember," he says, smiling, "I went around being terribly frank and odious after every play." At the same time, Martin points out, he was "reading and experimenting"—"I was thinking about Shaw; I was working on my ideas about diet and chastity."

In the spring of 1943 Martin, no longer attending classes at the academy, had his father to answer to. Other young men he knew were going into the armed services. Martin decided to become a pilot. "Everybody looked up to pilots," he explains. "It's probably a figment of my imagination, but they seemed so sure and secure. That seemed like a romantic profession." He offered himself to the Air Force and was rejected. He wrote to his father saying that he was coming home to be drafted, and returned to Newkirk. Jon was away at college. Mr. Beardson was living in the country. Martin moved in with relatives, an aunt, an uncle, and two cousins.

Although they had their differences—he was critical of his aunt's deference to his uncle's "whims" and believed she was "spoiling the baby"—Martin liked her: "I could talk to her. We would discuss things like music and art. I remember she liked one of my drawings so much she was going to show it to a friend of hers who had a gallery. I got so excited, I went upstairs and worked and worked on it. I got so excited," he repeats with self-annoyance, "I ruined it completely. I was carried away—I worked till I wore out the paper!"

With his uncle, Martin's relations were not so good. "I couldn't talk to him at all. His idea of philosophy was Dale Carnegie and Edgar Guest! He was the penny-saved-penny-earned type. He had that smug, self-satisfied look—you see those men on the streets, those well-dressed clerks with briefcases who think they've really done something important!" Martin speaks with a studied tolerance of the baby of the family, but says he "adored" his cousin Angela. And he "fell head over heels" for one of her friends, Kathleen: "I had seen her at the Beach Club once. I thought she was the most beautiful girl I ever saw in my life. I didn't think I would ever get to meet her."

In June 1943 Martin received his draft notice and was classified 4F. That came as "quite a shock." He had had his fears and doubts about Army life. Still, he had "wanted to be accepted like everybody else." He became profoundly depressed. In about September of that year, with his aunt's encouragement, he entered psychoanalytic treatment. He was given a choice between two therapists, a husband and wife, both practicing analysts, "but I preferred her. He wasn't much! I remember seeing him come marching into my father's hunting club in his riding breeches one day," Martin remarks with superiority and amusement. "He stumbled on one of the stairs leading into the lounge." What did that indicate? "That he wasn't as unaffected by life as one might expect. He wasn't such a man! I personally think he was gay as a Christmas tree!"

With his rejection by the Army, too, Martin's future career was again in question. He evinced an interest in textile design and, with his father's help, found a position in this field.

In the next six months Martin quit his job to study art; quit art school "because I didn't like being taught"; played the piano, painted, read; escorted Kathleen and Angela to parties and to the movies, and, at the insistence of his father, took another job, this time as a clerical helper in a factory.

In February 1944 he quit his job and enrolled in Hopper College. "I decided I wanted to go to Princeton, so I enrolled at Hopper for a few hours a day to prepare myself for entrance." Why Princeton? Oh, I had an exalted idea about being a Princeton student. My hero at Studor, Jed Horton, had gone to Princeton, and I had hopes of meeting him there. I was going to take a liberal-arts course—I had nothing in particular in mind—I was just at loose ends. There was a lack, a lack in my life."

He had been feeling increasingly "hemmed in," he continues. Newkirk was "dull." He felt "thwarted" in his social life. Kathleen? "She wanted to neck," he says shortly—"she went on to 'greener fields.' She was the most gorgeous thing when I first met her," Martin comments, "but when she started having sex experience, her looks just went with the wind! Her hair became stringy. She'd had that lovely glow about her. It was gone!"

His relations at home, too, were becoming increasingly strained. Martin liked to improvise "storm sequences" on the piano. "My uncle didn't care for the music I played." Martin had been buoyed and impressed by the play *Tobacco Road* and wanted to take his cousin Angela to see it. "My uncle objected. I had a fight with him right there at the dinner table. I said there was a lot of beauty and reality in it."

Martin was "writing a book—a kind of fictionalized diary. It was supposedly about my life. 'Grandma ran a house of ill repute in Albany . . .'" he quotes. "When I'd get bored with the legitimate part of the book, I would put in things like that. I would write that the whole football team would come to my house to visit me, and I would make suggestive remarks about that. This book was going to be full of observations about people and life. I was going to be very successful in this book, and make a lot of witty observations, and get rich. His uncle, fearing that Angela might see it, burned it. Martin said nothing to his uncle about this—"I just started on something else. I liked to work at night—I did my best work at night," Martin says. "My uncle objected to my typing at night."

Martin's psychoanalysis was going badly, too. He liked his analyst, he says. "She was a remarkable woman. She was very good-looking. She looked," he puts in brightly, "like Alice B. Toklas's friend! She had great intelligence." But analysis had not been for him. "In the end analysts are in business. Their business is to cater to the majority."

Martin had gone into treatment "because I thought it would help me in my social life. I felt so feverish and nervous, and I looked so awful! I wanted to be more aggressive. . . . I wanted to be better-looking. . . . I thought if I went things wouldn't bother me so much, and I could be more spontaneous. I wanted to be a success." But there were some things to which Martin felt bound; he wanted "success" on *his* terms. "We reached a stalemate on sex.

"It wasn't a question, to me, of relations with girls or with men. I was working on my own ideas. . . . I just didn't want emissions. Anyway," Martin continues, "when it came down to essentials there was always that insistence that I was wrong in my ideas, and I have never admitted that. I *know* my carnal life was a direct result of the kind of life I was forced to live. My father pressuring me—'Learn a business!' Not having money—my surroundings—the cultural aspects—everything about that city was so bleak, and I know that nothing will drive your thoughts into common carnal channels more than a life that doesn't present any ease or beauty or variety. . . ."

Martin had been in analysis for about nine months, visiting his doctor twice, and sometimes three times a week when he became "tired, fed up. . . . It went on and on, and she said so little, and I got so bored I just kept depending on my dreams. Finally I said I was considering seriously leaving town. She said yes, she could tell by my dreams. One day I simply walked out. I walked out on everything. I was standing in the bus station with sixty dollars in my pocket and I bought a ticket on a bus going south, and then hitchhiked. I went south, I guess, because I had been thinking about *Tobacco Road*." This was early in June 1944.

Martin spent the next few days hitchhiking and walking, sleeping in bus terminals, tourist camps, or roadside rooming-houses. "I followed my impulses. I would hitchhike for a while, then take a bus for a short distance. I wandered the back roads a lot. I sat around. I watched people. . . . My mind was just eating up all those new impressions! I was so engrossed, all my worries seemed to leave me. I felt so free. I felt so relieved, I thought: 'Good Lord, here I've been so hemmed in!' "

He came to a college town and wandered onto the campus. He saw a group of houses built around a quadrangle. By the looks of things he judged these to be girls' dormitories—"the places were wide open with people wandering in and out." He decided he wanted to play the piano. "I had visited girls' dormitories before, and I knew there was usually a piano, so I walked into one of the houses and sat down and began to play." No one paid any attention to him, he continues. The "tone of the piano was tired—it was out of tune." He got up and walked out.

He walked into another house: "This time the house mother came over. 'Are you waiting for someone?' she asked. I said: 'Yes.' She asked me: 'Who?' " He had been lofty, provocative, he recalls with amusement. "I told her: 'I can't tell you. I want it to be a secret.' I think I told her the piano needed tuning, too."

He realized that his behavior seemed strange: "I figured she was thinking that I was a jilted suitor, and that I had come back to make trouble." He realized, too, that his appearance was strange: "I was wearing the same blue jeans and jacket as when I left home—I didn't take any other clothes. All I had was a pair of barber shears sticking out of my breast pocket. I took those so I could keep my hair cut short: My hair was too heavy. I don't like a lot of bulk. I was wearing a crew cut," he comments, "but I had been chopping at it; by this time it was pretty ragged."

The house mother left him. "It was very quiet. There was a kind of inhibition in the atmosphere," Martin says. "I didn't like the piano anyway, so I left. I walked out and sat down on some steps in the quadrangle. I saw a police car drive up. They went into the house. I got up and walked over to the chapel to look for another piano. I tried one piano downstairs in the basement, but it was no good. I was looking for a big piano—something with a beautiful tone. I was in the mood for a Steinway, or even a Bechstein. I went into an upstairs room and found another one."

By this time, Martin continues, "I was very excited. My mind was very clear. I wasn't afraid, I was very stimulated. I was playing my pseudo-Bach, and I heard a rumbling downstairs, but I wasn't particularly concerned. I kept right on playing. Finally some young men came up —I found out later they were naval students taking special courses in the school, and they started to hang around and talk to me. I knew they were holding me there for the police and I said: 'A harmless little boy wants to play the piano!' "

Soon the young men were joined by girl students—

"quite a group gathered," Martin points out. "They were keeping me there by questioning me. I knew it, but I didn't care. Somebody asked me where I learned to play the piano. I said my mother was a concert pianist. I started pulling out a cigarette. Some girl put a cigarette in her mouth—I think she wanted me to light it for her, but I didn't. I just handed her the matches very indifferently. Then the police came. They put me in the car, fingerprinted me, and put me in a cell. I was charged with loitering."

Martin was arrested on a Friday. Except for the "horrible food and the confinement, I didn't mind. I rather liked it," he says airily. "I was very interested in the people, and I was the youngest one there, so everybody was interested in me. They asked me questions. There were several colored people—they seemed so simple and dignified and benign—Nature's children! It seems," Martin comments, "that the ones who have enough character and imagination in this world to let off steam in some way—they are the ones that land in jail."

On Monday morning Martin was handed back his barber shears and what was left of his sixty dollars and released. He paused only long enough to eat and get a shave, then spent what was practically the last of his money on bus fare to a famous university in a neighboring state. He was broke after paying for his evening meal and shelter for the night, but not yet bitten by this. He remained strangely ebullient. There had been hours of hardship, and moments when terror had flickered, but nothing terrible had happened. He was buoyed by his new-found freedom, by a sense of lightness, a limpid anonymity, as if in escape from "all those pressures at home" he had propitiated his angry body, shedding his unhappy self, and indeed was approaching that "new healthiness, stronger, sharper, tougher, bolder, and merrier than all healthiness hitherto . . ." of which he was to read in Nietzsche.[4] Martin today points to this brief period, despite its poverty, as a prime example of the validity of his theory: that, given favorable conditions—above all, freedom from "undermining pressures"—he could "rear" his Superman; he could realize that "transvaluation of values," that "order of rank" wherein "the most far-reaching accomplishments are possible."

"I was getting sunshine and fresh air. My diet was very simple and I was well and alert and happy. I was absolutely continent, and it came spontaneously—I simply wasn't conscious of my body at all. I thought," Martin continues, "that maybe I would take a job and some courses in the university."

The next morning Martin went to the office of the college. "I created a background on the spur of the moment, and I said I wanted to stay and take up mathematics in the fall, but I needed a job in the meantime." He was put to work as a truck-driver's helper, distributing books and supplies to the various buildings. That day he shared the truck-driver's lunch. (He had neither asked for nor been proffered an advance in pay.) That evening he had no dinner. He doesn't recall where he slept. In the morning he went to the courthouse. "I just stood around—I asked maybe five or six people: 'Where can I get some money for food?' I was hungry and broke," he says, "and I was doing something about it." He was directed to the City Welfare Department. There he was given five dollars. As he stepped out of the building he found an officer waiting for him.

[4] Friedrich Nietzsche: *Gaya Scienza*, Fifth Book, Aphorism 382.

"They put me in jail. I didn't mind," he says. "My job was too dull. I was held for investigation. The jail was nice and clean—there was even a bathtub there, but the place where they put me was empty—there were no people around. I was so bored I whistled and whistled—I just lay on my cot and whistled." He smiles. "I got the jailer so nervous he put me in another section with some fellows who had broken into a house." Martin observed them with interest. "They were rowdy young men. They had a fight. I think it was a mock fight to give one of them the excuse to move into my cell, because he took his blanket and moved in. I stayed away from him. I was sticking to my idea of chastity, but the experience," Martin says, "unnerved me." He slept badly. He dreamed. And in his dream he had an emission. In the morning, when he was released, his mood had changed completely. He felt weak and ugly again. He spent three of his five dollars on a bus ticket to Irwin. That evening he sat in a station. His funds were low. The feeling of poverty settled over him. He was depressed, and then sexually excited. He permitted a man to "pick me up." Afterwards, he says, "I felt awful. I lay awake all night. In the morning I thought it had been a *horrible* experience; I wanted to kill myself. All that progress, everything I had built up since getting away from home, lost! He bought me a breakfast, and then he took a bus. I began to hitchhike. His bus," Martin says with hatred, "passed me on the road."

In the city of Orlando, Martin made two or three attempts to get a job, but his efforts were halfhearted. "Anyway," he remarks, "nobody would have me. My clothes were a mess. I looked terrible—I looked so beat!" He wandered. He found a piano in an empty classroom in a high school and sat down to play. "Nobody bothered me." Then he "walked around again." Broke, hungry, depressed, he "deliberately passed a police station several times hoping they would take me in, then went around the corner and sat down on a stoop. Finally a policeman came along.

"I was half dead from exhaustion. I was so beat, I could only say yes and no. I was so dull they must have thought I escaped from an asylum. That was all right with me, I liked the idea. They put me in a cell with seven others—it was a big cage in the middle of a room. During the night it was cold. Some of the men were drunk. I slept on an iron cot. There were no blankets, no mattress—just the metal strips. The next morning when a cop came in and questioned me I thought if I kept it up maybe they *would* send me to an asylum—I took the word 'asylum' literally," he remarks. "The cop asked me: 'Where are you going?' I said as dully as I could: 'I don't know.' He said: 'You're a faker,' or words to that effect. I said: 'I don't know.' After I had some food I felt a little recovered. In court," Martin says, the judge delivered a lecture—" 'We don't want any vagrants here!' All for little me!" As Martin left the courtroom someone handed him two dollar bills. He hitchhiked to the home of a relative not far away and there, he says, he gave such an "entertaining" account of his adventures that "even my nights in jail didn't shock her." He rested. His clothing was laundered. He was provided with new jeans and shirts. "She *did* call my father, which I thought was underhanded." He hit the road again.

Martin estimates that at this time he had been on the road for roughly four weeks. The order of events during the next five or six weeks is confused in his mind. He traveled. He received occasional handouts—"I was more or less all right except when I wasn't eating." He steered clear of sexual entanglements, but in these straitened circumstances, he points out, it was difficult to control his excitement. At one point, he recalls, he wired his father: "Frankly I am starving. Send money care Western Union." His father sent twenty-five dollars, "but the money was slow in coming. I slept in a field that night. I felt like throwing myself off a bridge."

He worked as a bus boy for a few days and was fired. He became a bell hop in a resort hotel, but quit because "I couldn't get along with the other boys." One of them had made a remark "implying I was inferior." He had been enraged when another "made a derogatory remark about one of the Negro maids—he said it so loud she heard him." Martin had sprung to her defense— " 'What's wrong with colored people? My family has them to the house frequently: we dine with them' "— and promptly fell into a depression. Most difficult was his rage and anxiety in the roughhouse competition for calls. The one time he got ahead of the others, he says, "I had to brag about the tip. I had done two jobs. I said it was for one. And then I was depressed because I thought I had made them mad."

In another community Martin tried his hand at dishwashing. "I hated it." He made his way to Everett, a large metropolis, where he walked in the city park. "I was absolutely broke. Done in. My clothes were thin. In the evening it got cold. I walked until I literally dropped —I slept on a gravel path." The next morning a well-dressed man gave him some loose change and suggested a rendezvous later in the day. Martin agreed, "but I was afraid. I didn't keep the appointment."

He bought some cheese and crackers, ate them, and then found a place to wash his hands and face. He wandered down Ditmark Avenue. There among the gyms and frankfurter stands, the hock shops and Army and Navy stores, in the windows of dingy restaurants, he saw several signs: "Dishwasher wanted." This war-time shortage of kitchen help was to provide Martin's meager subsistence for the next three or four weeks. He rented a room at four dollars a week. "I would work until I could pay my rent and have a few dollars left over for food, and then quit."

Between short bouts of work Martin prowled the city. He "thought about Shaw and continence, but in my straitened condition, that was a cry on dying ears. My fantasies were completely out of control. I thought that I could control it, so I wouldn't have emissions, I wouldn't go all the way. I was avid for experience and I was scared to death—in fact I'm always scared. I walked and walked, and I would be hoping and hoping, and I would be scared to death."

At some point during this period Martin sent his father a postcard: "Having a wonderful time." Shortly afterwards he wrote that he wanted to come home. He received a railroad ticket by return mail. His father was "calm, matter-of-fact. No, he didn't lecture me. I told him I was anxious to get a decent job, that I wanted to try to settle down. I couldn't stand that other life," Martin remarks. "I felt myself sinking—I was afraid I would kill myself. Poverty was driving me to too many horrible things." After about two weeks of rest Martin moved into the Sparling, an inexpensive residence hotel for young men, and became an employee in an import-export establishment where his father had got him a job.

Martin remained in Newkirk for about nine months. All the old difficulties beset him. His hotel was "shoddy." Street noises kept him awake. He brooded on his "poverty." He was angry. He masturbated. He was "weak," "ill."

He was so miserable about his appearance that "I couldn't even take a shower. The showers weren't private, and I was squeamish about being seen naked." On the job, "all I did was stuff envelopes and pound pavements. I despised everybody, everything, and I couldn't stand myself. . . ."

Only one thing saved his sanity during this period, Martin believes—his frequent trips to the "water closet." There, in an unrestrained, haphazard catharsis, on small slips of scratch paper that he carried in his pockets, he set down for an unknown reader "my book, my record . . . the subjective, neurotic and otherwise outpourings of a sorely beaten and muddled brain . . . that is too old for its breeches and has already turned slightly senile. . . ."

"It is terrible, terrible, having to run to the WC every five minutes. Not to relieve my body," he wrote, "to relieve my mind. I hide in the little cubicle and write notes to you, reader. This is written in a water closet on company time. This is Bartlett, Radin, Smith and Coons, Importers. I am not an importer. I am a runaround boy. I am I, a boy actually having reached pretty damn near my majority which is . . . 19. . . . I know why it is called the Whooping can—I mean where I am writing this. People throw up in here."

And on other occasions: "Everyone is coming in here now. I had better get the hell out. They are probably looking for me. The Importer-Gestapo—though I doubt it. . . . But I cannot leave the WC. I am afraid. I look so degenerated compared to everyone in the office. . . . They are all whispering behind my back that I certainly take an extra long time in the john. And I do. I have to. I have to tell you everything. . . .

"This morning at the office they looked at me like the [illegible] on company time that I am. Why don't they give me something to do? . . . Some day I will bring a machine gun and get rid of the whole gang, from the manager down to the runarounds. I am sick of all of them. Yesterday I asked my father for my Victrola and typewriter and camera and safety box with my lewd writings in it, and oddly enough he acquiesced. If you give me a rope I'll make this whole damned book the corniest kind of melodrama. . . ."

And: "I cannot be accused of insanity when I say I hate my job. For I do. I hate it, I hate it. I have contempt for it, and I hate it. . . . I paste and copy and work the mimeograph and stamp letters and run messages . . . and pound all the marble floors and all the cement walks . . . and stand on the hard linoleum in the office, and my feet sweat, and I don't change my socks . . . and my feet itch and my head aches and balds in spots, and my feet get sore . . . and I crave everyone else's estate. . . ."

He wrote of his sexual conflict: ". . . I fear sex like poison. I have been in its foggy arms too often. It makes me tolerate too many hideous things. . . ."

"I am afraid I will end up in the movies again. I am afraid to go to bed. I will toss and turn and . . . destroy my optimism. I have not got enough enjoyment out of the day. . . . I must fall into bed dead tired. . . ."

". . . I don't want to be sober. I want to be drunk on

my repressed sex life, the life which pounds to escape my body . . . while another and superb part prevents. The arguments and fantasies they both construct in my oversized cranium are absorbing. So much so that I fall downstairs, stuff office supplies in my pockets and run into automobiles. . . ."

"In a war nobody wins. We all turn into animals. Look at the vituperative, revengeful people of France. Look what war is letting loose over there—people mauling trollops, and weak charactered collaborators who might work just as hard for us. . . . But the ticker tape is running all over the floor, and I am becoming sexually excited. . . ."

And: "Today my face is all puffy and pasty looking, a resulting hangover from yesterday's debauch. My face looks older, my neck is puffy. People look at my morose looking face with the nervous . . . smile, and they can all see how goodlooking I would be if my mind wasn't such a mess. I despise these laughing people. Now I must go through the tedious process of getting back the pressure inside my body, the pressure that makes me think of suicide and tries to pull me out of my job and find a place of rest for me. . . . It is the dullness of the job that ruins my existence."

He punished himself: ". . . I am a terrible ass, a terrible ass. It gives me pleasure to revile and defile myself. If I defile myself with words perhaps that will prevent me from harming myself physically. . . ."

And resolved, and made promises to himself: "Now I am announcing for the umpteenth time the beginning of another great episode in my perpetual battle against the sex urge. I must win it. Winning it invigorates and uplifts to an enormous, unqualified extent. This battle I must win, I must win, I must, must, must. For ten years and more now I vow . . . I will lead the clear, transparent life of a virgin with its deep cool pools that hold unadulterated and effortless genius. . . ."

". . . People half my size could always beat me up. Now . . . when I am looking very healthy and virile, people twice my size are afraid of me. . . ."

"From now on I can look anyone in the eyes and fathom out their souls, while my own remains enigmatic and virginal to them. They will be consternated, cowed, and led deftly by my strong hand. . . ."

At lunch one day he wrote: ". . . A lot of people are looking at me. Everyone around the counter regularly takes me all in. They should only glance at me and be satisfied with that impression, for when they stare it consternates me and I cease to be cute and handsome in a second. Perhaps I am exaggerating. Now that I look again no one is watching me. But when I get up everyone will be interested. I will strut for them and make them think I am the world's richest boy, with my expensive and conservative oxford flannel suit, my fine shoes, soft shirt and fine tie that droops rakishly and darkly down my front. And my short hair makes them think . . . I am a great tennis player who won the . . . championship in 1940, but became fatalistically dissipated and lost out in the finals. . . ."

He wrote of George Bernard Shaw: ". . . The world is so intent on classifying that it is getting to be a hell of a job to be original. Effortless originality is rejected and left to starve or charge on itself. . . . I love Bernard Shaw, and everything he writes I passionately believe.

Everyone else is secondary crying in the wilderness with very brief open spaces, but he is all open space . . ." but he quarreled with him, too: "Bernard Shaw claims that genius will come to light no matter how many years clumsy society will suppress it. I am a genius. I say he is lying. I have come too near swords (complete frustration!) to seriously [illegible] words of his."

Food was an intense preoccupation. And money, attractiveness, and girls: "Spiel is seldom real—merely a mental meal— . . . Perhaps I should not eat lunch before I write. A full stomach encourages so much contentment that I do not even wish to wiggle a pen. . . ."

"I love, crave and glorify pickles, chopped egg, deviled egg and pickles. It rescues me from my depressions, at least my food depressions. Eating makes me think of money and money makes me think of the girls my brother goes with. . . .

". . . My head is not too muddled or suicidal. . . . I am going to be a superb physical attraction in a few months, what with my intended virginity and my writing. . . . I wish to write out every neurosis in every cranny of my brain. . . . My face and body will take on the serene, powerful attitude of my mind. . . . I must save ten thousand before I am thirty. At thirty I will invest my ten thousand at five per cent and live on fifty a month. . . . I will then . . . write best sellers, and marry the richest girl in the world. Fooey. I do not mean what I say. I am tired. . . . I am also sitting on the horns of a dilemma . . . and cannot escape the thing that keeps me awake. . . ."

And: "I can no longer get a thrill out of being called brilliant, a genius. I much prefer the girl who comes rushing up to me and says, 'Oh, you are wonderful!' I melt inside at that moment, and acquire goose pimples and a rosy complexion on the outside. . . ."

He wrote about his "beautiful cousin, Angela." About another "young girl I like," he wrote: "I would not want her to think I didn't wish to see her, but tonight my voice is so weak, and my personality so unsure that I dare not call her for fear of the great prickly heat that will overcome me, and tire my eyes. . . ."

With his "reader" he conversed with split-second changes in mood: "I have only a half hour with you today. A half hour every day at lunch. Not a half hour for you to read though. . . . Please don't get antagonized . . . I welcome your stares. I hope you acquire the pith and image my book holds. You should know me better when I am through my travail. And I am much better than most of your friends. . . .

"When we talk that is sensual. It is the first step in Seduction. No matter what we talk about I am trying to seduce you. . . . I am also trying to seduce myself into thinking you should read this. . . ."

". . . I want to say so many things before I am finished with your attention. You must listen. No, you don't have to, but please do. No. I don't want to beg you either. You may be an awful rotter—a stupid ass whom I wouldn't care for, or who would look on me as vermin. . . . But I am approaching a confession, something that will make another hundred dozen throw me aside. Good. I want to get rid of all the stew balls and closed minds. . . .

"Forgive and forget me, and I beg you—and do not like to beg. It is violent and embarrassing to my heart, the poor thing, my heart flutters and bounces all day from begging. I beg people to speak to me—any kind of trash.

But not for long can they speak. I will monopolize the conversation. . . . My personal account is bloody red, and all on the debit side. . . ."

". . . You believe you are best, but you are not. But then again . . . you may be a young, passionate girl with avid stare that frightens people and sends great hulking men into embarrassing fidgets. I do not do that, but I would like to. I cannot look great hulking men in the eyes, or women, or children. Everyone is great hulking to me. Even you who I cannot see or feel. You are terrifying. I have a superb imagination which has already rotted out the inside of my stomach, and in it you are a great hulking monster eating me alive. For after I put down my words and cease burning—and though I am much better when not . . . burning, I am nevertheless a bit dispassionate. But it won't last. . . . I have to go back to writing or hogging the conversation. I must have every piece of the talking, and people must admire my brilliance, and laugh at me, for if I can't talk I must rock my chair, and drink liquor, and rub spots in the rug and pull apart the houseplants, and burst out in . . . pimples. My body is bad enough. . . . My mind is corrupt and demented. . . . There are too many unsymmetrical designs. . . . People smile behind their unpleasant masks, and their smiles make me laugh hysterically, and cry when I reach home and my room where the walls are covered with castle photographs and pretty women and expensive furniture. . . .

"I seldom have money. . . . My father always hesitates before giving me some. . . . Tomorrow I am going to let you in on my notebook which is the most passionate affair ever printed. I chase down all the words at the office and kill the hot blood that rises every time I stamp an envelope. . . . I wrestle with sex continually. . . .

"But I . . . had better stop. For you must resent my getting personal. So personal as to say, 'You must resent my getting personal,' and so into night in which you can hear me still whining that you must resent my saying that you must resent my saying we are really in the darknes. If you don't understand what I mean I believe I'll leave us there. It is pleasant and doesn't hurt anyone till we knock our heads together or against a stone wall. That is my relation to you, dear reader. If you are like the people I see outside my window you are equivalent to a stone wall. My head is the lightest kind of balsa wood—very soft molly coddled and impressionable."

In the spring of 1945 Martin handed in his resignation and told his father: "I'm going back to Everett." It was Martin's belief that if he could live more anonymously, away from family and from Newkirk with all their associations, he would be better able to tolerate "some undemanding part-time job," in the meantime dedicating himself to the solution of his deeper problems. His father had been disappointed, Martin recalls with an edge of pain. " 'I wish you had talked this over with me before making your decision,' " he had said. " 'We were going to try to make a career for you.' I couldn't help it," Martin says. "I had to try to save myself. The monotony was getting me. My mind was a sinking fair. I felt as if my brain was being beaten into a stupid ape shape. . . ."

This time, with a suitable wardrobe, with money in his pocket (he had saved about one hundred and eighty dollars), and with the understanding that so long as he made a sincere effort to help himself, his father would supplement his income, Martin felt that he was making a more propitious entrance, though that feeling was somewhat marred by the nature of his travel accommodations. His father had provided him with his railroad ticket but, characteristically, Martin remarks: "he bought me an upper berth."

Within a few days after his arrival in Everett, Martin was robbed. He had taken a room at four dollars a week in a grubby hotel on Allison Street. "A man sent me a note. He said he wanted to see me. I put a note under *his* door: 'I'm not in the mood.'" When Martin returned from his evening walk, both his money and the man had disappeared from the hotel. This experience, like a slap in the face—though Mr. Beardson replenished Martin's funds—was so to demoralize him that "everything was ruined—I got off to a terrible start."

In the next five and a half years Martin was to hold three jobs, the first during the summer of 1945 for about three months, as a typist for from three to four hours a day; the second, for nearly two years, as a half-day clerk and errand boy in a large museum; the third, as a part-time messenger, from about November 1949 to September 1950. He was to move ten times, not including several hitchhiking trips and a visit home. For a short time Martin remained in a stripped and abandoned rooming-house—"I slept in one of the bathtubs"—from which the other tenants had moved, or had been evicted. He was to "take a crack at panhandling," but that was "morally too exhausting." What Martin did not yet know of cynicism, of sordidness and brutality, and of the preying and preyed upon, he was to learn in this time.

Once Martin "picked up" a Marine captain. "He was drunk. He demanded my electric razor. I offered him five dollars instead. He hit me and took it anyway. . . .

"Two truck-drivers came to my room. I left immediately afterwards. I left them there because I knew if I stayed they would beat me up. They took my radio and my pawn tickets. It was all I had in the world."

Martin has been "picked up," too—twice by city detectives. "This is a town," he says with bitter irony, "where handsome, well-fed, strong men are paid to go into the poverty-stricken sections offering starving people food, and then arresting, humiliating and jailing the ones who accept."

In one of the rooming-houses where he lived he made the acquaintanceship of Jack, a university student. "I wasn't interested in him sexually because I don't like effeminate men. I guess he was too much like me—he was always so anxious and depressed, he got on my nerves."

One morning as Martin went down the hall he noticed that Jack's door was ajar. "I felt there was something peculiar right away. I looked in. There was a light on. It was right above him, and I thought I could see him under the light. I went in. Then I saw him. He was hanging from a pipe that covered an old gas light, and he had used one of his ties to hang himself, and there was this light on over his head. . . .

"I couldn't get over that! It was like the end of the world, this boy hanging, with this peculiar glow all around him. . . . I saw him everywhere, hanging there like a doll. I moved to another room, but it didn't do any good. . . . That cured me for a while; it seemed so final —death. I have thought about suicide so much myself. Even when I was a kid, even if I had a comparatively good day, I would think about killing myself. . . ."

"MARTIN BEARDSON *must survive!*" he has written. "MARTIN BEARDSON *is important!* As each is to himself, so is the world important! . . . IT is the only way out: SEXUAL CONTINENCE. . . ."

And: "Ladies and gentlemen. . . . Stop wringing your hands. You are living in a jungle. A leopard is in the tree above you, a snake, a crocodile and a worm and scrofulous toad are crawling over your feet. On a level with your eye, putrifying vermin. . . . We are . . . entangled in the undergrowth. We are beasts. We will destroy each other. . . . Do you mind if I don't join you? I am crawling through this jungle with you and the other stray dogs. Do you mind if I keep my distance . . . ? I am going to taste the coconuts that fall in my path and gaze at the sky. I will not . . . lie with you, male or female. . . ."

Scrawled in huge letters on the walls of Martin's room are injunctions such as the following: " 'MINIMUM OF EFFORT: MAXIMUM OF ERROR,' SAYS NIETZSCHE. FIND OUT *what* IS BAD FOR YOU!" A few days later Martin will write: "MY *virtue* IS MY ONLY INCLINATION!!! I WILL *not* BE CONFUSED ANY MORE BY NIETZSCHE!!!"

Yet, given a period of continence, there are other dangers. There are always dangers. Martin is prone to deception. "I get too encouraged, I feel so free and strong. That's when you have to be so careful. . . ." One evening when he had been continent for nearly a month, Martin went for a long walk. In front of the Galaxy Cafeteria, a hangout for derelicts and toughs, "a young tough asked, 'Have you got your harmonica?' " Another remarked contemptuously: " 'Why are you talking to him? He's a queer!' " Both then turned belligerently to Martin: " 'You're a queer, aren't you?' "

Normally Martin would have run away, "but I felt like facing the world. I said: 'Yes, I'm a queer.' One of them gave me a kick. Then I did this ridiculous thing—I put up my ridiculous fists." Martin was so badly beaten that hospitalization was required. When he got out of the hospital, "I couldn't control myself. . . . I went through a whole series of debauches. I was weak and sick for months."

Always it is deprivation that Martin blames for his plight. Poor in health, poor in strength, poor in money, poor in position, it has always been the brawny boys who divested him of his powers. That, longing for "pure flight —it's an odd, entrancing feeling, like 'Lost in the Stars and Drifting Along,' " Martin explains. "It's tied in with some pure, clean, wistful, longing existence—" That, longing for this, he should be "dragged through the mire!" Martin despairs.

Martin would like to turn from this feud, to find another way. He turns again and again to those other symbols, concepts and promises—Gandhi's conquering of "the yammering of the flesh"; Shaw's vegetarianism and "ideal love" for Ellen Terry; the travail of Christian searching for the Celestial City, and the escape of Tannhäuser from carnal Venusberg. Finally there is Nietzsche's "eternal justice," "the eternal wheel"—the promise of return at last to that "pure," "joyous," "childlike" state, "neither striving nor denied," but "innocent in all its instincts. . . ." But Nietzsche is so subtle; Martin has not yet succeeded in unraveling the riddles within Nietzsche's riddles. And Martin cannot surmount his rage.

On the day the death of George Bernard Shaw was announced, Martin wept. And as if in Shaw had been em-

bodied the promise, the method, and the exemplification
of the success he wanted, he now wept for his mother,
too. It was now, as if acknowledging her death as well,
that Martin described his last visit with his mother.

"I was so shocked—she looked so terrible— It was the
first time I saw her looking very sick. I bent down and
kissed her, and then I stood at the foot of the bed and
cried. . . . I thought: 'This is the end of her attention
to me. . . .'

"Life would have been so different," he sobbed. "Now
Shaw is gone— My mother is gone— This filthy, shoddy
life! I am living my father's life!"

November 1950

AFTERWORD

SINCE COMPLETING these studies I have been asked again and again: "What has happened to these men? How did their stories come out?" Unlike fictional stories, these go on and on.

After his last arrest, in the fall of 1950, Martin made an impassioned plea. If only his father would free him from his "degrading poverty," from the necessity of his "common, monotonous job," he could solve not only his sex problem but, ultimately, the problem of earning his living. With relief from tension-producing circumstances that drove him to excesses, he would be better able to mobilize his resources. He would grow stronger. He would pour his energies into writing and painting and, as it takes money to make money, and as nothing succeeds like success, he was sure that some day his endeavors would bring him both prominence and cash.

Mr. Beardson agreed to place Martin on a modest monthly allowance. Martin moved once more, then settled down to another "regime." At the end of one year he went to work again, but only for a short time. After a few unhappy weeks Martin quit his job, and his full allowance was resumed.

In the three years since that arrangement first went into effect, Martin has made no appreciable progress in achieving the "complete continence" that he believes would transform him, lifting him to heights of health, grace, and creative production. That, naturally, Martin believes, is because he works against obstacles. He has not yet been given enough. His allowance, he points out, provides for only his fundamental needs. But there have been some peripheral changes that are worthy of note.

Martin seems somewhat more relaxed—less headlong and hectic—than during the months of our formal interviews when he was going to work every day. He has not moved again. He explains it this way: that's because he was lucky enough to find a comparatively quiet room, and because his room overlooks a quiet garden instead of an active street.

Although there have been sexual episodes, he has not been arrested again. And, Martin says, he is neither so driven toward nor so slow to recover from "a sexual debauch," though every emission, he adds, still brings its wake of fury and misery.

His central idea remains: the loss of "vital forces" is a devastation, the preservation and transformation of "vital forces" into health and art the only way to salvation. That he has been engaged in creative pursuits is evidenced by the mounting piles of new writings that litter his room, and by the stacks of canvases that fill the walls and stand along the floor.

"One day," Martin recalled, "I was so upset and excited I was afraid I was going to fall into a complete fatalism—you know, neglect my diet, and *fly* into sex. I got myself home, and I began to paint. Michelangelo," he interpolated, "thought that painting jeopardized his soul. That day I thought: 'Quite the contrary!' I started working and it all went away, but if I have had an emission, then my soul suffers. My work *and* my soul suffer. Then everything suffers."

And Martin continues his studies. Bernard Shaw remains a paramount symbol in his scheme. During the spring of 1952 Martin was reading Stendhal with enthusiasm. In July 1953 Martin said impatiently of Stendhal, whose *Notebooks* he had recently finished reading: " I don't think I'll use him! He can't be sound. He was constantly getting himself involved in cheap little carnal affairs. But Chekhov!" he added. "When Chekhov writes about love, he is writing about your whole life; he's writing about everything you have ever longed for or dreamed of."

And though Martin has not yet succeeded in unriddling Nietzsche, he clings to that concept of "the wheel"—of "eternal justice," and "the eternal return." "Because," he says with gaiety, "it has been proven! Einstein topped them all! He proved it scientifically! All of his theories about the inner relationship of energy and matter—his whole time-space continuum comes to that. Einstein proved the inevitability of everything when the atom bomb went off!"

That these stories do not end is even more strikingly demonstrated by Miller's remarkable resiliency. Although Miller pleaded for a long sentence when he gave himself up to the police in July 1951 and then sank into a period of depression and confusion, by March 1952 he was planning an appeal for clemency. He still believed that he himself had destroyed his eyes, but he wrote to members of the institute and to me: "I've made my peace with God. God has forgiven me. . . ." Six months later, in September, he wrote that the visiting prison physician, and other doctors who had examined him, had succeeded in convincing him that "what I did [to my eyes] was in no way responsible; the loss of sight was due to natural causes." Although he had sixteen more months of his sentence to serve, he was hopeful of an early parole, and he asked for intercession by institute personnel and myself. Miller was in a distant state. An organization for the blind in that area was doing whatever was possible in his behalf. Beyond writing him an occasional letter or sending small gifts, there was nothing more that any of us could do. Two months later Miller wrote again to staff members of the institute, many of whom are blind themselves, this time in the voice of a warning prophet:

". . . Seasons are changing. Population is growing to the extent where our badly depleted soil . . . means less and less of badly needed food for our people. Gratuities and donations will become less as time goes by. People are becoming increasingly more selfish, hard and cold toward their fellow men. We as a people are bent on total war, and total war is now inevitable and a sure bet. . . . You must think constructively. . . . It is almost impossible for sighted people to survive . . . let alone blind people, with no water and little food to go around. . . .

"Because I am interested in your organization and your members," he continued, "I would like to offer a suggestion. I make this suggestion . . . because of my fondness for you." Miller went on to propose that the institute "purchase a large farm about one hundred miles from Lundberg or Freetown." His reasons for choosing these locations: ". . . good roads, good transportation, better soil conditions, especially in the Freetown area, where the soil is very productive, and above all the water supply is good. This," he pointed out, "is more important than good-looking buildings, for we must bear in mind in . . . our next war . . . money will be of no value." In addition, ". . . in the Freetown County area most old farmers took good care of their farms"; there were "quiet and beauty," and taxes were lower than in the state where the institute was located, "and where so many of the farms are soil depleted and ruined away."

Miller developed his idea further. This was to be a "community" for the blind, and it was to consist of "a thousand acres or more—not less." He outlined a training program: every man, woman, and child was to be taught "plant therapy," as well as poultry, fruit, vegetable, and dairy farming. The community could also sell handicraft objects made in occupational therapy. He urged his correspondents on with the proposition that "there are many blind farmers . . . poultry, fruit, vegetable . . . throughout our land. . . . Let's teach the blind to be self-sufficient on the farm. . . ."

Enclosed with this letter was an elated little note for me: he was devoting all his time to the study of plant therapy. "If nothing else, I am hoping to become a good florist. . . . Also, I may become an instructor somewhere. . . . I shall fight hard for a come back. I have found that the loss of my sight has become more of a nuisance than a handicap. . . ."

After a few months Miller got the early parole he had wanted, and, under the ægis of a large organization for the blind, he was permitted to go to another state. There he was put through a course of training "to see what work I like to do," and once more Miller was writing:

". . . I have a nice little apartment with a little kitchen in it, a nice little gas stove and an electric ice box. I have a little radio, braille typewriter and talking machine. . . ."

The last time I heard from Miller he had joined a large evangelical organization that includes in its doctrine the belief that with the second coming of Christ, the righteous living and the righteous dead will become immortal, but for the wicked there will be no resurrection for a thousand years. He had been given work among other handicapped members of the flock, had been baptized, and was once more contemplating a marriage.

I have little further news about Johnny Rocco. When Johnny began his studies at the psychological clinic, it seemed best that I begin to withdraw from the picture. But in December 1952 I learned that Johnny was still going to his lessons, that "he enjoys them very much," that he thought "Miss Young is a very nice person," and that "he has a new hobby—raising tropical fish." In February 1953 Johnny himself wrote again:

. . . I hope this letter finds you and your family in the best of health. As for my self, I am fine—I am in ~~scool~~ *[struck out] school, doing my homeword and learning Quite a bit. Things are going along fine. . . .*

He was still interested in his new hobby, and thanked me for a book about the care and breeding of tropical fish which I had sent him.

It has come in very handy. I use it in my school work and it has taught me a great deal about fish.

Tomorrow is my day off so I am taking Maudie to see "Peter Pan."

I would like to say more but I can't think of anymore to say. . . .

Best of luck,
John

JEAN EVANS, OCTOBER 1953

A NOTE ON THE TYPE

This book was set on the Linotype in ELECTRA, *designed by W. A. Dwiggins. The Electra face is a simple and readable type suitable for printing books by present-day processes. It is not based on any historical model, and hence does not echo any particular time or fashion. It is without eccentricities to catch the eye and interfere with reading—in general, its aim is to perform the function of a good book printing-type: to be read, and not seen.*

JEAN EVANS first attracted wide attention through her remarkable "portrait-interviews," from which the form of *Three Men* grew. She was born in Winnipeg, Canada, in 1912, and her earliest writing, mostly poetry, appeared in the *Los Angeles Saturday Night* and other small publications while she was still in her teens. At seventeen she became a girl-of-all-work on a Southern California weekly that had bought two of her sonnet sequences.

She came to New York in 1933, and from 1935 to 1937 she was a researcher for *Living Newspaper*, a production of the Federal Theatre Project. In 1940 she became a feature writer for the magazine section of the newspaper *PM*. It was then that she began her "portrait-interviews," of which "Bummy Davis, Who Yearned for Glory," "The Case of the Ancient Individualist," "Joseph to Whom the Virgin Appeared," and "Portrait of a Killer" were outstanding and attracted the favorable attention of professional psychologists.

She received the New York Newspaperwomen's Club Award for the best feature of 1945; a research foundation grant in 1946 for experimentation with the case history as a literary form; and Guggenheim Fellowships in 1950 and 1951. The result was the present book, of which J. McV. Hunt, past President of the American Psychological Association says, "These *Men* are magnificent."

VINTAGE BIOGRAPHY AND AUTOBIOGRAPHY

A free catalogue of VINTAGE BOOKS *will be sent at your request. Write to* Vintage Books, 457 Madison Avenue, New York, New York 10022.